THE PROBLEM OF LEMURIA

THE SUNKEN CONTINENT OF THE PACIFIC

BY
LEWIS SPENCE

AUTHOR OF
"THE PROBLEM OF ATLANTIS," "THE HISTORY OF ATLANTIS,"
"THE MYSTERIES OF BRITAIN, " THE MYSTERIES OF EGYPT,"
ETC.

THE BOOK TREE
SAN DIEGO, CALIFORNIA

Originally published 1932
Rider & Co.
London

New material, revisions and cover
©2002
The Book Tree
All rights reserved

ISBN 1-58509-090-5

Cover layout and design
Lee Berube

Printed on Acid-Free Paper
in the United States
by LightningSource, Inc.

Published by
The Book Tree
P O Box 16476
San Diego, CA 92176

We provide fascinating and educational products to help awaken the public to new ideas and information that would not be available otherwise.
Call 1 (800) 700-8733 for our *FREE BOOK TREE CATALOG*.

TO
CHARLES RICHARD CAMMELL
AND
IONA CAMMELL
Who love the traditions of Atlantis
and Lemuria.

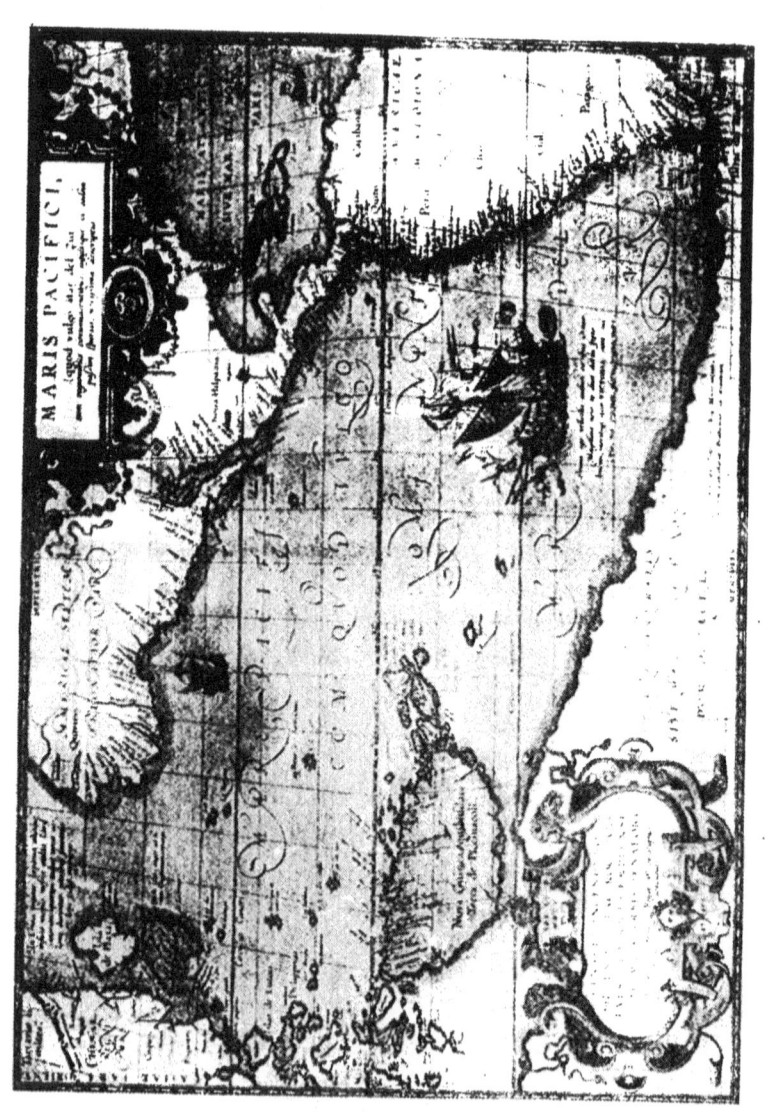

MAP OF THE PACIFIC, 1589, SHOWING HYPOTHETICAL CONTINENT SOUTH OF NEW GUINEA
From Ortelius' Theatrum.

INTRODUCTION

This book presents evidence that an advanced civilization once existed in the area of the Pacific Ocean in ancient times and, except for a few remnants, has since vanished due to cataclysmic activity. It is Spence's counterpart to his acclaimed book *The Problem of Atlantis* (also published by The Book Tree). Spence admits that proof for the existence of Lemuria is less prevalent than for Atlantis, but claims it is just as solid. The research in this book covers all available evidence known for Lemuria by the author and bears out the fact that such a place must have existed.

The main "problem" of Lemuria is that the Pacific Ocean covers such a vast area and that Lemuria existed within this area such a long time ago. Yet Spence does a brilliant job in tracing the available clues we have back to where Lemuria was located and in showing us what it was like. He reveals supporting evidence from many disciplines including geology, archaeology, mythology, biology, linguistics (including word origins), and the transmission of various customs.

In writing this book Spence was clearly ahead of his time. Modern research into Earth's cataclysmic activity is taking on new and more complete proportions. A larger picture is taking shape in which Spence's theories on both Atlantis and Lemuria fall into place almost perfectly. What we've been learning about the Earth's past is both fascinating and chilling, since many scientists are convinced that a pole reversal or shift of the Earth's crust could happen at any time. This is due to the cyclical patterns of this activity that researchers have unearthed. Such events do not occur "right on schedule," but seem to vary between the range of 4,500 to 10,500 years—most often occurring somewhere near the middle. According to some researchers, the last big cataclysm (not ice age) was just over 6,500 years ago. Indications of another one coming include a huge, continent-sized iceberg, and one a bit smaller, breaking off from our polar ice caps in the years 2001 and early 2002, respectively. The ice caps could be starting to slip, and of this we should be completely aware.

Most know that wooly mammoths have been found frozen almost instantly and perfectly preserved in northern Siberia, containing plants and fauna from a much warmer climate in their stomachs and sometimes mouths. A comet did not do this. It is true that a comet would cause immediate atmospheric problems, as in the case with the extinction of the dinosaurs, but it would not pick up entire land masses and move them to colder areas. A slippage of the Earth's crust and/or pole reversal would do this, causing huge, terrible winds and awesome floods. Such an event would go far in explaining not only the sudden loss of Atlantis and Lemuria, but also for the Great Flood legend that is found in virtually every culture worldwide. Much of the terrain would change.

Based on the research of Spence and others, we can safely assume that mankind has lost, on more than one occasion, an advanced degree of civilization almost overnight—and the few survivors have repeatedly been forced to start over again with almost nothing. The work of Michael Cremo, among others, reveals various technological tools and gadgets discovered in strata dating up to millions of years old, but modern scientists tend to dismiss or ignore these items because they "don't fit in" with accepted archaeological data. Yet history, as we know it, is beginning to change.

The recent discoveries of advanced underwater cities off the coasts of India (30 miles west of Surat) and Cuba (4 kilometers off the western tip of the island, covering a seven and three-quarter-mile area) confirms this, since each has been initially dated to be over 6000 years old. If this is the case, then both cultures predate what we *thought* was the birth of human civilization. This is staggering in itself, yet these cultures could be far *older* than 6000 years. Radio carbon dating in India puts the site at about 9500 years old and the city off Cuban waters, being 2,200 feet under the ocean's surface, makes it likely that anything this deep is extremely old—possibly older than the Indian city.

In light of these recent findings, this book should be read carefully, with fresh eyes and an open mind.

Paul Tice

PREFACE

THE most effective way to destroy a hypothesis is to advance it dogmatically and in that manner of pompous assurance and intolerance for the views of others which compares so evilly with the attitude of honest conviction. In these pages, then, as in my similar works on the problem of Atlantis, I will not attempt to hector the reader into an acceptance of what must after all remain a theory until such time as adequate and final proof is forthcoming, but prefer to place before him such considerations as I have been enabled to collect and such arguments as appear to justify the case for the former existence of a Lemurian Continent in a candid and, I hope, a logical manner.

The whole Lemurian controversy is greatly more complex than that associated with the Atlantean theory. In the first place it has not received nearly so much consideration, save in the sphere of geology. The racial and archæological data necessary to its assumption are much more scanty, and the vastly greater area involved assists its general obscurity. Although the insular vestiges of the sunken continent or continents are almost immeasurably larger than those of Atlantis, the lapse of time during which they have been inhabited by races of comparatively recent immigration has helped to destroy any remains, architectural or cultural, which may formerly have existed.

But the peoples who followed the Lemurian population in the occupation of those areas, either while they were still in a fragmentary continental state, or in their later insular phases, have not failed to retain a considerable measure of tradition the nature of which is scarcely to be mistaken for mere invention, and of this testimony I have taken the fullest advantage, preferring it, indeed, to evidence of seemingly greater weight, for example that associated with geology, which appears to me somewhat chaotic because of the grave divergences of its witnesses.

In proving that the myth of Lemuria is almost precisely similar to that of Atlantis I believe I have been enabled to simplify consideration of the whole question, and have made a discovery of some moment, and in indicating what is probably the geographical position of its several remnants and especially of its oldest and most important cultural centre, I feel I have cleared the way for intelligent discussion. The proof that a native white race once dwelt in the Pacific area and that its vestiges are still to be found there, is, I am convinced, of the highest moment to the whole study of a difficult question.

L. S.

34, HOWARD PLACE,
  EDINBURGH.
7th September, 1932.

CONTENTS

CHAPTER I

THE LEGEND OF LEMURIA 17

Tradition of a vast Pacific continent—Difficulty caused by poverty of ancient records concerning this— Critical summary of facts and hypotheses set forth— Proof of submergence in Pacific—Evidence from geology and archæology—Origin of the name "Lemuria"— The myth of Hotu Matua—Conclusive evidence regarding submergence and elevation of Pacific Islands—Islands which rise and sink—The Lost Davis Land—Traditions of Easter Island—Native legend of former extensive archipelago—Mystery of Ponape, "The Venice of the Pacific" —Theory regarding a former empire in East Central Pacific—Polynesian culture.

CHAPTER II

THE ARGUMENT FROM ARCHÆOLOGY 27

Most vestiges of Lemurian civilization submerged— Ruins exist which cannot be referred to Pacific races— The Prehistory of the Pacific—Monuments "beyond the powers of present inhabitants"—The pyramids of Hawaii—Island temples and statues—Pyramids in Tahiti —Megalithic monuments in Fiji—The Prehistory of New Zealand—The ancient race of the Moriori—Terraced buildings and hill-forts—"A higher civilization than the Maori ever reached"—Ancient drainage system of New Zealand—This implies an organized government—The monuments of Melanesia—Building in New Caledonia and the New Hebrides—Origins of Melanesian masonry "lost in antiquity"—Micronesian monuments—Wonders of the Caroline Islands—"Houses of the Ancients"—Ruined city of Metalanim—Vast megalithic walls—How were their stones laid ?—Ancient engineering feats—Empire, of which Metalanim was the capital, now submerged— The forty temples of Malden Island—How did Malden Island support life ?—The statues of Raivavai and Hivaoa—The Mystery of Easter Island—Its gigantic monuments and statues—Centre of a vast empire now submerged—The legend of Hotu Matua—Signs of a sudden cessation of work—How the statues were moved—The monuments imply a condition of great luxury—Easter Island thousands of leagues from anywhere—Must have been centre of great civilization on an archipelago now submerged—Legends of continents and archipelagoes in Easter Island—Fleets of vessels necessary for the carriage of supplies—The mysterious script of Easter Island—Summary.

CHAPTER III

THE TESTIMONY OF TRADITION 47

Evidence from Oceanic myth regarding former existence of Lemurian continent—Two descriptions of tale relating to disaster—Myth which tells of devastating flood—Legend which records catastrophe either by volcanic action or earthquake—Belief of ancient Hawaiians that their god Kane destroyed the world by fire because of the sins of his people—Story bears strong resemblance to that of myth regarding the destruction of Atlantis—The gods reorganised the world and created the first man and woman—Body of tradition whence this myth is taken " a most valuable relic of the mental status, religious notions and historical recollections of the earlier Polynesians "—Remnant of legend discovered in Society Islands—Legend of the chaos of a previous world—A Hawaiian chant of the deluge—The Pacific Paradise—A Marquesan myth of a sunken continent—Polynesian expeditions to find lost lands—Flood myths of the Pacific—The Myth of the ocean god—Myth of the Menehune, or white dwarf-folk—" A great continent stretching from Hawaii to New Zealand "—A sorcerer's prayer connected with flood traditions—Why the Menehune left Hawaii—The phantom island—Struggle between the gods of fire and water—The god Tangaroa controls migrations—The god Maui—The legend of Easter Island—Land of the dead beneath the sea—The Polynesian war between the gods and titans—" Po " the Polynesian Atlantis—Its myth substantially the same as that of Atlantis—Attitude of the ancient world to such catastrophes—Summary.

CHAPTER IV

THE EVIDENCE FROM MYTH AND MAGIC 64

Polynesian myth eloquent of cataclysm—The nature gods of Polynesia—Oceanic deities—Polynesian gods created before dispersal from the sunken Fatherland—Cult of the volcanic goddess, Pele—Maui associated with the floods of the Pacific—The Oceanic story of the flood—Parallels with the Atlantis myth—Deluge caused by

CONTENTS

human sin—Polynesian myths of destruction had their origin in an older Lemurian tradition—This myth conserved by a fair-haired people—The Place of the Dead is the submarine world—The myth of the goddess Pele eloquent of formerly existing continents—Terrestrial disturbance the keynote of Oceanic myth—Summary.

CHAPTER V

THE RACES OF LEMURIA 73

Late arrival in Oceania of the Polynesians—Evidence and tradition of the existence of an indigenous fair-haired race in the Pacific—This race for the most part decimated or absorbed, yet its remnants still persist in many Oceanic localities, especially in New Zealand, the Gilberts, the Solomons and Hawaii—Whence did this fair race come ?—The Negrito race of the Pacific—Its presence there an argument in favour of former continental conditions—Legends of the Oceanic fair race—Their alleged supernatural and magical capacities—A modern Maori account of them—Were they the remnants of the Lemurian race ?—New Zealand legends of early immigrations—A New Zealand ogre story—Names of some Pacific Islands eloquent of subsidence—Madame Blavatsky on Lemuria—Rudolf Steiner's Lemurian writings—Colonel Churchward on *The Lost Continent of Mu*—Mr. K. Browning's *Lemuria and Atlantis*—Unsupported nature of their testimony—Jacolliot on the lost continent of the Pacific—Variety of the Lemurian races—Did the white race of Lemuria come from Asia ?—Objections to this theory—Did the Lemurian fair race reach Europe ?—Haeckel and Lemuria—A Californian contribution to Lemurian lore—Summary.

CHAPTER VI

THE TESTIMONY OF CUSTOM 111

Types of Oceanic custom not referable to a common basis—American analogies with Oceanic custom more valuable than Asiatic—Culture of the Gilbert Islands—Origin of taboo in a submerged locality—Ancient origin of the family in Polynesia—Fair women respected as a superior caste—Women in Polynesia generally regarded as " polluted "—Sufficient traces of customary principle to account for insistence on taboo by a governing class—Descent of Lemurians into savagery—Colonel Churchward's theory—A " relative barbarism "—Little to be gleaned from customary evidence—Summary.

CONTENTS

CHAPTER VII

THE PROOF FROM ART 119

Fenellosa's theory of a widespread Pacific Art—Its unique character—Its nature and type—Pre-Polynesian—Fenellosa's hypothesis implies an ancient land-connection between Oceania and Asia—The origins of tattooing—Its significance—"Evolution" of the art of tattooing—Bornean and Polynesian systems—Tattooing on the North-east coast of America—Ideas underlying the process—Its social and medical affinities—Tradition that it was taught by a fair people in the Underworld—Its associations with early writing—The symbol of the frigate-bird—Summary.

CHAPTER VIII

THE GEOLOGY OF LEMURIA 128

Geology not the sole test of the existence of a former Lemurian continent—Striking diversity of opinion as regards its chronology—Consensus of opinion in favour of the Lemurian theory—Outline of geological time—The "standard" geological view—Problems associated with elevation and depression—Huxley's statement—Theories of Hutton, Von Ihering, Pilsbry, Baur, Speight, Arldt, Scharff, Hershey, Burckhardt and Macmillan Brown—Insular evidence of subsidence and emergence in recent times—Disappearing and reappearing islands—the strange case of Tuanaki—Haeckel's hypothesis of Lemuria—Alfred Russel Wallace—His early agreement with and later rejection of the Lemurian theory—Criticisms of Wallace's attitude by Hartlaub and Starkie-Gardiner—Blandford's conclusions—Sir Archibald Geikie's non-committal summary—Eruptions in the Pacific—Earthquakes chiefly found on its coastal fringes.

CHAPTER IX

THE GEOLOGY OF LEMURIA (continued) 147

Darwin's theory of coral reefs and atolls—Its relation to subsidence—Proofs of subsidence—Criticism by Geikie, Murray and Agassiz—Macmillan Brown's belief in subsidence—His justification of Darwin's hypothesis—Wegener on Lemuria—"No room for a submerged Lemuria in the older sense"—Guppy on the Fiji Islands—Summary of above views—Balance of authority on the side of Lemurian hypothesis—Consensus of opinion that Lemuria foundered about the end of the Secondary Period—Positions of Oceanic races coincide with its geographical divisions—This induces belief that they may have effected an early settlement in Pacific while partially continental conditions still prevailed—Possible Oceanic land-masses—Where is the island of Sarah Ann ?

CONTENTS

CHAPTER X

THE EVIDENCE FROM BIOLOGY 163

Biological evidence of Hutton, Macmillan Brown and Wallace—Wallace's inconsistencies—The American-Australian connection—The ornithology of New Guinea—Evidence from the Sandwich Islands—Wallace's evidence much too confused to invite acceptance—Guppy on Hawaiian floras—Heilprin's and Lutley Sclater's testimony—Summary—Body of biological proof too contradictory to permit of rational conclusions.

CHAPTER XI

THE CATASTROPHE AND ITS RESULTS 181

Need for inspiration in arriving at scientific conclusions—Continental character of Lemurian land-masses apparent—The cause of catastrophe—General Jourdy's theory—"The Continent of Diamonds"—A series of gaseous explosions—Colonel Churchward's similar theory—Slow disintegration the probable cause of submergence—Emigration from Lemuria—Submergence, earthquake and volcanic action brought it about—Resemblances betwixt Asiatic and American culture—Did Asia "discover" America?—Did Polynesians settle in America?—Polynesian culture in America—Settlements in Peru—American traditions of a great flood—Lemurian settlement suggested by resemblance between architecture on Easter Island and in Peru—Further resemblances between traditions of Easter Island and Peru—Government and customs the same—Summary.

CHAPTER XII

LIFE AND CIVILIZATION IN LEMURIA 201

Descriptions of civilization in Lemuria to be gleaned from analogy alone—A Stone Age civilization—This does not imply savagery—Governed by a caste of fair white people—Their arcane knowledge—Occult tradition respecting Lemuria—Vast difference in racial type of its inhabitants—The food supply—Pacific systems of writing—The script of Oleai—The Easter Island script—Its origins—Attempts at translation—Its books or tablets the preserve of the priesthood—Obviously developed in the Pacific area—Not Polynesian—Thomson's translations—Character of Lemurian civilization—Its great cities, religious centres and ports—Virtual slavery of its masses—Must suppose a priesthood, a commercial class and a clerical class, and standing army—Probable luxury of its ruling class—Resemblance of the whole to the civilization of Incan Peru—A continental land between Easter Island and Peru must be posited—Reasons for this belief—Davis Land, near Easter Island, probably the original Lemuria—Summary.

CHAPTER XIII

ATLANTIS AND LEMURIA 222

Was there communication between Lemuria and Atlantis ?—Not necessary to infer direct communication between them—Rather a drift and flow of culture by a slow process—Can the " Atlantis Culture-complex " be applied to the circumstances of Oceanic culture ?—Certain of its elements found in Oceania—Easter Island a link—Head-flattening—In Oceania are found certain "items" of the Atlantis culture-complex coming from the American side—Cut off from such customs on the Asiatic side—The complex, at its most consistent, almost in a straight geographical line—This implies the existence of a much earlier civilization in America than had previously been accepted—The Maya civilization—Its Antillean origin—Summary.

CHAPTER XIV

CONCLUSIONS 235

Self-evidence of the Lemurian hypothesis—Common basis for the myths of Lemuria and Atlantis—Resemblance of all myths of submergence—" Sin " as a " reason " for submergence—This " reason " of secondary importance to the fact—Yet the myth is the proof of the submergence—Summary of the whole evidence—Conclusions following its compression—The original Lemuria.

LIST OF ILLUSTRATIONS

MAP OF THE PACIFIC, 1589	*Frontispiece*
	FACING PAGE
THE OUTER WALL OF NANTAUACH, METALANIM, AT PONAPE	24
THE PYRAMIDAL STRUCTURES OF MALDEN ISLAND AS THEY WERE IN 1825	36
PICTURES OF STATUES AND NATIVES FROM "THE VOYAGE OF LA PEROUSE"	40
NAVEL-STRING TOWER AT EASTER ISLAND	84
HAECKEL'S SUGGESTED SITE FOR LEMURIA IN THE INDIAN OCEAN	136
THE PACIFIC OCEAN WITH PROBABLE ARCHIPELAGIC LAND-BRIDGES DOWN TO HUMAN TIMES	142
THE LEMURIAN CONTINENTAL LAND-MASSES, ACCORDING TO THE AUTHOR	160
THE HOUSE OF THE VIRGINS OF THE SUN, CUZCO, PERU	188
SECTION OF WALL ON PLATFORM AT VINAPU, EASTER ISLAND	188
PHOTOGRAPH OF THE SCRIPT ON THE TABLET IN THE MUSEUM OF SANTIAGO, CHILI	208
A "MARAE" OF TAHITI AS REPRESENTED IN "THE VOYAGE OF THE DUFF, 1799"	226

THE PROBLEM OF LEMURIA

CHAPTER I

THE LEGEND OF LEMURIA

NO episode, perhaps, in the endless narrative of human romance exercises a spell so enthralling as that which tells of lands ancient and cultured submerged by catastrophe in the deep gulfs of ocean. The sentiments aroused by the glowing fictions of the East, the glamour cast by the chronicles of magic and the supernatural, pale before the curiosity which the mere mention of sunken Atlantis or Lemuria invariably excites.

For those marvellous lands, unlike the fabled Lyonesse, or the Garden of the Hesperides, were the actual scenes of human occupation and endeavour in which were enacted histories the most extraordinary and rites the memories of which yet linger in many an ancient faith and ritual. Their architectural remains, so far from being the wreck of legend, even now litter the abysses of the sea, awaiting discovery by processes of archæology as yet unguessed.

The tradition of a vast continent once occupying a large area of the Pacific basin has long exercised a charm of attraction compelling in its fascination. In some respects its geological history is more definite than that of sunken Atlantis, still the whole consideration of its historical probabilities opens up questions greatly more complex and difficult of approach. This is owing not so much to geological doubt, as in the case of Plato's marvellous island, as rather to the poverty of ancient record and because of the vast oceanic spaces which must be scanned by the scientist in gathering the data essential to a proper comprehension of the problem.

But if much remains to be understood, the moment has surely arrived when a review of the entire circumstances of Lemurian probability should be essayed. This, in the light of partial knowledge, cannot but be of an imperfect nature. Even so, a critical summary of the facts garnered by scientists and the views set forth by numerous searchers may serve as a timely impetus to the progress of a study which cannot but cast a vivid and illuminating ray upon the mysterious past of our race. Nor will it be profitless to consider and debate the opinions of those adverse to the hypothesis.

It had been proved that Pacific islands have disappeared within living memory, and that land-masses of comparatively large area have been drowned beneath Pacific waters within the last few centuries. Moreover, a mass of tradition far too widespread to be void of significance, much too clamorous and important to be dismissed by the wave of a conservative hand, renders it abundantly clear that the peoples of the Pacific possess the historical memory of not one but several masses of sunken land which were probably the decaying remnants of far-flung continents.

The probable area and locality of Lemuria, or of the several land-masses which composed it, the dates of its floreat and of its disappearance are questions which can be answered at present only approximately, and will be dealt with in their appropriate places.

The name "Lemuria" was given to the vanished continent of the Pacific by Philip Lutley Sclater, the naturalist, in the belief that within its area the Lemurs or lemuriod type of animal was evolved. It was speedily adopted as a striking and apposite title for the continental mass which many geologists believed had formerly filled a large part of the world's most extensive maritime basin. Quite early in the controversy regarding its site and existence it became apparent that Lemuria had behind it no great or picturesque myth, as had Atlantis, its northern counterpart. No classical writer among the Greeks or Romans had outlined its history or alluded to the circumstances of its disappearance, as did Plato in the case of the submerged island-continent of the Western Ocean.

But this does not imply that traditions of equal cogency and credibility with those handed down by the classical recorders of the destruction of Atlantis are lacking, for the unwritten chronicles of the aboriginal populations of the Pacific archipelagoes bear witness in inherited tales and myths to the existence in former ages, near as well as remote, of vast land-masses occupying either the actual site of the island-clusters on which they dwelt, or in close proximity to them.

For example, the myth of Hotu Matua, found in Easter Island, tells of a culture-hero arriving there with his followers after the submergence of his native land, and the peoples of Melanesia, Polynesia, and other areas bordering upon the Pacific possess similar traditions of a vanished continent no less striking or less replete with the authentic in their particular details than the Platonic narrative of Atlantis. In this place a brief quotation from the collection of Hawaiian legends of Mr. David Hyde Rice, of Kauai, published by the Bishop Museum, Honolulu, may serve as significant of the character of many oceanic myths of the kind. Says Mr. Rice in his *The Menehune, a Legend of Kauai* : " The belief of the Hawaiians of ancient times was that there was one great continent stretching from Hawaii, including Samoa-holokoa (Rarotonga) and reaching as far as New Zealand, also taking in Fiji, and there were some lowlands in between these higher lands. All this was called by one name, Ka-houpo-o-Kane, the solar-plexus of Kane."

Evidence of the most conclusive kind exists to show that certain Pacific islands have sunk and risen again within the historic period. There is, indeed, the clearest evidence of alternate subsidences and elevations. The phosphate islands, Makatea in the north-west of the Paumotas, and Ocean Island and Nauru in the west of the Gilberts, have gone down and re-arisen several times, as we shall see. The Gilberts themselves, along with the inner Ladrones, Carolines, Marshalls, Ellice and Austral groups have lost their volcanic energy and are even now in process of subsiding.

The Solomons group in some instances reveals a tendency to rise. Many insular localities in the Pacific exhibit terraces of recent elevation, all of coralline formation, whilst Mono, south of Bougainville, shows in its sedimentary strata evidences of a long period of submergence. Quite recent elevation of an almost startling kind is exemplified in the southward portion of the New Hebrides. Fifty years ago the Presbyterian Mission ship, the *Dayspring*, lost her anchor in deep water off the island of Tanna. To-day it rests on the summit of a hill which has taken the place of the depths where it was lost.

In the New Hebrides, remarks Professor Macmillan Brown, one can see land forming beneath his eyes, especially through the volcanic process. The local place-names in Tanna, in the New Hebrides, are eloquent of eruption which has been proceeding for ages untold. All over this group the word for fire appears in the names of islands or districts, and volcanic steam and smoke veil every landscape.

Elevation is, indeed, presently obvious throughout the whole Asiatic side of the Pacific, from the Aleutian Islands in the north, to the Antarctic, while, corresponding to it, is a curve of subsidence forming the atoll depression of the great oceanic waste. On the coast of Tanna there is a harbour which was named Port Resolution by Captain Cook. To-day its depths have been so elevated that it is a harbour no longer. The natives actually believe that the island of Araki on the south-east coast of Santo has moved from Hog Harbour in the north to its present position, and a certain chief declares that he actually beheld it do so, population and all! Another chief in Tongoa vouches for having seen it sail into the neighbourhood of his own island and then move farther to the east, to the position it now occupies.

The odd thing is that its inhabitants, in language and custom, resemble the people of Hog Harbour. It seems possible that an islet sank in that locality about the same time that another rose off Santo, and that the people of one migrated to the other. The signs of comparatively *recent* elevation and former subsidence are markedly visible over the entire New Hebridean group in volcanic and coral action, as are the presence of shells at a high altitude on the one hand, and sedimentary strata over and beneath coral formation on the other. Moreover, its Melanesian inhabitants must have migrated thereto at a period when the islands were nearer each other, for, as a race, they have never essayed the crossing of oceanic spaces.

Even in Polynesian or modern times there must have been subsidence of land on a large scale. The Polynesians were driven westward, not eastward. The trade winds, for three-quarters of the year, blow steadily from south-east to north-west, and constitute the chief medium for the wholesale transference of peoples by sea. The westerly winds, which blow for the other quarter of the year, are much too broken by calm and tempest, to account for deliberate migration, for which, moreover, well-equipped expeditions are essential. The Polynesian race was driven westward by the slow and continuous subsidence of the archipelagoes on which it dwelt in the Central Pacific. The traditions of the Maori are eloquent of great eruptions and subsidences in Hawaiki, the original seat of their race, and Polynesian homogeneity in race and custom is the best proof of origin in a single continent or archipelago to which the race must have penetrated at a period when continental or semi-continental conditions were still possible. Indeed, in many of their traditions, their first Pacific home, Hawaiki, is a land submerged beneath the sea, in which the spirits of the dead must plunge, should they wish to return to its sacred soil.

The Polynesian part of Oceania presently exhibits an extraordinary sparseness of land. Navigators have crossed it for hundreds of miles without beholding more than a few insular specks of soil. Why, then, did the Polynesians leave their continental home and push outward into the Oceanic waste ? Was it not because they found or knew of continents existing there at the period of their dispersal ?

But we have more than mere surmise to go upon in discussing the possibility of the existence of very considerable land-areas in the Pacific which must have undergone submergence only a few centuries ago. The logs of the navigators of the seventeenth century contain more than one allusion to Pacific land-masses of large extent, now no longer visible. In his *Description of the Isthmus of Darien*, published at London in 1688, Wafer describes how, when sailing in the ship *The Bachelor's Delight*, in lat. 27° 20′ south, the latitude of Easter Island, " to the westward, about twelve leagues by judgment we saw a range of high land which we took to be islands. . . . This land seemed to reach about fourteen or fifteen leagues in a range, and there came thence great flocks of fowls." *The Bachelor's Delight* was commanded by John Davis, a Dutchman in spite of his English name, and had just experienced a severe submarine shock, which proved to be the earthquake of Callao of 1687.

Thirty-five years later the Dutch Admiral Ruggewein sailed along the same latitude in search of " Davis Land," but could not locate it or discover any signs of it. But, to compensate for his disappointment, he discovered Easter Island on Easter Day. In 1771 Gonzalez, a Spanish navigator, likewise sailed in search of Davis Land, and, like his predecessor, came upon Easter Island. This island resembles not at all the land which Davis and Wafer saw, as Beechy, who visited the island in 1825, declares, so that it is positively certain that an island or archipelago of considerable extent foundered in this area of the Pacific at some time between 1687 and 1722.

But there was evidence forthcoming long before the date of Davis's discovery that land had vanished in this region. Juan Fernandez, in 1576, went out of his course when sailing between Callao and Valparaiso, and encountered what he believed to be the coast of that great southern continent which so many of the seamen of his day dreamed of. He saw " the mouths of very large rivers . . . and people so white and so well clad and in everything different from those of Chile and Peru," that he was amazed. His ship was small and ill-found, and he resolved to return, meanwhile keeping what he had seen secret. But he died without fulfilling his purpose. As late as 1909 the ship *Guinevere* reported a reef in about 95 long. east and 85 lat. south, which may be the remains of the land Fernandez saw.

There are several well-authenticated instances of the entire submergence of islands in the Pacific during last century. In 1886 the island of Tuanaki, to the south of the Cook group, disappeared. Two natives of the Mangaian group had landed there and remained upon it for some time, and reported to the missionaries at Mangaia that its people were anxious to embrace Christianity. The missionary schooner was dispatched to the island under the guidance of these native sailors, " but it never found the island, and no one has seen it since, although up till recently there was at least one native living in Rarotonga who had lived in it and one who had visited it. Had the two Mangaians not landed on it and reported it to the missionaries, would anyone ever have known of the submergence of it and its people ? There might have been a vague rumour, easily believed and easily discounted, and that would have been all the record," remarks Professor Brown.

The traditions of Easter Island maintain that it was once the hub or centre of a large, scattered archipelago. The culture hero, Hotu Matua, was forced to land on its shores, says legend, because of the submergence of his own island, Marae Ronga, to the west, where " the sea came up and drowned all the people." There are numerous reefs round Sala-y-Gomez, a rocky islet about three hundred miles east of Easter Island, and the natives tell how this islet was once a large archipelago, of which a certain Makemake was the prince. When Hotu Matua came to his death-day he ascended a volcano in Easter Island and looked out towards the west, calling to the spirits who hovered over his submerged home. The legends of Easter Island are full of reminiscences of other neighbouring islands now drowned beneath the surface of the Pacific. The immense dry-stone monuments of Easter Island, says Professor Brown, could not have been raised by an insular people, but must have taxed the capacity of a great contiguous archipelagic empire, maintaining thousands of people.

But other mysterious cyclopean ruins besides those of Easter Island are to be encountered in the widely-scattered archipelagoes of the Pacific, and equally important are the theories of submergence associated with them. By far the most important and perplexing of these sites is that at Ponape in the Caroline Islands, lying between the Equator and the eleventh north parallel, some 2300 miles from the coast of Japan. The deserted city of Metalanim, the ruins of which cover 11 square miles, stands on the south-eastern shore of Ponape. The site is covered by massive walls, stupendous earthwarks and great temples, intersected by miles of artificial waterways, from which circumstance it has received the name of " The Venice of the Pacific," as we shall see when the course of the argument arrives at its discussion.

At a conservative estimate tens of thousands of labourers must have been engaged in the work of building construction at Metalanim. The island at its best could never have supported more than twenty thousand people, and of these not more than one-fifth would be able-bodied men, therefore it is only reasonable to suppose that labour must have been recruited from outside areas. Professor Macmillan Brown suggests as a solution to this difficulty that the Caroline archipelago is the remains of a vast island-empire, the greater part of which subsided beneath the waves of the Pacific centuries ago. Yet within a radius of 1500 miles from this as a centre there are not more than fifty thousand people to-day.

A thousand miles to the west of Ponape, Professor Brown found on the little coral island of Oleai, with six hundred inhabitants, a written script still in use, quite unlike any in the world. It is still used by the chief of the island, and was formerly employed on Faraulep, an islet about 100 miles to the north-east. On the east coast of the island of Yap, about 500 miles west of Oleai, there is a village called Gatsepar, the chief of which still levies tribute annually on islands hundreds of miles away. When Professor Brown asked the natives who brought the tribute

THE OUTER WALL OF NANTAUACH, METALANIM, AT PONAPE

why they continued to do so, they replied that if they neglected this duty the chief of Gatsepar would shake their island with his earthquakes and the sea with his tempests. This would seem to imply, thinks Professor Brown, that the chief's ancestors built " an empire to the east of Yap, and when some intermediate islands had gone down, the others continued still to look to the ruler in the west as the holder of all power, natural and supernatural."

Is there any evidence of similar submersion of organized archipelagoes farther east? Polynesia covers a greater space than most of the larger empires of the world have covered, and is occupied by a people more homogeneous in physique, culture and language than the people of any one of the great empires. In handicraft, social and political organization and religious belief they retain the remains of a very high type of civilization, and it is obvious that they have been segregated from other races for a space of time so prolonged that an indelible and easily distinguishable mark has been set upon them. " We can scarcely avoid the conclusion," says Professor Brown, " that they have lived unitedly under one government and under one social system for a long period : and that the slow submergence of their fatherland has driven them off, migration after migration, to seek other lands to dwell upon, each marked by some new habitat, into which they were driven by the gradual narrowing of their cultivable area. . . . All the indications point to an empire in the east Central Pacific having gone down."

It is thus sufficiently obvious that a very striking body of proof for the former existence of continental conditions in the Pacific can be appealed to, over and above the mere geological testimony, and it is well that those who are disposed to rely upon the results of geological research alone should bear this in mind.

The proofs to be adduced in this volume of the former existence of Pacific continents supporting a very ancient culture or cultures are in many cases of equal cogency with those already cited, and a much larger body of analogical evidence has further been drawn upon to assist the general thesis. But sufficient evidence has, I believe, been presented in this introductory chapter to show that we are not dealing with matter of phantasy or the dreams of imagination, but with a very actual and ponderable theory indeed.

CHAPTER II

THE ARGUMENT FROM ARCHÆOLOGY

SCATTERED over the surface of the Pacific are the ruins of monuments the origins of which have been, since their discovery by Europeans, a subject of considerable perplexity to archæologists. Some of these can certainly be referred to the activities of builders of the Polynesian race, to Melanesians and to other peoples presently resident in the Pacific area, and it is obvious that no very great length of time has elapsed since their construction. With such this inquiry has little to do. But other ruins and remains exist which cannot be referred to the races of the Pacific as we presently know them, or even to their ancestors. It is with these ruins, the remains of an older people, with which we are primarily concerned here.

Agreeing with authorities of weight that the land in the Pacific area has been subsiding for countless centuries, and that it continues to do so, the writer is compelled to the opinion that the older vestige of a Lemurian civilization must naturally be submerged at a very considerable oceanic depth. As the continental mass or masses gradually sank, so would their inhabitants be forced to build at an ever-increasing altitude, until at last no space was left them except those mountain-peaks which now compose the insular clusters of their several archipelagoes.

But evidence is not lacking that older forms of construction and more early types of artifact than the Polynesian are to be discovered practically over the entire length and breadth of the Pacific basin. It has, for example, been established that certain islands of the Hawaiian group were inhabited before their volcanoes had ceased to be active and the land had assumed its present form. The legends of this archipelago, as we shall find later, infer a native belief that its Leeward group was inhabited before its volcanoes became extinct.

When in 1822 the first wells were dug at Honolulu, excavation was carried through some eight or ten feet of surface loam and underlying volcanic sand, when a coral bed of some eight feet in thickness was encountered and cut through, under which fresh water was reached. In this coral formation were found embedded a human skull and other osseous remains. In 1858 when the harbour of Honolulu was dredged, under a heavy deposit of mud and sand, a pan of coral rock was struck which it was found necessary to remove. The thickness of this averaged about two feet and beneath it was a deep layer of black volcanic sand, embedded in which was found the pointed end of an ancient spear and a worked stone. A year later, at Molakai, a human skull was discovered in a stratum of volcanic mud in such circumstances that its great age was obvious.

Guppy states that in the island of San Cristoval in the Solomon group, stone implements of Old Stone Age types are frequently dug up which bear no relation to Polynesian workmanship, and it is known that an ancient trade in such implements, especially those formed from jade or obsidian, was at one time carried on in New Zealand and New Caledonia. Professor Seligman says that fragments of worked obsidian have been found wherever search has been made in the south-eastern portion of British New Guinea, but that this substance is not now made use of by the natives. But the prehistoric archæology of Oceania is not as yet sufficiently advanced to permit of more than general statement concerning its facts. There is, however, sufficient evidence in existence to demonstrate that Oceania was certainly inhabited in Neolithic times, using the term in its European sense, that is to say at a period before the coming of the Polynesian and Melanesian races.

The stone monuments of Polynesia, at least those of the more archaic type, are, as the late W. H. R. Rivers wrote, " quite beyond the present powers and implements of the people, and in most cases the inhabitants do not know when

THE ARGUMENT FROM ARCHÆOLOGY

or by whom these objects were made." The same may be said regarding the great stone terraces and hewn stone statues of Easter Island, that isolated refuge of man in the far eastern Pacific, whose massive stone houses disposed in rows, great platforms from 200 to 800 feet in length and monolithic images, some of which are as much as 30 feet high, bespeak a most advanced type of method in mason-work. The platforms on which these statues were placed resemble the bases of pyramids, and huge pyramids of stone are still to be found on the desert plains of Hawaii, 7000 *feet above the sea*. In Neckar Island, 450 miles distant from Honolulu, stone idols and stone walls are to be found, and the Marquesas group is peculiarly rich in stone constructions resembling those of Easter Island. The foundations of temples have been discovered in Pitcairn Island, and the existence of rude statues at Raivaivai in the Austral group, has puzzled travellers because of the fact that in none of the surrounding islands does any trace of masonry exist.

Tahiti has also its pyramids, or *maraes*, that of Opoa in Raiatea composing a pyramid which measures at the base 267 feet by 67 feet and at the top 250 feet by 8 feet. It is partly faced with hewn stone which has been finished with edged tools. On Penrhyn Island is a megalithic stone circle, while in Samoa the monument of Fale-o-le-Fe'e constitutes a mystery which, says Stair, still remains unsolved. Fiji likewise possesses important megalithic monuments and in the island of Rotumah stone tombs exist, so ponderable in their masses that archæologists are at a loss to comprehend by what means they were got into place. The fact that some of these are in the form of dolmens is eloquent of their very ancient origin. The remains of pyramidal structures and irrigated terraces are also to be found in Fiji.

The prehistory of New Zealand is important to the general consideration of Pacific archæology, for its Maori settlers found on their arrival some thirty generations ago that the islands were already inhabited by an older race, the Moriori, of a physical type entirely different from themselves. These people built irrigation terraces, hill-forts, and stone-wall refuges, the vestiges of which remain and which have no resemblance whatever to Polynesian work. They were also notable artists, particularly as regards carving, both in wood and stone. In the district of Pelorus Sound are to be seen the traces of an old agricultural population which must have dwelt there in considerable numbers. These people were also terrace builders, facing their embankments with stone, so that they had the appearance of great staircases. The territory in which they formerly lived is now, for the most part, covered by forest in which their cave-dwellings, cut out of the solid rock, are frequently discovered. At the period of the arrival of Captain Cook their ancient plantations had been strewn with gravel brought from the beaches and there was little ostensible to reveal their former presence in the area.

Moreover, many strange inscriptions testifying to their occupation are still to be observed at Takiroa, Pareora and elsewhere. J. Van Haast, so long ago as 1879, indicated the interest of these inscriptions and referred them to " a far higher civilization than the Maori ever reached." The general appearance, both of their artifacts and their larger constructions, makes it clear that their craftsmanship had relations with that of the megalithic builders of the Polynesian area, and that these latter were not Polynesians is obvious enough from a comparison of Polynesian work with their own.

In New Zealand, too, the ancient drainage system recently discovered in the Awanui swamp is worthy of notice. These drains are 5 feet wide by 5 feet deep and were dug, thinks Macmillan Brown, at a time when the peninsula north of Auckland was still an island, the Manukau Harbour having a straits connection with the Hauraki Gulf, so that the peoples of the far north would be shut in.

" One thing we may be certain of," he writes, " is that those miles of drains were not dug without huge supplies of labour to draw upon, nor without an organized government that could plan extensive schemes for the relief of over-population and could command the armies of labour that were needed for the achievement of such schemes.

THE ARGUMENT FROM ARCHÆOLOGY

The great fortified *pas* found all over both North and South Islands indicate the same state of affairs. Their huge trenches and earthworks, that remind us of the entrenched methods and engineering of the war just finished, meant armies of toilers highly organized by efficient command. The cyclopean *maraes* of the Marquesas, Society Islands and Rarotonga, and the great stone cities of refuge, and the huge stone-enclosed fishponds of the Hawaiian group, have the same implication."

In the neighbourhood of these drains a curious carved lintel was discovered, which is not of Maori work, and affords evidence of a large and flourishing population having a leisured class. Says Professor Brown:

" It is to be classed by itself, not merely for the spearhead scroll of its open-work carving and its saurian finials, but for the grotesque figure that with outstretched hands holds the two limbs of the carving in place and forms its centre and bond. The stern-piece is especially a masterpiece of lace-like tracery that has no compeer for refinement of outline, except in the rood-screens of mediæval cathedrals in Europe or the ivory carved fans of Canton. Its safety from fracture is generally secured by making the pinnæ of the *pitau*, or fern-frond, the solid bonds between the fragile curves of the spirals. But so much more delicate is the tracery of the stern-piece that the artist has to give a solid backbone to it by two tusk-like nuclei that curve through three-fourths of its length and are usually gripped near the point by an arm protruding from above."

The finials of this lintel represent crocodiles' heads. The rock and cave-paintings found in the South Island of New Zealand also exhibit evidences of a non-Maori race.

Entering the area of Melanesia, comprising the huge island of New Guinea, together with all the islands and archipelagoes extending from it to the east and south-east as far as Fiji and New Caledonia, we also find many vestiges of stone monuments relating to an ancient population. In New Caledonia are to be found large ramparts of stone, dolmens, carved symbols and other evidences of ancient occupation, of the origin of which the present native population know nothing. In the New Hebrides, however, dolmens are still in use for sacrificial purposes and Santa Maria in the Banks Islands is covered with numerous stone walls built of large blocks of basalt. Rivers believed the stone-work of Melanesia to be very ancient, and thought that the earth-mounds of Santa Maria had been raised by a people whose origin was almost lost in antiquity. Even in New Guinea, at present one of the most backward areas in the world, discoveries have been made of fragments of pottery and stone and obsidian implements which differ entirely in type from those used by the the present inhabitants. Stone circles are also found in New Guinea, as well as stone carvings of birds and other smaller objects. Irrigation terraces are to be encountered there, as well as in the Solomons and the New Hebrides, and in many cases these are still made use of for the growing of taro.

But it is when we come to that part of Oceania known as Micronesia, comprising the area north of Melanesia and east of the 180th meridian of east longitude, that we find perhaps the most surprising evidences of the former presence of an ancient population. Especially is this the case as regards the Caroline Islands, lying between the Equator and the eleventh north parallel, some 2300 miles from the coast of Japan. It is strange indeed to find in this remote and isolated part of the world the remains of gigantic monuments and cities eloquent of a populous past. In the Ladrone Islands are still to be seen the remains of pyramids of slender construction which are known to the natives as the "Houses of the Ancients," and which appear to have been built for burial purposes. Yet much more amazing is the wealth of antiquity discovered in the island of Yap in the Carolines, which is littered with the relics of a vanished civilization, embankments and terraces, roads paved with regular stone blocks and large council-houses with high gables and lofty carved pillars.

But by far the most important and perplexing of these sites is that at Ponape in the Carolines. The Caroline group lies between the equator and the eleventh north parallel, some 2300 miles from the coast of Japan, which occupied the islands shortly after the outbreak of war in 1914.

The deserted city of Metalanim, the ruins of which cover eleven square miles, stands on the south-eastern shore of Ponape. The site is covered by massive walls, stupendous earthworks, and great temples, intersected by miles of artificial waterways, from which circumstance it has received the name of " The Venice of the Pacific."

The entire island of Ponape is littered with huge basaltic blocks which must have been brought by raft from a distance of 80 miles, and from similar blocks have been built the massive walls of the harbour and the embankments of the winding canals, many of which are from 80 to 100 feet in breadth. The outer cincture which surrounds the city is partially submerged, and this has given rise to the idea that the land on which Metalanim was built has subsided in later times. But this seems improbable, as the colossal breastworks which line the canals are all above low tide, and it is plain that the buildings have been erected on artificial islands constructed on the foundation of the natural coral reef. It is evident that the city was built on the eastern coast of the island, so that if it were attacked on the land side escape could readily be effected by sea, and it is equally plain that the waterways were constructed to enable rafts laden with stone to be brought close up to the artificial islands on which the larger buildings were raised.

The city of Metalanim was enclosed on one side by the land and on its maritime side by three extensive breakwaters of basalt, the whole occupying an almost rectangular area. At the north-west corner a sea-gate gave entrance to vessels and rafts of considerable dimensions, and this was carefully guarded by a large breakwater consisting of immense courses of the basalt characteristic of the site. The water-front to the east is faced with a terrace built of massive blocks about 7 feet in width, above which frowns the vast retaining wall of the enclosure of Nan Tanach, " the Place of Lofty Walls," the remains of the great gateway of which still tower to the height of about 80 feet. A colossal staircase leads to a courtyard littered with fragments of fallen pillars which encircle a second terraced enclosure with a projecting frieze or cornice. The dimensions of the outer enclosure are about 185 by 115 feet, and the thickness of its walls measures about 15 feet. Within the inner enclosure lies the great central vault or " treasure-chamber " of a legendary dynasty known to local tradition as the Chan-te-leur, or " Kings of the Sun."

The nature of the building material at the disposal of the ancient masons who raised Metalanim exhibits the difficulty presented by the erection of large edifices on an artificial foundation. The immense basaltic crystals they employed must have been almost unworkable with the primitive tools at their disposal, and as the megalithic masses dealt with were usually five-, six-, and eight-sided, the structures of which they are a part frequently present a " bristling " appearance. Some of the walls and platforms are only faced with these huge crystals, the space between being filled with small coral.

Nan Tanach, the hub of the city, though situated in the north-east in a corner of the breakwater, seems to have been the nucleus whence the numerous canals radiated throughout the whole ghostly length of the place. It is surmised that the great blocks of which it is built were put in position by means of an inclined plane—a slope of tree trunks greased with coconut oil. The process of hoisting may have been assisted by the use of ropes made of green hibiscus bark and levers of hardwood.

Excavation of the tombs discovered on the site has revealed the presence of axes formed from shells, beads made from shells rubbed down, resembling the wampum or shell-money of the American Indians, and wristlets and other ornaments made of the same material. The axes were almost certainly of a ceremonial character and could scarcely have been employed for dressing wood or stone. In front of the great staircase leading up to the central courtyard of Nan Tanach and its altar-tomb are immense basaltic crystals placed on end, traditionally assigned to the making of the Polynesian beverage known as kava.

It is surpassingly difficult to hazard a guess as to the

THE ARGUMENT FROM ARCHÆOLOGY 85

racial identity of the builders of Metalanim. A survey of the evidence would not seem to point to a Polynesian people as its founders and architects. In any case it is obvious that the Caroline Islands at the period of the occupation of this site must have supported a very much larger population than they do at the present time.

Judging from four skulls found on the site, Christian and Kubary believed Metalanim to have been founded by a negroid race. But conjectures based on so limited a collection of crania cannot be regarded as satisfactory. A Polynesian origin might seem to be indicated not only by the presence of the great kava vessels already alluded to, but by certain customs and traditions which still flourish among the native population. The hereditary chieftainships are held by paternal descent, and that the Polynesians were acquainted with megalithic architecture is witnessed to by their remains in Apia, Tonga, and the Society Islands. It seems, therefore, the most simple solution of the problem to ascribe the building of Metalanim to a people of Polynesian stock. But there are features in the architecture of the city which render this view extremely difficult of acceptance. The Polynesian architect had a tendency to ignore walls and to confine his whole attention to a roof supported by pillars. The solidity of the walls at Metalanim would lead us to infer that they were erected by someone acquainted with the principles of a much earlier architecture.

The mystery of Metalanim was certainly not rendered any clearer by the description of it by Dr. Hambruch of Hamburg, who visited it in 1908–10. He believes the buildings to be little more than 200 to 250 years old, and that their erection was ended by the coming of American missionaries in the nineteenth century, whose presence was held to have defiled the sacred site. So much information was tendered him by a local chief. But manifestly it would have been impossible for the sparse population then inhabiting Ponape to have raised such vast structures, which, indeed, are fulfilled of every sign of antiquity.

Nor do the large measurements of the skulls or fragments

thereof fit in with the theory of a Negrito population which at that late period occupied Ponape. The local legends, too, are averse from the conclusions of the writers alluded to. They tell of two divine men, Olochipa and Olochepa, who brought the stones of the ruins from the northern part of the island " by magic," making them " fly through the air." These stones are larger than any found at Tiahuanaco, or other Incan Peruvian sites. Some of them must be 80 tons in weight and occupy places in walls more than 80 feet high. Leaving aside altogether any explanation of how they were put in place by a possible scanty Negrito population, it is obvious that such a vast labour could only have been undertaken by a power backed by large imperial resources and having a population of many millions. The nearest continental land-mass, New Guinea, is at present 1500 miles distant, and it is out of the question that Metalanim was built by immigrants from that quarter. These, the world's most titanic stones, stand as mighty witnesses of an equally mighty empire of the ancient past.

If Metalanim was built by Polynesians, as Professor Macmillan Brown alleges, it must have been so at a most early date, and indeed his idea that it was rests almost solely on his theory that the Polynesians entered the Pacific at a primeval period. His ancillary arguments that Polynesian kava vessels, the custom of father-right and building in stone are also found in Ponape do not assist the general argument very greatly. The Polynesian custom of kava-making may have been an inheritance from an older race. Indeed it has no associations with any of the continental mainlands which border upon the Pacific, and is clearly indigenous to that area. Father-right is not a solely Polynesian custom and would necessarily be the ruling ideal in an ancient civilization which had emerged from barbarism. And where else do we find in Polynesia megalithic structures of which absolute proof exists that they were built by Polynesian hands, save those at Afia and Tonga ?

Rapa ? Easter Island ? The self-same difficulty applies to these, and Professor Brown is forced to admit a non-

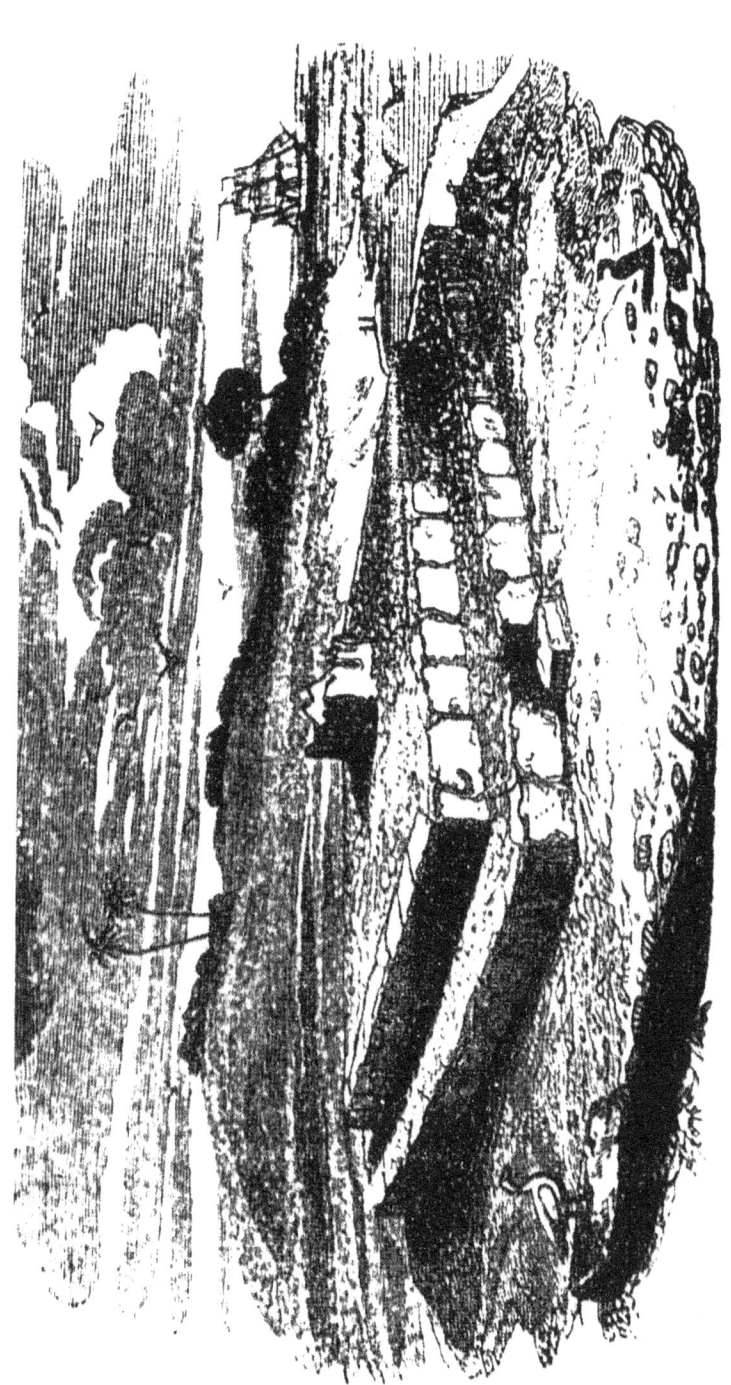

THE PYRAMIDAL STRUCTURES OF MALDEN ISLAND AS THEY WERE IN 1825
From *Byron's Voyage*.

THE ARGUMENT FROM ARCHÆOLOGY

Polynesian element in the erection of Metalanim. This he attributes to Asiatic influence. Polynesian architecture takes no account of walls, and these, Professor Brown argues, are Asiatic. They must be of prehistoric Japanese origin, he thinks, as Japanese bronzes have been found deep in the coral below the forest in the Mariannes and a Mongolian element is visible in the Ponape face, though a " Caucasian " type is also to be found. But elsewhere, he says: " Oceanic warriors came in their canoes from Polynesia and carved out a great empire in Micronesia that has now sunk under the waves ... and then Japanese architects gave them the idea of solid walls and water and streets such as they had already seen on the coast of the sea of Japan." With all due regard to an interesting if somewhat elaborate theory, it appears simpler to believe in the erection of Metalanim by a people much more archaic, the " Lemurians," especially as Professor Brown himself lays stress on the extreme antiquity of the site.

Malden Island, north-east of Manihiki, near the Cook Islands, is situated in an area where considerable subsidence is known to have taken place. It contains many remains of temples, among others what has been described as a parallelogram of coral stones, with a pillar erected in the middle of a single stone, seven feet high. At least forty such buildings occur on the island, showing that it was a sacred region and that the neighbouring land from which its devotees came must have disappeared, for the inhabitants of such a comparatively small island could surely have had little use for shrines so numerous.

Among other remains it contains a truncated pyramid with a lower terrace, resembling those of Tonga, save that this is not so carefully chiselled. It is 50 feet long and 25 feet broad and some of its characteristics are comparable with those of the masonry of Metalanim, showing that its architects must have belonged to the same school. The work could not have been accomplished without drawing upon a considerable reservoir of wealth and labour, as in the case of the ruins on Ponape. Furthermore, it has been found that the paved roads leading from the pyramid-temples stretched in the direction of the sea and were covered with coral debris, so that the level of the sea must have changed since these roads were made.

The place is incapable of supporting human life, there is no fresh water, and the coconut trees it once contained must quickly have perished without yielding their produce. The people who built the temples which required so much labour could not have existed on the island in its present foodless state. In all likelihood they inhabited archipelagoes within easy reach of it which have since been submerged.

The small island of Raivavai, or Vavitao, is the most southerly of the Austral group, which is between three and four hundred miles to the south of the Society group. This island, or rather islet, contains great stone statues and other ruins which must have required an organization of considerable power with a large population behind it to erect. In the other islands of the group there is no indication whatever of rough stone monuments of the kind.

Moerenhout, a French merchant, who visited the island about a hundred years ago, says that it is one of those where are to be found such " singular monuments " as in Pitcairn or Tubuai, the shrines of the Polynesian gods. The figures are well executed, the ears are large and pierced, and the lower parts of the bodies deformed and monstrous. They were, he thinks, statues of inferior divinities or great men, or had been erected to " perpetuate the memory of the most extraordinary phenomena, of the most terrible catastrophes known in the land, *as the destruction of the mainland.*"[1]

Now certain such statues are to be found in Easter Island and are known, as Professor Macmillan Brown and Mrs. Scoresby Routledge practically prove, to have been intended as guardians of the land against the sea, magical presences whose office it was to act as a preventive to oceanic encroachment and further submergence.

Two of the statues at Raivavai represent a round-headed type with long ears, flattened noses, and deep-sunk eyes. The legs bear a strong resemblance to those of many of the Maya statues of Central America in their

[1] Italics mine. L.S.

THE ARGUMENT FROM ARCHÆOLOGY 89

shape, the foot-gear seems to be the same, and in this they resemble the Easter Island statues not at all. Nor do they resemble facially the people of the Austral Islands.

There is no great stone sculpture, as apart from architecture, to be found between these islands and the Coast of Asia. Whence did their makers come ? The odd thing is that these statues once evidently stood in a great stone *marae* or temple known as Atorani, or " Built to the Heavens." They are carved out of volcanic tufa, are respectively about 12 and 9 feet high and must be each 15 to 20 tons in weight.

In the Island of Hivaoa, in the Marquesas group, are stone images also wholly unlike the present native type, with flattened cylindrical skulls, capacious mouths and stout legs, as in Raivavai. There are also to be found there remains of large pyramidal temples and rectangular altars of great stones ornamented with carved images near the remains, wellnigh indistinct, of processional avenues, obviously of great age. Three avenues flanked by great stone seats lead to a throne and sacrificial altar. It is difficult to understand how the people of so small an island could have quarried and transported stones so huge, some of which are many tons in weight.

Far to the east in the Pacific rises the lone island known as Easter Island, regarding which Professor Macmillan Brown and others have of recent years afforded the necessary data for a thorough comprehension. This relatively small island is thickly covered with the memorials of a forgotten race, which it must have taken the labour of tens of thousands of men working over many years to construct. Many of the burial platforms consist of scores of immense stones ranging in weight from two to twenty tons, all shaped and tooled in the hardest basalt. " No architect of the historical civilizations," says Professor Brown, " has ever reached a conception so magnificent for immortalizing the past." This civilization, he believes, was brought to an end by catastrophe, probably by the submergence of a vast empire, the inhabitants of which found a refuge in Easter Island. But the most striking thing in the island is the existence of numbers of huge statues, or of torsos of human heads and shoulders, standing on its barren moorlands. These were formerly capped by huge hats of red stone and were probably images of dead chiefs and princes. Some are as many as 70 feet high and depict a type still to be found in Easter Island. Professor Brown believes them to be the images of a race of conquerors and the 50 or 60 tons of conglomerate out of which some of them have been fashioned must have been enormously difficult to place in shape without mishap, so brittle is it.

The burial platforms which surround the island are, on the other hand, of the hardest basalt. The legend of Hotu Matua casts some light upon the secret of Easter Island. This culture-hero, when the empire of which he was a chief was submerged, was told by his king of the existence of Easter Island, and with his followers set out to discover it. Arriving there in their canoes, Hotu Matua at once commenced the organization of his society. The native name of Easter Island implies " navel " or " centre " of the Universe, and it is probable that at one period it was the nucleus of a large archipelago. It is equally likely that Hotu Matua came from a similar archipelago 300 miles to the east, long since submerged.

Professor Macmillan Brown tells how he personally found numerous signs of the sudden cessation of work on the vast statues, " as if a tremendous blast of poison-gas had asphyxiated all the workmen." Tools lie about as if they had been thrown away on a sudden impulse and some of the great torsos are in an incomplete state. It would seem as if catastrophe had visited the island without warning.

The manner in which these statues were conveyed over stony and uneven surfaces for a distance of twelve or fifteen miles presents a problem of extraordinary complexity. The probability is that the deep grooves or runs which still appear on every slope were made use of in this connection and that the statues were placed on large toboggans in the shape of cradles or canoes on two keels and hauled over these runways. There is a tradition in the island of the former existence of an aerial gravitational tramway from the top of an eminence down to a great

PICTURE OF STATUES AND NATIVES FROM *THE VOYAGE OF LA PEROUSE*

platform nearly a mile off, on the coast, and another from the same height reaching to a spot nearly two miles distant. On the ridge of the height are circular holes drilled deep in the rock, and into these, says tradition, were wedged high circular beams from the top of which huge ropes were stretched. By means of these the statues on their sledges were passed by gravitation to the site where they were to be erected. The ropes were oiled, to prevent friction, by the juice of yams, but where the wood was found to construct the beams and where the fibre was procured to make the hawsers in an island which is practically without timber, presents a further puzzle—which can surely be solved only by the supposition that the necessary material was conveyed from a continental afforested region not very far distant.

Whence, asks Professor Brown, did the luxury come that is implied in the monuments? There are usually good local reasons for the existence of civilized development. Thus Egypt owes everything to the rich deposits of the Nile and Assyria to the irrigational possibilities of its vast rivers. But Easter Island, situated a thousand miles even from the merest speck of land, is not only without local advantages, but is separated by thousands of leagues from the ancient empires of America, and is far out of all commercial tracks. Its canoes never venture for more than a mile of two from land, and how without commerce, and all the organization it implies, could sculpture and architecture on such a large scale become possible?

The island contains no fresh water except in the craters and its very vegetation has a hard struggle for existence. Tradition says that Hotu Matua, its pioneer, took a hundred and twenty days to reach it, and that his home was situated in a land so hot that in summer vegetation was shrivelled up by the heat. There is also reason to believe that Easter Island was formerly ringed round by an archipelago and it may be that Sala-y-Gomez, a rocky islet 800 miles to the east of Easter Island, is the remains of that Davis Land discovered by John Davis, the Dutch captain, in 1687, and which has since disappeared. It is environed by reefs and the sea in its vicinity is comparatively shallow. The natives of Easter Island say that their great god, Makemake, was its Prince. It was evidently from another such archipelago towards the east that Hotu Matua came. Indeed the traditions of Easter Island are replete with legends of other islands and archipelagoes not very far distant from their home. One of these to the west was spoken of as " a land of temples," and that it was part of an ancient continent, upon which large Cyclopean buildings had been erected, seems a good deal more than probable.

As we have seen, there are indications of at least three vanished empires in the north-west Pacific alone, that which had Ponape as its centre, that area a thousand miles to the west of it, where the little coral isle of Oleai still stands, and that 500 miles still farther west, which probably had the island of Yap for its nucleus. Toward the east evidences of sunken archipelagoes or land-masses are also to be encountered, of which Easter Island appears as one of the least, though by no means the least important.

Professor Macmillan Brown believes that when the archipelago which surrounded Easter Island was submerged it went down as an imperial unity. Hotu Matua, the culture-hero of Easter Island, he thinks we must assume, was either ruler of a large circle of archipelagoes or subordinate ruler of the western alone, and had journeyed to the greater land in the east to report on affairs in his own particular region. That he was preparing for an attack by certain enemies on his Easter Island retreat Professor Brown thinks possible. Who were those enemies, and where in the waste of ocean did they dwell ? The island, judging from the mass of stone-work it contains, must have housed thousands of toilers, whom it certainly did not maintain by its products. Its food-supply must have come from elsewhere and doubtless " it was the policy of the masters to make the labourers wholly dependent on them for their sustenance." The cessation of the food-supply would certainly precipitate revolution among the thousands of artificers on the island, cannibalism followed, and was, of course, accompanied by a chaotic condition. The small number of women

THE ARGUMENT FROM ARCHÆOLOGY 43

brought by the labouring colony was the cause of a sudden collapse in the numbers of the population. In the event, a handful of people found themselves on an almost barren islet, thousands of miles from anywhere, and wretchedly subsisting on rats and a poor and variable fish supply.

Professor Brown believes that Hotu Matua's host of artisans were of Marquesan and Maori stock. The surviving population, he thinks, gives that impression. But that the entire Easter Island art and polity is not of Polynesian origin but is rather a survival from a much older civilization I hope to demonstrate at a later stage when the whole body of proof is a little more apparent to the reader. He makes it clear that fleets of large vessels were a necessity for the carriage of supplies to Easter Island with its hordes of workmen. Hotu Matua established order after the isolation of the island through the instrumentality of taboo, which by its mysterious decrees restrained the almost foodless workers from the extremes of anarchy. The *rongo-rongo*, or collection of traditions brought by him from the east, were, as we shall see, chronicled in a mysterious script which still exists, but which none can now precisely decipher. There was no need for such a script on an isolated island which one could traverse in a few hours. It was obviously intended in the first place to serve the needs of administrative communication over extensive areas, as did the quipus or knotted string records of the Peruvian Incas.

Let us summarise the foregoing evidence and see if it reveals any conclusions of value regarding the presence of a race in the Pacific area who may have inhabited its ancient continental regions. Let me repeat that we are not here concerned with Polynesian or Melanesian remains, or the traces of peoples of comparatively recent immigration into Oceania, but with those which will assist the theory of the presence there of a much earlier stock.

It must, of course, be obvious that if a continental mass sinks, most of its architecture sinks with it. We cannot expect to find its temples and palaces on the mountain-tops which still rise above the sea, save in certain rare instances.

We find that the Oceanic area was certainly inhabited in the Old and New Stone Ages, as the discoveries at Honolulu, San Cristoval, New Zealand, New Guinea and many other centres prove.

W. H. R. Rivers, a sound authority, believed the more archaic monuments of Polynesia to be " quite beyond the present powers and implements of the people," and in most cases of unknown origin to them.

The existence of rude statues in the Austral group has puzzled travellers because no trace of masonry exists in the surrounding islands.

In many of the archipelagoes, pyramids, dolmens and stone circles which were not the work of Polynesians have been found. Some of these, to observers like Stair, " constitute a mystery."

The Maori settlers of New Zealand found an older race in the islands, the Moriori, of a physical type quite different from themselves, who built forts and terraces which bear no resemblance to Polynesian work.

Van Haast testifies that their inscriptions reveal the evidence of " a far higher civilization than the Maori ever reached." Their work had a relationship with that of the archaic masons of the present Polynesian area, who were not of Polynesian stock.

In Melanesia many vestiges of stone monuments relating to an ancient population are to be found, of the origin of which the present population is ignorant. Rivers believed the masonry of Melanesia to be very ancient, and thought that the earth-mounds of Santa Maria had been raised by a people whose origin was " lost in antiquity."

In Micronesia are to be discovered the most surprising evidences of a population of great antiquity. In the Ladrone Islands are the remains of pyramids known to the natives as the " Houses of the Ancients." The island of Yap is littered with the relics of a vanished civilization.

The deserted city of Metalanim, in Ponape, the ruins of which cover eleven square miles, must have been built from materials brought by sea. A portion of it is partially submerged. The dynasty which ruled it is now " legendary." It must have supported a large population, as tens

THE ARGUMENT FROM ARCHÆOLOGY

of thousands of workers must have been employed in its construction. Yet the island, as it is at present, could never have supported more than 20,000 people. It is probably the remains of a vast island empire, the greater part of which has subsided beneath the waves of the Pacific.

Much the same problem is offered by Easter Island, which was, thinks Professor Macmillan Brown, a place of refuge for the survivors of a great continental catastrophe. It may have been the nucleus of a large archipelago. Its monuments reveal signs of the sudden cessation of work, and it would seem that catastrophe visited the island without warning. The timber employed in this woodless island must have been brought from a continental afforested region not far distant.

The art and organization of Easter Island could not have been developed without commerce, and the island is at present far from the track of commerce. It contains no fresh water except in the craters.

Sala-y-Gomez, a rocky islet 800 miles to the east, may be the remains of that Davis Land discovered in 1687, and which has since disappeared. The traditions of Easter Island are replete with legends of other islands and archipelagoes not very far distant from their home.

There are thus indications of at least three vanished empires in the north-west Pacific alone, their probable nuclei being on Ponape, Oleai and Yap. Easter Island furnishes another example of a place of refuge from similar possible subsidence. Professor Brown believes that the archipelago which surrounded it went down as " an imperial unity." Hotu Matua, its culture-hero, he thinks, was either its subordinate ruler or King of a much larger circle of archipelagoes. The mysterious script of Easter Island was assuredly invented to facilitate communication over extensive areas.

From these collected facts, what outstanding results do we glean ?

(1) We find that Oceania was inhabited in the Old and New Stone Ages before peoples of Polynesian and Melanesian race entered it ; that is, at a period when, according to geologists of eminence (as we shall see), continental

conditions were still prevalent. In many cases finds of prehistoric remains have been discovered in areas where subsidence has taken place, either in the mass still represented by an insular remnant, or in an area near at hand.

(2) The archaic monuments of Polynesia and Melanesia have been classed by sound authorities as beyond the powers of the Polynesian and Melanesian races.

(3) Isolated structures and sculptures are found in certain islands, no trace of masonry existing in the neighbouring isles. This seems highly suggestive of the ancient erection of sacred enclosures on elevated sites which have since subsided so much as to appear as mere islands.

(4) The conditions on Yap, Ponape and Oleai are particularly eloquent of the erection of buildings and the floreat of a civilization either whilst continental conditions still persisted or shortly after their cessation. We thus find proofs of at least three vanished empires in the northwest Pacific, and of one in the vicinity of Easter Island. The existence of others will be indicated in the chapters on the Geology of Lemuria.

CHAPTER III

THE TESTIMONY OF TRADITION

WE have now to consider the evidence for the former existence of a Lemurian continent or continents and their destruction which may be gleaned from the myths and sagas of the present peoples of Oceania, and which may reasonably be regarded as of the nature of traditions handed down to them by the remnants of the Lemurian races. This mainly consists of two descriptions of tale—that which tells of a devastating flood, or of conditions associated with flood and consequent submergence, and that class of legend which speaks of volcanic action or cataclysm by earthquake. These records are fairly numerous, and I shall endeavour to render my account of them as embracive as possible.

The ancient Hawaiians believed that their god Kane destroyed the world by fire, on account of the wickedness of the people then living. This resembles the story which tells of the destruction of Atlantis by the gods for a like reason, and surely points to a similar catastrophe in the Pacific. The gods then organised the world as it at present exists, and created the first man and woman. Fornander, in his great work, *The Polynesian Race*, refers to the body of traditions whence this myth is taken, though " obscured by time and defaced by interpolations," as "still a most valuable relic of the mental status, religious notions and historical recollections of the earlier Polynesians " which has been widely disseminated throughout all the Polynesian insular groups.

In the Society Islands the remnant of a legend was discovered by Lieutenant Bovis, and published by him in an article in the *Revue Coloniale* for 1855. It states how: " In the beginning there was nothing but the god Ihoiho, afterwards there was an expanse of waters which covered the abyss, and the god Tino Taata floated on the surface."

Says Fornander: "It is to be regretted that no more of that interesting legend has been preserved. It has the ring of the true antique, ere the primal myth was shattered into fragments. M. de Bovis translates Ihoiho with ' le vide,' the empty space, as a better rendering of sense than ' image de soi même.' I know not if the Tahitian word Ihoiho has also the sense of ' le vide '—a void, empty space—but it certainly has the meaning of the ' manes, ghosts or remains of the dead,' and in the legend was probably a trope expressive of a dead and perished world, the wreck of which was covered by water; and the god Tino Taata, which I think M. de Bovis correctly renders by ' the divine type or source of mankind,' floated on the waters.

"It is with some hesitation that I thus correct a writer whose article shows him to have been well-informed, exact, and cautious. But the expression, ' le vide,' seems to me misleading. Through all the Polynesian cosmogonies, even the wildest and most fanciful, there is a constant underlying sense of a chaos, wreck, *Po*, containing all things, and existing previous to the first creative organisation; the chaos and wreck of a previous world, destroyed by fire according to the Hawaiian legend, destroyed by water according to the Samoan legend; a chaos, ruin or night, *Po*, in which the gods themselves have been involved, and, only in virtue of their divine nature, after continued struggle, extricated themselves and re-organised the world on its present pattern."

The following is a Hawaiian chant from the *Kane* cycle of myths, which unquestionably refers to cataclysm:

> "O Kane, O Ku-ka-Pao
> And the great Lono, dwelling on the water,
> Brought forth are Heaven and Earth,
> Quickened, increasing, moving,
> Raised up into Continents.
> The great Ocean of Kane,
> The Ocean with dotted seas,
> The Ocean with the large fishes,
> And the small fishes."

Let us remember that such chants were composed and sung in an oceanic insular area where no continents are now known, or have been for centuries. Their antiquity is proved by the fact that the legends coeval with them speak of monsters of extraordinary size, living in caverns and spreading terror among the inhabitants of a land where nowadays the largest reptiles are no bigger than the common house lizard. " They are," remarks Fornander, " an heirloom from the time when the people lived in other habitats where such large reptiles abounded."

The land in which the older population of the Pacific dwelt is described in the traditions of Hawaii as Kalana i Hauola, that is " Kalana with the life-giving or life-renewing propensity," or a fount of civilization and religious dispensation, as another of its names, " the land of the divine water of Kane," goes to show. One of the ancient chants says of it :

> " O Pali-uli, hidden land of Kane,
> Land in Kalana i Hau-ola,
> In Kahiki-ku, in Kapakapa-ua a Kane,
> Land with springs of water, fat and moist,
> Land greatly enjoyed by the god."

The *Aina wai Akua a Kane*, or, as it is more generally called in the legends, *Aina wai-ola a Kane*, " the living water of Kane," is frequently referred to in Hawaiian folklore. According to traditions this spring of life, or living water, was a running stream or overflowing spring, attached to or enclosed in a pond. It was beautifully transparent and clear. Its banks were splendid. It had three outlets; one for the god Ku, one for Kane, and one for Lono, and through these outlets the fish entered into the pond. If the fish of the pond were thrown on the ground or on the fire, they did not die ; and if a man had been killed and was afterwards sprinkled over with this water, he soon came to life again. In the famous legend of " Aukele-nui-a-Iku " the hero visits " Kalana i Hau-ola " and, by the aid of his patron god, obtains water from this fountain of life, wherewith he resuscitated his brothers who had been killed a long time before.

It was associated with the idea of the fall of man, and the temptation of woman by the serpent, and that this was brought about by the eating of apples is made clear from a sacrificial hymn current in the Marquesas group which made reference to " the red apples eaten in Vavau." The likeness to the Hesperidean myth is thus very marked.

We also find frequent allusion in the myths of Hawaii to " the island hidden by Kane " and peopled by his direct descendants, where food grew without the necessity for cultivation, and where there was no sickness nor death. When its inhabitants grew old and feeble they were transformed into spirits and they became gods and dwelt in the clouds. This is surely the tradition of an insular fatherland now submerged.

In another chant of the Marquesans relating to the creation of the earth, it is stated that the then known world extended from Vavau to Hawaii. If this be not a folk-memory of a previous continental condition, what is it ? In still another Marquesan chant of the deluge it is said that *after the flood* the ribs of the earth and the mountain-ranges of Hawaii and of " Matahou," an unknown region, rose up and extended far and near over the sea of Hawaii. In this connection it is to be noted that the legends of New Zealand also refer to a country called " Mataaho," which had been destroyed by a flood. That these chants were composed under entirely different conditions from those prevailing in the Pacific area to-day is obvious enough.

Expeditions for the discovery of the old lost lands of the Pacific were set on foot by the Polynesians themselves in modern times, precisely as the English and Dutch sought during the seventeenth and eighteenth centuries for " Brasil " or " Buss " or other foundered islands in the Atlantic. In the Marquesas group numerous expeditions have from time to time been set on foot, up to fifty years ago, in search of the traditional land of bliss and mystery, and as lately as the commencement of the nineteenth century the Nukahivans were wont to fit out voyages of exploration in their canoes in search of a traditional country called Utupu, said to be situated to the westward of their archipelago, from which the god Tao first introduced the coconut tree.

Myths of a great flood in which the majority of mankind perished are common in Polynesia. Writing of the Fijians, the Rev. Thomas Williams, one of the best authorities, says :

" They speak of a deluge which, according to some of their accounts, was partial, but in others is stated to have been universal. The cause of this great flood was the killing of Turukawa—a favourite bird belonging to Ndengei —by two mischievous lads, the grandsons of the god. These, instead of apologizing for their offence, added insolent language to the outrage, and fortifying, with the assistance of their friends, the town in which they lived, defied Ndengei to do his worst. It is said that although the angry god took three months to collect his forces, he was unable to subdue the rebels, and, disbanding his army, resolved on more efficient revenge. At his command the dark clouds gathered and burst, pouring streams on the devoted earth. Towns, hills, mountains were successively submerged ; but the rebels, secure in the superior height of their own dwelling-place, looked on without concern. But when, at last, the terrible surges invaded their fortress, they cried for direction to a god who, according to one account, instructed them to form a float of the fruit of the shaddock ; according to another, sent two canoes for their use ; or, says a third, taught them how to build a canoe, and thus secure their own safety. All agree that the highest places were covered, and the remnant of the human race saved in some kind of vessel, which was at last left by the subsiding waters on Mbenga ; hence the Mbengans draw their claim to stand first in Fijian rank. The number saved—eight—exactly accords with the " few " of the Scripture record. By this flood it is said that two tribes of the human family became extinct. One consisted entirely of women, and the other were distinguished by the appendage of a tail like that of a dog. The highest point of the island of Koro is associated with the history of the Flood. Its name is *Ngginggi-tangithi-Koro*, which conveys the idea of a little bird sitting there and lamenting the drowned island. In this bird the Christians recognize Noah's dove on its second flight from the ark. I have heard a native, after listening to the incident as given by Moses, chant ' *Na qiqi sa togici Koro ni yali*,' ' The Qiqi laments over Koro, because it is lost.' "

At Raiatea, Society group, the legend runs that one day Rua-Haku, the Lord Rua, the Ocean God, was asleep at the bottom of the sea, when a fisherman came along that way with his hook and line. The hook got entangled in the hair of the god, and the fisherman, thinking he had caught a fine fish on his hook, pulled up so vigorously as to bring the god to the surface. Enraged at being thus disturbed in his sleep, the god threatened instant destruction to the unlucky fisherman; but the latter, having implored the god's pardon, was told to repair to a coral bank or islet called *Toamarama* for shelter, while the god vented his displeasure on the rest of the world. The fisherman did as he was told, and took a friend, a hog, a dog, and a couple of hens with him to the islet. After that the ocean commenced rising, and continued rising until all the land was covered with water and all the people had perished. Then the waters retired, and the fisherman returned to his former home. Other versions of the event exist at Tahiti, but equally distorted.

Fornander summarises the Marquesan legend of the flood as follows: " The chant opens by saying that the Lord Ocean, *Fatu-Moana*, was going to overflow and pass over the dry earth, but that a respite of seven days was granted. It then speaks of the animals who were to be reserved from the Flood. Then speaks of a house to be built high above the waters; a house with stories, with chambers, with openings for light, stored with provisions for the preservation of the various animals. The animals then are fastened with ropes, tied up in couples, and, with one man before and one behind, marched off to this big, deep house of wood. Then the family enter, consisting of four women and four men. The men's names are given ' *Fetu-moana*,' apparently the father and master of the family, *Fetu-tau-ani, Fetu-amo-amo,* and *Ia-fetu-tini.* A turtle is then sacrificed; the family retires to rest amidst the din, confusion, and crowding of the confined animals. Then the storm bursts over them; the rain is pouring fearfully, and gloom prevails; all on earth is displaced and mixed up by the waters.

"The second part opens with a description of the waters retreating, and mountain summits and ridges appearing, the grounding of the house, and the command of the Lord Ocean for the dry land to appear. The head of the family, encouraged by the sight, promises to sacrifice to the Lord Ocean seven holy and precious things and seven sucklings. Then a bird, called *te teetina o Tanaoa*—from its name apparently of a dark colour—is sent out over the sea of Hawaii, but after a while returns to the vessel. The wind sets in from the north. On a second attempt the same bird alights on the sand of the shore, but is recalled to the vessel. Then another bird, called *te Teetina o Moepo*, is sent out over the sea of Hawaii. It lands on the dry land and returns with young shoots or branches it had gathered. The land is now dry, and the great ridges of Hawaii and of Matahou are fit to dwell on. In the third part reference is made to the debarkation of men and animals.

"In the Hawaiian group there are several versions of the Flood. Some indicate the decay and corruption of the original legend in a similar manner to the Fiji and Raiatea legends above referred to; but one legend approaches nearly to the Marquesan, though greatly shortened in details as I obtained it. It relates that in the time of *Nuu* or *Nana-Nuu*, as he is also called, the Flood—*Kai-a-Kahinalii*—came upon the earth and destroyed all living beings; that 'Nuu,' by command of his god, built a large vessel with a house on top of it, which was called and is referred to in the chants as *He Waa-Halau-Alii o ka Moku*, 'the royal vessel,' in which he and his family, consisting of his wife, *Lili-Nae*, his three sons, and their wives, were saved. When the Flood subsided, 'Kane,' 'Ku,' and 'Lono,' entered the 'Waa-Halau' of 'Nuu,' and told him to go out. He did so, and found himself on the top of Mauna-kea (the highest mountain on the island of Hawaii), and he called a cave there after the name of his wife, and the cave remains there to this day, as the legend says, in testimony of the fact."

A Hawaiian song on the subject of the deluge contains the following significant passage :

> " O wake up, here is the rain,
> Here is daylight,
> Here the mists driving inland,
> Here the mists driving seaward,
> The swelling sea, the rising sea,
> The boisterous sea of Iku.
> It has enclosed (us).
> O, the foaming sea,
> O the rising billows, O the falling billows,
> O the overwhelming billows,
> In Kahiki.
> Salvation comes
> From this death by you, O Lono."

A chant of the ancient Hawaiians known as that of Kamahualele, an astrologer, states that the seer Kaialea " went round the land, separated Nuuhiwa, and landed on Polapola, dividing and separating the islands," surely a reference to cataclysm. Another Hawaiian legend tells how Kamapuaa, quarrelling with the goddess Pele, the patron divinity of volcanoes, tried to put out her fires by floods from the sea.

The collection of Hawaiian myths by Mr. David Hyde Rice, of Kauai, published under the auspices of the Bishop Museum of Honolulu, refers to a legend of the Menehune, or white dwarf-folk, who built stone temples and carved in wood and stone. Says Mr. Rice :

" The belief of the Hawaiians of ancient times was that there was one great continent, stretching from Hawaii, including Samoa, Lalakoa (the Hawaiian version of Rarotonga) and reaching as far as New Zealand, also taking in Fiji, and there were some lowlands in between these higher lands. All this was called by one name, Ka-houpo-o-Kane, the Solar-Plexus-of-Kane, and was also called Moana-nui-kai-oo, the Great Engulfing Ocean."

A sorcerer's prayer, he tells us, contains further references to this tradition, which is known as " Ke Kumulipo," or " the tradition that comes from the dark ages."

" The great flood came, Kai-a-ka-hina-alii, the sea-that-made-the-chiefs-fall-down, submerging all the lower lands, leaving only specks of higher land, now known as islands, above the waters. After the Deluge there were three peoples—the Menehune, who were dwarfs or pigmies, the Kenamu and the Kenawa; a great part of these other peoples were destroyed by the Menehune. One of the chiefs of the Kenamu had come to Hawaii from Kahiki."

"Contrary to common belief, they were not possessed of any supernatural powers; but it was solely on account of their tremendous strength and energy that they were to accomplish the wonderful things they did."

These Menehune not only raised great stone temples, but brought the stones from a distance, passing them on from hand to hand, as did the Scottish Picts of Folklore in many a legend. They also carved images, and built fish-ponds surrounded by cyclopean walls. They seem to have been much the same in type and effort as the people of Easter Island. Like them, too, they made run-ways down high hills, and had similar amusements.

But their King discovered that they were marrying Hawaiian women, and as he wished to keep the race pure, he decided to leave the islands. Accordingly the people were drawn up in battalions and journeyed onward, whence is unknown.

Another legend of these Menehune tells how they sought the Phantom Island, " the home of the Menehune and Mus." It was a floating isle called Kuehelani, which moved about in the ocean by night. But the angry goddess Pele, patroness of the volcanoes, set it on fire, the blaze being quenched by her oceanic sister Namakaokai. This island is said to have been three days' canoe sail to the north-west, and the entire myth is obviously an account of migration from a subsiding or volcanic area to another.

Professor Macmillan Brown strikingly remarks on the everlasting struggle for supremacy between the gods of fire and water in Pacific ocean legend, a struggle which recalls that of Poseidon and Pallas Athena in Atlantean story. He says:

" It is little wonder then that the Hawaiians seem almost

to have monopolized amongst the Pacific Ocean peoples the mythology of vulcanism. Pele as a volcanic deity seems to have no rival. She and her relatives tower above all other divine or heroic impersonations of the phenomena of catastrophic movement of the earth's crust. For they have specialized in these, as the gods and demigods of no other region have. They have no relationships to other phases of nature except the oceanic, and that in the Pacific is closely related to the volcanic; there is, of course, the fundamental antagonism between fire and water; but over and above this the everlasting struggle in this ocean between its deep waters and the fires underneath is patent to the most primitive imagination. Poseidon, the Hellenic god of the sea, was also a deity of volcanic phenomena; he was the earth-shaker in Homer. For the Ægean Sea impressed the ancient mind by its earthquakes and hot springs as by its demand for maritime enterprise in the people who lived in and around it. The relationship of sea and earth movements is even more intimate in the greatest ocean of the world."

According to legend, says Fornander, the Hawaiian group of islands at the time of its discovery by Polynesians, consisted only of the two islands of Hawaii and Maui, the other islands of the group not having yet arisen from the sea. Yet, before the death of their discoverer, it is said, they not only arose from the ocean, but became wooded, watered and fertile and were allotted as the homes and principalities of his children!

It was said of Maui, a god of the Maori, that he hauled up the Tongan Islands with his fish-hooks. Returning to Bolatu, the island of immortality, he vaunted of its beauty, and his son Atalanga and his companions went in search of it. They found it, but soon longed again for the divine region they had left, which, however, they could never find again.

As Professor Macmillan Brown shows, Tangaroa, the plutonic god, is an amalgam of Jupiter, Neptune and Hephaestus. He hauls up the earth from the sea-depths, and is regarded as the deity of subterranean fire. But his dominant phase is as a god of the ocean, and an upheaver of islands. It is significant that in Mangaia he is represented as fair-haired and that all his children are fair-haired, which is as much as to say that he is the god of a fair-haired race, which was thought of as dwelling in a remote land, to reach which the spirits of the dead must plunge into the sea.

Mariner, who lived in the Tonga group from 1806 to 1813, regarded Tangaroa as the controller of migrations and the patron deity of the fair-haired and virtuous. He gave to his people the command: " be your skins white like your minds," which surely indicates the existence of a cult of superior wisdom and advanced ethics fostered by a white people in the Oceanic region.

There is evidence in the Pacific area, too, of the presence of a religious cult and ritual designed for the control or amelioration of volcanic and seismic outbursts through sacrifice and taboo. The people of Java cast fowls, cloth, and money into the crater of a volcano in order to pacify its presiding spirit, and in the Celebes children were thrown into volcanoes to prevent eruptions. Even in New Zealand during last century the body of a great chief was exhumed and cast into the crater of Tongariro when a disastrous landslide occurred there.

Says Professor Macmillan Brown: " Strangely enough, it is the same form of Maui's name that has found its way right through Micronesia north of the Equator to Yap, one of its westernmost islands and nearly 3000 miles to the north-west of Tanna. Mathikethik is the Yap form. The demigod went out fishing with his two older brothers; at first he fished up taro and other crops; but at last his hook stuck in land and he hauled up the island of Fais, some 200 miles to the north-east of Yap. The chiefs of this latter island keep the people of Fais in abject subjection to them by threatening to destroy the hook of the demigod, which they say they have, and by making them believe that Fais would sink again into the ocean if it were destroyed. In Micronesia, from the Ellice group away to the south-east to the Pelews in the north-west, there is little even of exotic mythology of vulcanism, and what little there is, is chiefly of the movements of islands up or down in the ocean, but largely of subsidence. In the Pelews the people were descended from giants of powers far beyond those of their posterity; these were the Kalits, and they came from spirit islands that are now submerged, all but their cliffs. The megalithic buildings in Ponape were erected by these. Micronesia, all but the northern islands of the Mariannes, has evidently seen no great eruptive phenomena during human occupation. The Ruk Archipelago, Ponape and Kusaie are mainly volcanic. But most of the archipelagoes are coralline, and are doubtless due to the subsidence that alone appears in their legends. Even the Gilberts, whose islands, all but Ocean Island, are practically level with the water, speak of a time when their ancestry had far more extensive areas of land to live upon."

Nor, in a review of the evidence of tradition for submergence, must we forget the myth of Easter Island, already alluded to, which described the arrival of a culture-hero, Hotu Matua, from a probably submerged continent. This chief left his native land to the north-west of Easter Island 120 days before his arrival there. His King, Haumaka, had dreamt of the islet, and sent six prospectors to search for it. They arrived before Hotu Matua, and when he came informed him that they intended to return to the archipelago, Marae Renga, or Marae Toiho, whence they had been dispatched by the royal command. But Hotu Matua informed them that a search for it would be fruitless, as, since they had sailed, the sea had submerged it and drowned all the inhabitants.

From this sunken land came Makemake, the great god of the Easter Islanders. He is a marine deity, physically composed of a combination of the shark, the frigate-bird and a man-eating mammal, and thus obviously the invention of a people who inhabited a locality where the sea was regarded as a dangerous and devouring monster, prone to violent and savage outbursts, and levying a toll on human life.

The circumstance that Easter Island was known to its inhabitants as "the navel of the world," would seem to indicate that it was formerly ringed round with archipelagoes which have gone down, one after another. They were probably combined in one empire under the easterly power known in local legend as Motu Motiro Hiva, Easter Island acting as the mausoleum and perhaps the religious Mecca of some of all of the insular groups once in contiguity with it, and now submerged. In all likelihood its several coasts were shrines set apart for the archipelagoes opposite to them, as Professor Brown seems to think. Probably that to the east first erected religious platforms on Easter Island, that to the south coming next in importance, or in time, for there the ahus are of the most excellent workmanship. That the dominant power was situated in the east seems to be proved by its supplying the great god Makemake, the supreme deity of the islands.

The Maori myth of Maui says that he found fire on the land he had fished up, which at the same time was populous with men. The fire burned him, and in his pain he leaped into the sea to cool himself. When he came up again, he had the White Island, now in the Bay of Plenty, on his back.

Maui, like gods in other mythologies, made a descent into the land of the dead, which is in some Polynesian legends regarded *as a submerged land beneath the sea.* In some insular groups if the dead wished to join their ancestors, they plunged into the ocean. He has also relationship with the flood-myths found so plentifully in the Pacific.

Another god who essayed the descent to Hades was Mataora, who desired to bring back his wife Niwareka, who had fled thither because he had beaten her. He found the land of Po a place of nightless sunshine, "where women are never beaten," a contrast to the upper-world, the "home of evil." His wife's people who dwelt there had all fair skins and flaxen hair. Their noses were straight, unlike those of most Polynesians, and they had taught the Maoris tattooing, weaving patterns, and wood-carving. That this myth applies to the remnants of an old civilization whose peoples dwelt in a remote, or submerged, island can scarcely be questioned.

Lemuria, like Atlantis, had its Poseidon, but one who was much more furiously disposed than the oceanic deity of the Atlantic, earthquake-begetter as he undoubtedly was. His memory is repeated in the person of the early Polynesian god Whiro, a cyclonic deity, resembling the Hurakan or "Hurricane" of the Indians of Central America. But Tahitian myth represents him as rising from his cave at the bottom of the sea when the winds threatened sailors and compelling the boreal forces into quietude.

One of his avatars is as a god of the under-world and partner of Whakaru, the earthquake god, in tormenting mankind with eruption and cataclysm. Latterly he was regarded as a fiendish disturber of man's peace, analagous to the Titans, an under-world power who tried to destroy the work of the immortal gods.

The war he and his associates waged against the higher gods is known as *Te Paerangi*, or "the destruction of Heaven," the grand attempt of the Titans to wreck the Pacific continents. We recall that the intention to wreck a hypothetical Athens, that is, the civilized city of Pallas Athene, arose from her quarrel with Poseidon, god of Atlantis, although, of course, chronology does not support the historical side of the saga. Here we have in the Pacific a set of circumstances almost parallel with the myth as " euhemerized " by Plato.

Only we have in " Po," the Polynesian Atlantis, a land already submerged, and regarded as the country of the dead, whereas in Atlantis we behold the theatre of a rebel or disaffected civilization, to which a more righteous if hypothetical Hellenic civilization is opposed, still existing above the level of the sea while threatening a mythical Grecian culture. The story in its essence and details is the same, only we here observe it at a different phase of development. " Po," or Lemuria, as a country of the dead or drowned, attacks its insular vestiges after its destruction. Its wicked denizens are now transformed into demons. In the case of Atlantis it is the Militarist or Bolshevist elements which design the downfall of " Athens," the symbolic metropolis of all the virtues, while the island-continent they occupy is still in being.

In the result Atlantis sinks, as " Po " or Lemuria submerges, and for the same reason, that its inhabitants had

THE TESTIMONY OF TRADITION

brought upon themselves the wrath of the gods because of their want of social discipline and wickedness. But the myth, as Professor Macmillan Brown seems to imply, is not an allegory in which the powers of winter are considered as attacking the " civilization " of summer, even had such a myth been imported from the cold north, as has been suggested by some writers.

Such an allegory could scarcely have applied either to the climatic circumstances of the Southern Atlantic or the Pacific, where the rigours of the cold season are far to seek. Its significance as a saga of the seasonal triumph of the winds is less in question, perhaps. As Professor Brown surmises elsewhere, it is much more likely to represent the clash of the terrestrial or earth-born forms and the celestial powers. But it has a further and more definite meaning above and beyond that.

It represents not alone the defeat of the powers of volcanic and seismic might, but, in its more " refined " and sophisticated version, the destruction of human elements who refused to recognize the " way " of the gods, that path of righteousness which had been laid down by them for humanity. This is clear enough in the case of Atlantis from the Platonic account. And what is true of Atlantis, must, as I have shown, be posited of Lemuria also.

I do not mean to infer that the celestial powers destroyed Atlantis and Lemuria because of their moral infirmities. What I mean to convey is that the peoples of the ancient world construed visitation by earthquake or volcanic eruption and consequent submergence as of the nature of dire punishment, as savages still do. Out of the result arose the myth explanatory of catastrophe. But it was, in both cases, a myth which, like all myths, is eloquent of actual historical fact as well as allegorical reasons for divine punitive action.

Thus the discovery of an actual parallel betwixt the myths of Atlantis and Lemuria is valuable not as destroying any historical material accruing to those continents, as some might think, but rather as illustrating the attitude of the ancient world to such catastrophes. Lemuria does not alone constitute a mythical parallel to Atlantis. The myths are the same, but that similarity arises out of the tendency of ancient or barbarous ethic to devise a similar cause for the disappearance of a continent or continents in the Pacific and the Atlantic. All over the world catastrophe is caused by the vengeance of the gods for evil-doing, but that does not imply either that the catastrophe never occurred, or that the likeness of the reasons advanced for it makes it any the less probable. The land seaward of what is now Brittany was at one time submerged. Legend attributed this to the vicious life of a princess. Yet geology proves that submerged it was, despite the mythic ætiology attaching to it.

Summarizing the testimony of tradition concerning Lemuria and its disappearance, we find that two descriptions of tale exist, one of flood and submergence and the other of volcanic disturbance or earthquake. Myths of definite chaos and of the destruction of the world, known as Po, occur in Hawaii and Samoa, while other myths speak of a paradise land " the fount of civilization and religious dispensation " since lost or " hidden," because of sin, either on the part of an individual or the general populace.

The Marquesans believed the early world to extend from Vavau to Hawaii, or about the breadth of Australia. The legends of New Zealand refer to a country called Mataaho which had been destroyed by a flood. The Fijians had traditions of a deluge and the people of the Society Islands a very definite myth of such an occurrence. The Marquesans told a story resembling that of the ark, as did those of Hawaii. According to Mr. D. H. Rice the Hawaiians believed in a former continent stretching from Hawaii, including Samoa, and reaching as far as New Zealand, also taking in Fiji, called Ka-houpo-o-kane. It sank, and left only its mountain-tops as islands, which were inhabited by the Menehune, an aboriginal race of dwarfs, who seem, as we shall see later, to have been the same as the fair race mentioned in many Oceanic myths.

The struggle between fire and water is a marked feature of Oceanic myth. Its chief Plutonic god is fair-haired,

THE TESTIMONY OF TRADITION

and inculcated the motto to his folk " be your skins white, like your minds," thus indicating the existence of a cult of superior wisdom in Oceania practised by a fair race. The megalithic buildings of Micronesia were raised by Titans resembling those of classical myth. The people of Easter Island came from a submerged area. Among the Maori and other peoples of Oceania the country of the dead is beneath the sea, the land of a fair-haired folk, who practised weaving and wood-carving.

Lemuria, like Atlantis, had its Poseidon, Whiro. He wages war against the higher gods as did the classical Titans against the deities of Olympus, a parallel in a sense with the myth of Atlantis. In the event Po or Lemuria submerges, as does Atlantis. The myth evidently signifies the punishment of human elements who refused to recognize the " way " of the gods.

It is thus evident that a mythic idea similar to that underlying the belief in the destruction of Atlantis, and for a similar reason, had a widespread acceptance in the Pacific area.

CHAPTER IV

THE EVIDENCE FROM MYTH AND MAGIC

EVEN in its bare outlines Polynesian myth is eloquent of conditions of cataclysm. In the chapter on " The Testimony of Tradition " those myths and tales which deal with submergence were reviewed. In the following pages we have to do with those traditions which speak of deities or heroes whose acts and whose cults seem to provide evidence of a similar kind.

It is essential for our purpose that we take particular notice of those myths which deal with the primeval gods, the builders, the creators. The Maori make Rangi the sky-father and Papa the earth-mother, the eastern Polynesians call Atea the creator, the Hawaiians Wakea the father, and Haumea the female producer.

The secondary phase of Polynesian mythology introduces the gods Tane, Tangaroa, Tu and Rongo, the third Maui and his mother Hina, demiurges of the forces of nature, who, with the goddess Pele, and her husband Kanepuaa, are responsible for earthquakes and volcanic eruptions. Beyond this, we encounter a popular mythology in which taboo and totemism play leading parts, and are found side by side with animal stories and the like.

One of the most dreaded of the Hawaiian deities or genii is Kihawahine, who is represented as a mermaid, or a woman as regards her upper part, and a water-lizard below. The terror engendered by this monster appears as symbolic of the dread of the Hawaiians for the power of water. The shark is the hero of legends equally terrifying. Yet it claimed human relationship—a myth evidently explanatory of a people submerged, the belief entertained that they still survived in fish form beneath the waves.

The shark and his human friends or worshippers were supposed to keep up an amicable intercourse, and many were the stories related of the intervention of this marine creature at periods of human stress. Some of these sharkmen were humans until they touched the sea, when they were immediately transformed into fish.

Professor Macmillan Brown believes that the great gods of Polynesia were created before the dispersal of their worshippers from the sunken fatherland Hawaiki. He writes:

"One of the most striking things about Polynesian spiritual culture is that whilst its lower elements have taken their own development in each group, its greater gods and heroes are practically the same over the vast oceanic area occupied by the race; not merely the names are identical, but their natures, functions, and histories. It looks as if there were at least two strata in the religious formation of the central and eastern Pacific, and both of them were laid and inter-related before the Polynesian people broke up into its constituent elements and spread by migration all over the ocean. For the lower stratum, that of ancestral worship and *tapu*, though it is greatly diversified in its developments in the various groups, is identical in its nucleus and fundamental characteristics. Though it has some exorcistic features, it is on a far higher plane than the Melanesian system, being essentially religion and not mere magic. It probably belongs to the ancient palæolithic immigration into the centre of the ocean that came before pottery began to be made on the continent it left, before the spindle was invented, before the bow had begun to be used in warfare and before the art of fire-making had advanced from the highly elementary and difficult fire-plough to the fire-drill. The higher religious culture that created the great gods and heroes and the wonderful mythological fabric probably came in with the megalithic conquerors who in later neolithic times introduced the advanced arts of house-carving, canoe-building, net-making, warfare and fortification; these are all masculine arts and stand in striking contrast to the feminine arts and those that belong to the domestic circle. Had this conquering immigration that laid the foundations of the powerfully feudalistic society of Polynesia brought its women with it, it would have raised the domestic arts to the level of the masculine, and the position of women above the cruel oppression of the *tapu*. The uniformity of the whole culture through an oceanic area 5000 miles by 5000 makes it axiomatic that both these immigrations came into the insular and oceanic fatherland, Hawaiki, before by its subsidence it drove the amalgamated people in all directions in search of other islands to settle on."

What might be called the cult of the volcanic goddess Pele lasted longest in Hawaii, where, indeed, the territorial circumstances afforded it every opportunity to flourish. To her shrine by the fire-lake of Kilauea the people brought offerings in the hope of averting her wrath. The priestess of Pele, in debating with the missionaries who accused her of destroying the island, admitted that " formerly we did overflow some of the land, but it was only the land of those who were rebels or very wicked people."

The struggle betwixt the volcanic and oceanic powers is well illustrated in the myth of Pele. No deity of the seismic variety anywhere is invested with such appalling might. In Polynesia the strife betwixt the earth and sea has such vivid recollections for the people that the myths it has evoked can only be of age-long character. The everlasting war between the Titans of the earth and ocean has stamped Polynesian myth more potently than has any other agency which arouses the popular imagination of a race. Although of relatively late provenance, it would seem that the idea of Pele may have been ancient in the germinal sense, a very venerable myth resurrected. Maui is the older volcanic or seismic deity, but his myth and cult became overlaid by those of Pele.

Her struggle was fundamentally with her sister Namakaokahai, the Ocean. Maui was more universal, less local. In Tonga and Samoa he is the earthquake god and their people attribute all seismic disturbance to his attempts to turn as he lies beneath the earth. They make a great noise to keep him quiet. In the Celebes the natives attribute earthquakes to a subterranean pig which rubs itself against the piles whereon the earth rests. This is certainly not a Polynesian idea. Ndengei, the Fijian god of earthquake, has a serpent form, but as a general rule the Oceanic explanation of seismic disturbance is referred to a god and not an animal, as in the case of the myth of Atlantis.

The legend of Maui as a bird which possessed the secret of fire is reminiscent of a land of volcanoes. Maui, we remember, fished up the earth from the bottom of the sea. He has the power of transforming himself into a bird of brilliant plumage, and in one story this bird pulls the canoe of the migrating folk across the ocean. As Matuika he is the personification of the fire-drill, just as a similar bird is in Mexico and Central America, for fire is frequently symbolized as a bird by "barbarous" peoples. He is, indeed, a mixture of the fire-bird and the oracular fowl which leads on a migrating people to its goal, like the Picus of the Latins and the Uitzilopochtli of the Aztecs. He undertakes to find fire in the Underworld, rather than, like Prometheus, in the heavens, sure evidence that he belonged to a volcanic region.

But Maui, if not the oldest among the fire-gods of Polynesia, is also associated with the floods of the Pacific Ocean. It is also by his aid that people seek the dead in the land beneath the sea, where the folk have all fair skins and indulge in the arts of tattooing and wood-carving and weaving. His mother advised certain underworld folk not to seek the earth, as " the world is now full of evil," the ancient refrain of all myth which deals with sunken lands. Sin sinks Atlantis, Ys, and Lyonesse, and submerges Lemuria.

But we must examine the older volcanic gods of Oceania. In *The Lore of the Wharewananga*, edited by Mr. Percy Smith, is told the story of a flood accompanied by earthquake. The gods meditate destruction. The god of ocean, Kiwa, and the god of tempests, Tawhirimatea, threaten to overturn the earth to its foundations, and the earthquake god Whakaru and Mataaho intend to dismember the earth-father Papa into archipelagoes. Maui intervenes, however, and insists that the land he has fished up shall remain as a dwelling for himself and his folk.

Mataaho, " the maker of earthquakes," is a more ancient seismic deity. Whiro, the god of wind, arrived at an agreement with Whakaru, the god of volcanoes, to work woe upon the world of men. From the surface of the ocean he betook himself to its depths, or, rather, was compelled to hide himself in them by the more beneficent powers. This would seem to imply that part of the ancient myth concerning earthquake in the Pacific was associated with a deity whose powers of evil found their opportunity through the sins of man. Everything, indeed, points to the conclusion that in the Oceanic area we discover the vestiges of a myth parallel with that of Atlantis—the destruction of a continent or continents because of the sin of their inhabitants.

It is indeed remarkable that flood myths, almost without exception, allude to the sin of the people as the cause of the deluge. The Biblical flood, the destruction of Atlantis, the Babylonian deluge, the destruction of Ys and Lyonesse, flood myths in Mexico, Peru, China, and practically everywhere are accompanied by the assertion of popular sin. Childish mischief or drunken carelessness is in some cases the cause, as when the top of a well is left uncovered.

The idea underlying flood myths is obscure and probably very ancient. It can scarcely be that it relates to the purification of the earth by water, for in more than one mythological system the earth is destroyed cyclically by other mediums, fire, wind, or a fall of burning resin. The likelihood is that the flood myth in its more sophisticated form was a story of long and probably composite ancestry founded upon many actual human experiences.

But this does not account for the inevitable statement that the deluge was caused by human sin. May we not account for this prevalent view as follows : the moon was regarded as the great source, tank or reservoir of all moisture. She was also thought of as having a marked influence on sexual affairs. Any undue indulgence in sexual pleasure among a people would then be likely to

THE EVIDENCE FROM MYTH AND MAGIC

interfere with her normal hydrostatic condition, and precipitate disaster by flood. We know that undue sexual indulgence is considered by some primitive peoples to interfere with the fertility of the earth, probably because it is believed to disturb the lunar functions in regard to rain.

Without pushing this theory, or suggestion, too far, we must also take into account the undoubted abhorrence of primitive people for sexual indulgence. It is regarded as intrinsically dangerous, both personally and tribally, and is usually hedged about by an extraordinary number of taboos, the infraction of which may, to the primitive mind, result in fatality. Innumerable, indeed, are the myths and tales that " sin " or indulgence of a flagitious kind results in destruction. Primitive peoples regard the infringement of taboo as a crime of the most heinous character, for the good reason that it upsets or disturbs the whole balance of terrestrial and cosmic economy. The lust of a princess deluged Ys, the orgulous pride and material inclination of a people submerged Atlantis.

But this does not imply that if the cause be rooted in mythic or customary belief that the deluge itself is legendary. Whatever the catastrophe, one may be sure that it would be attributed to sin or the breaking of taboo on the part of an individual or a people at large. Tollan, the capital of pre-Aztec Mexico, fell because of the wickedness and deterioration of its folk. In reality it was attacked and sacked by the wild tribes of the plains, but in the minds of its priestly caste these would have been sent to destroy it by a deity outraged by the lack of conformity on the part of its inhabitants with tribal or religious law. Troy was given over to the furious Greeks because the gods were displeased at the rape of Helen. When its last safeguard, the Palladium, was stolen by Odysseus, its fate became automatically certain, according to the opinion of its pious hierophants. In a similar manner reasons were supplied for the destruction of Atlantis and Lemuria. The powers of nature, it was thought, were disgusted with their profligacy and loosed upon them the agencies of their wrath, the earthquake and the engulfing ocean. We have also seen how this idea ranges itself quite naturally with the Greek and Atlantean legend of a war betwixt the gods of heaven and the Titans of nature.

We must now examine the proofs, if any, that these Polynesian myths of destruction had their origin in an older Lemurian tradition, that they were indeed the folk-memories of an ancient cataclysm or series of cataclysms. This is indeed almost self-evident, having regard to the fact that by the time of Polynesian settlement in Oceania its greatest time of seismic violence must long have been passed. The records of Polynesian immigration into the Pacific area do not reach back many centuries, and it seems a most ample margin of time to allow for them. During the period which has elapsed only minor seismic movements have occurred within the area. At least no continents or great land-masses have been submerged within that stretch of time.

It remains as a logical consequence that the frequent allusion to continents formerly existing which are so common in Polynesian myth must be a legacy from an older race. Who this race was we are already aware. It was that fair-haired people whose traditions and racial remnants are still to be encountered in Oceania, the people whom, says tradition, dwell as the dead beneath the sea.

The proof thus appears to me as irrefragable as human proof can be. Indeed, I cannot well see how it can readily be traversed on any sufficient grounds. If it be argued that the Polynesian race has occupied the Pacific area for a hundred thousand years or any such length of time it will be found difficult to substantiate such a theory in view of the lack of evidence and of expert authority. This is the opinion of Professor Macmillan Brown, and it is with much regret that I find myself compelled to disagree with that able, learned and amiable scholar, whose books have cast such a flood of light upon Pacific history and to whom I cheerfully admit myself as fundamentally indebted for arguments and views of the most cogent value and appositeness.

Professor Brown himself provides the clue when he writes: " Hawaiki " (the primeval fatherland), " or as it

THE EVIDENCE FROM MYTH AND MAGIC

is in Mangaia, Avaiki, is, in many of the groups, not merely Po, or darkness, or night underground, but under the sea. The spirits of the dead have to plunge in order to get to it. In the smaller islands and in the groups of small islands in Polynesia they plunge westward, and in the groups of large area, northward or north-westward. The fatherland was evidently submerged. It was also volcanic, for in all but Hawaii the art of fire is procured from it, and in procuring it the world is set ablaze."

In Mangaia the goddess Miru, a volcanic deity, kept her oven well alight, so that the spirits of all but those who perish in battle might be consumed therein. But a demigod, Ngaru, brought down a deluge of rain and swamped the fires of the volcanic goddess. He was a deity of the underworld of sea, and in his warfare with its demonic shapes he grew jet-black. His fair-haired spouse Tongatea rejected him, but his grandfather Moko buried him so that he became white as snow. His own golden locks had been burned off in the fires of Miru, and, on the plea of his mother, Tangaroa presented him with a new head of black hair.

Here we observe the process of myth by which a fair god, the deity of a fair-haired folk, becomes dark-haired.

In one of the myths relating to the goddess Pele, we discover allusions to mythical or formerly existing continents. " Kahiki was land at the dawn of time," exclaims Paoa, the incarnation of Pele's magic fire-plough. Another goddess, returning to her own country called Kuaihelani, a floating island, finds it on fire through the agency of Pele. Kuaihelani was three days' sail to the north-west of Kauai Island, but there was another mythical land seven days' sail beyond it, the land of Nuumealani, or " the high altar." On this island Namaka, the seagoddess, took up a position to watch the depredations of her sister Pele, as she created volcano after volcano, pursuing her from island to island, until at last the goddess of sea and fire clashed in mortal combat.

It is not too much to say that the keynote of Oceanic myth is terrestrial disturbance, seismic, volcanic and diluvian. That being so, and having regard to the fact that the Polynesians arrived in Oceania after the period of greatest seismic stress, it does not seem a conclusion of error to refer their myths and tales of sunken lands and of forces which compelled their submergence to a mythology or tradition not only much more ancient than their own but of different origin.

The evidence from Myth and Magic, when cast into the form of a precis, reads as follows : Polynesian myth, the heir of the Lemurian, is eloquent of conditions of cataclysm. The secondary phase of Polynesian myth introduces deities responsible for earthquakes and eruptions. Its greater gods are practically the same over the whole oceanic area, and were probably developed before the Polynesian dispersal from the fatherland Hawaiki before its subsidence.

The struggle between the volcanic and oceanic powers is most marked in Polynesian myth. All the evidence points to the conclusion that in Oceania we discover the vestiges of a myth parallel with that of Atlantis. The myth of earthquake and submergence in the Pacific is associated with a god whose powers of evil found opportunity through the sins of men. The Oceanic continent was destroyed because of the sins of its inhabitants, as was Atlantis. Sin upsets the cosmic economy. Although the ideas has a mythical basis, this does not imply that the disaster is itself mythical. Catastrophe follows breaking of taboo because it is invariably attributed to the same.

It is self-evident that these myths of destruction had their origin in Lemurian tradition, as by the period of Polynesian settlement in Oceania its greatest time of seismic violence had long passed. No continents have been submerged since then, and it remains as a logical consequence that the numerous myths of continents formerly existing must be a legacy from an older race—the fair-haired native race of Oceania. It is also to be noted that Hawaiki, the fatherland of the Polynesians, is thought of by some of them as being " Po," or darkness, chaos, destruction, and as under the sea.

In the myths referring to the volcanic goddess Pele we discover allusions to mythical or formerly existing continents.

CHAPTER V

THE RACES OF LEMURIA

IN considering the question of the origin of the races of Lemuria it is necessary to glance in passing at the subject of Oceanic ethnic relationships, though any extended consideration of the subject is by no means essential. It is now generally understood that neither the Polynesians nor the Melanesians have occupied the Oceanic area for any very prolonged period. Indeed Mr. S. Percy Smith, a good authority, has laid it down that the Polynesian immigrants did not enter the area until some time about the beginning of the Christian era. This is in direct opposition to the belief of Professor Macmillan Brown, who thinks that the race has been settled in its present position for a space of almost one hundred thousand years. But the whole question is, in reality, rather finally settled by the traditional but well-authenticated genealogies of the Polynesians themselves, which, although they go back to a respectable antiquity, do not appear to stretch back for more than six hundred years.

We must then regard the Polynesians as practically new-comers in Oceania. With the theory which brings them from India, Java, or elsewhere, we have indeed little to do. It is more of interest to us to inquire whether they inherited or acquired any customs, beliefs or traditions from the still older inhabitants of the Oceanic region. The Polynesians were not Lemurians, but only the heirs of the Lemurian civilization and culture.

The nature of our inquiry therefore makes it incumbent upon us to try to discover any traditions or traces regarding the presence of pre-Polynesian peoples in Oceania which may still persist.

Practically throughout the entire length and breadth of

the Pacific Ocean, but more especially in its more easterly latitudes, there exist the clearest and most astonishing traces of a white, fair-haired race which owes nothing to European admixture. The legends of Hawaii, the New Hebrides and New Zealand are all eloquent of the past traditions of such a race, and numerous examples of it are still to be found in white and fair-haired natives who have not a drop of European blood in their veins.

That the majority of these people were massacred by the invading Polynesians seems to be a conclusion generally accepted. In the smaller islands they would, of course, quickly be killed or absorbed, and it is only in the more spacious localities like Hawaii and New Zealand that they could find refuges and hiding-places. These islands are especially rich in legends of them. In the former they were worshipped as gods, one of whom, Lono, departed, promising to return. When Captain Cook, a fair-haired Englishman, arrived in Hawaii, he was regarded as the god Lono returned. He was worshipped by the natives and provided with an abode in the Temple of Lono.

It is, however, in New Zealand that we discover not only the majority of the legends concerning a fair race, now regarded, like the Picts of Scotland, as a Fairy folk, but where we still find the most numerous living examples of this strange stock. The mountainous and afforested character of these islands has made it possible for them to survive. Traditions tell of the Pakepakeha, the Turehu of the Urewera Mountains, and the Karitehe of the Bay of Islands and Hokianga being driven by the Maori immigrants into caves and forests, but occasionally venting their vengeance on the new-comers in raiding expeditions in which they carried off their women and looted their homes.

In the mountain region of Urewera in New Zealand, the Turehu, a light-haired aboriginal race, have intermarried with the Maoris, and numbers of them are still to be found there. But the blond race par excellence is the Patupaiarehe, the purest of all. Mr. James Cowan, writing in the *Journal of the Polynesian Society* for 1921, states that the elders of the Ngatimaniapoto tribe have traditions of this fair-skinned people who originally dwelt in the Polynesian fatherland, Hawaiki. Their sacred places on Mount Rangitoto are still guarded, but such of the natives as succeed in penetrating to them are believed to be kidnapped by their spirits!

Mr. Percy S. Smith, in his interesting book *Hawaiki*, is opposed to the theory that these should be regarded as fairies or supernatural beings. They were, he thinks, a race who had more experience of a maritime life than the ancestors of the Polynesians. He further states, "All through the race, everywhere we meet with it, we find a strain of light-coloured people who are not Albinos but have quite light hair and fair complexions. With the Maoris this strain often runs in families for many generations. At other times it appears as a probable reversion to the original type from which this strain was derived. There are also traditions amongst the Maori of a race of 'gods' called Pakahakeha, who are said always *to live in the sea*[1] and are white in complexion—hence the name Pakeha they gave to the white man on first becoming acquainted with us in the eighteenth century."

The New Zealand myth of Mataora makes pregnant allusion to the presence of a white fair-haired race in the island. He chased his wife Niwareka into the lower world of sunshine in jealous rage and found her people with fair skin and flaxen hair, handsome of build and stature, and having straight noses. They taught Mataora woodcarving and the weaving of ornamental borders on garments.

In the Gilbert Islands, in Micronesia, there are legends of blond people called "Matang." In the Solomon Islands there is a considerable sprinkling of light-haired people, especially in Malaita and the islands surrounding it. In Omba the people are markedly light in complexion, so much so, indeed, that Captain Cook believed them to be lepers. In the Ellice group blond individuals are common, and all of those alluded to are indigenous and not European hybrids.

Some of the Polynesian gods are described as fair, with red or sandy hair and florid countenances. In Honolulu fair

[1] Italics mine. L.S.

individuals of unmixed blood are to be met with among the natives. In Mangaia, the most southerly of the Cook group, golden-haired children were sacrificed to the god Tangaroa.

Mr. Angas, an artist who travelled in the North Island of New Zealand in the 'forties of last century, encountered many fair natives. He wrote that: " In the very heart of the interior, light or golden-coloured hair may occasionally be observed . . . where no mixture with European races could have taken place."

According to Maori traditions, this blond race took refuge in the mountains and forests from the invasion of their Polynesian foes, making sorties on the new-comers by night, and gradually producing a sentiment of awe and uneasiness which gave rise to the belief that they were of supernatural origin. The names given to them by the Maori, besides those already mentioned, were Karokako, or " white," Pakehakeha, or " moonlike," Hekiton and Rahurangi, " fiery," and Patupaiarehe, or " puny."

In Hawaii the Menehune, or pigmies, are thought of as megalithic builders, like the Crions and Gourics of Brittany. Speiser, in his *Two Years in the New Hebrides*, waxes enthusiastic over the blond people of Takopia, " the golden godlike forms of the natives," who seemed to him " the living originals of some classical picture."

Towards the west of Oceania traces of native fairness grow fainter. This shows that it is more indigenous to the eastern part of the area. Had it passed through the Tropics with their dark races it would have decreased, an observation which practically disposes of the theory that the fair peoples of the Pacific came from India, Egypt or the Persian Gulf.

Professor Macmillan Brown of Christchurch, New Zealand, in his noted work *The Mystery of the Pacific*, provides numerous photographs of these fair Polynesians, for whose non-European ancestry he vouches. Some of these are fair, curly-haired children, whose mothers are as dark as negroes.

Whence came this fair Pacific race ? He believes that they may have come from North-eastern Asia, passing

THE RACES OF LEMURIA

down through archipelagoes now submerged. But their presence in the islands of the great ocean remains a mystery still unsolved.

I cannot subscribe to the theory of Professor Macmillan Brown that the Polynesians arrived from North-eastern Asia at an early date, and I fail to understand how he reconciles it with the belief that they formerly inhabited a continent now submerged, unless he contends that that submergence was relatively late. But he admirably sums up the argument in the following passage :

" Polynesia, with its Caucasian face, its fair skin, but slightly dyed in the tropics, its chiefships and feudalism, its patrilinear descent, its tendency to Imperialism, its megalithism, and its absence of pottery, that sure mark of the Old Stone Age which ended twelve to fifteen thousand years ago, points up to the coasts of Asia north-eastwards through Micronesia, with its partially Caucasian face, its blanching of the complexions of its young women, its kings and aristocracy, its father-right, its relics of great insular empires, its no-pottery, except in the far south-west in the Pelews and Yap, and its great cyclopean ruins ; but it is to an Asia that was still unflooded by the Mongoloids, an Asia that was as yet Caucasian and in parts blondly Caucasoid.

" And then the thousands of islands that now lie in the depths, with only a coral buoy to mark their submergence, rose high above the ocean and by their continuous series tempted early man in his dug-outs far out into the Pacific. When the Mongol broke out of his high Asian home and crowded eastwards on to the coasts of the great ocean it was too late ; the stepping-stones into the oceanic unknown had sunk, and only timidly the insular Japanese groped their way down the broken line of islets into the Mariannes and the northern Marshalls."

But did the Northern Asia of the age Professor Brown alludes to possess the said culture-complex in its entirety ? Where are its cyclopean monuments, was it egregious in kingship and aristocracy or father-right.

Another of the racial indications which reveal an argument in favour of the former continental conditions of

Oceania is the present disposal of the Negrito race within it. The early population of Micronesia was almost certainly Negrito in type, as in New Guinea and Melanesia, as the physical characteristics of its inhabitants show. But the Negrito was here absorbed, although legends tell of his early coming to the archipelago, legends which allude to little folk who sought refuge in the forests and inland parts from the later immigrants.

But it would have been impossible for a people so primitive as the Negritos to have negotiated the broad and usually stormy seas that separate these islands from the continent. They have never been a sea-going people, and the rafts and coracles they at present use would certainly have succumbed to the dangers of such a passage. It is thus obvious that they could have reached the present Micronesian islands only by way of land-bridges or by a solid terrestrial route. As the length of time since they can have settled there cannot be very great, geologically speaking, we are absolutely compelled to the acceptance of the theory that they made their way thence by land-route. In respect of this particular area there is, indeed, no alternative of hypothesis, and, furthermore, it plainly points to a quite recent submergence, either of solid land betwixt the continent and the islands, or the submergence of a large area which has left only insular vestiges. Also, it is clear, the existence of the great megalithic ruins of Ponape in this area can only be accounted for by submergence in late prehistoric times, after the coming of the Negritos and subsequent to the building of the said ruins, and is eloquent of a large imperial tract covering thousands of square miles where only small and scattered islands now lie.

Early as was the advent of the Negrito type, however, that chronology of its coming must be regarded as comparative, for it is clear that it has been strengthened in certain areas of Micronesia by still later immigration from Melanesia or New Guinea, thus providing additional evidence of recent submergence.

It is also clear that the land distribution of the Northwest Pacific was different when the Gilbert Islands were first peopled. Their inhabitants have traditions of their arrival there, some saying that they came from " Baneba," perhaps Ponape. Their " Otherworld " is supposed to be situated on Gilbert's Island. They probably came from the Central Pacific before either Negroid or Mongolian influence was brought to bear upon them.

Says Macmillan Brown: " It was long before Polynesian culture attained its full development in the Central Pacific, or was thrust out in all directions by the subsidence of its lands. That subsidence was probably part of the great movement which, in human times, filled up the primeval volcanic fissure of the Western Pacific stretching from the coast of Japan to Easter Island. And the subsidence of the Gilberts area must have been part of the same movement. From Japan to the Gilberts and onwards must have had, in early human times, a series of easy stepping-stones for man; even palæolithic man would find his way in his dug-outs across the north-east trades in the lee of what must have been high, if not mountainous islands, so little distant from each other as to be seen on the horizon."

In his *Fairy Folk Tales of the Maori*, a work which is well worthy the consideration of students of Comparative Folklore, Mr. James Cowan furnishes us with material which assists the theory that the blond so-called fairy folk of New Zealand were the remnants of a most ancient Pacific stock. They are spoken of as an *Iwi-atua*, or race of supernatural beings, and occasionally as of dwarf stature, though most of the tales told of them allude to them as of mortal height.

They were of much lighter complexion than the Maori, with hair of the dull golden or reddish hue often to be remarked among the Maori of to-day. They were averse from the habits of the Maori, his oven cookery and his custom of daubing himself with red earth. They were the guardians of sacred places, and, according to Mr. Cowan, were " the remnants of an immeasurably ancient fair-haired people who have left a strain of *uru-kehu*, or blondness, in most Maori tribes.

As in the case of the Scottish Picts of Folklore, they

were driven to the caves and mountains by the immigrant Maori, and became to the more powerful race an enchanted tribe, practising magic and possessed of powers of transformation and invisibility. The legendry of these Patupaiarehe in the North Island is associated chiefly with the forested peaks of the Waikato-waipa basin, the Cape Colville-Te Aroha range, and the hills about Lake Rotorua. They frequently were credited with the building of great natural features, like the lava-reef of Auckland Harbour. They tried to prevent the coming of the Polynesian Maori with incantations and enchantments.

By sleight of magic, they " flew through the air," not with wings, but, like the Irish Druids, by dint of their powers of levitation. Like the people of Easter Island, they had a marionette drama and magical houses or institutions. The legends concerning them are significant for us, says Mr. Cowan, because they describe the contact between the remote ancestors of the Maori and a people more advanced in culture. " In a number of Maori-Polynesian traditions the underworld, in other words the home of a strange race, is mentioned as the place of origin of various arts and crafts, such as carving and tattooing, and of occult knowledge."

Mr. Cowan supplies an account of the Patupaiarehe from the lips of Te Matehaere, an old Maori of his acquaintance.

" Long ago," said Te Matehaere, " the summit of yon mountain Ngongotaha, the peak-top called Te Tuahu a te Atua (' The Altar of the God '), was the chief home of the fairy people of this country. The name of that tribe of *Patupaiarehe* was Ngati-Rua, and the chiefs of that tribe in the days of my ancestor Ihenga were Tuehu, Te Rangitamai, Tongakohu, and Rotokohu. The people were very numerous; there were a thousand or perhaps many more on Ngongotaha. They were an *iwi atua* (a god-like race, a people of supernatural powers). In appearance some of them were very much like the Maori people of to-day; others resembled the *pakeha* (white) race. The colour of most of them was *kiri puwhero* (reddish skins), and their hair had the red or golden tinge which we call *uru-kehu*.

Some had black eyes, some blue, like fair-skinned Europeans. They were about the same height as ourselves. Some of their women were very beautiful, very fair of complexion, with shining fair hair. They wore chiefly the flax garments called *pakerangi*, dyed a red colour; they also wore the rough mats *pora* and *pureke*. In disposition they were peaceful; they were not a war-loving, angry people. Their food consisted of the products of the forest, and they also came down to this Lake Rotorua to catch *inanga* (whitebait). There was one curious characteristic of these Patupaiarehe; they had a great dread of the steam that rose from cooked food. In the evenings, when the Maori people living at Te Raho-o-te-Rangipiere and other places near the fairy abodes opened their cooking-ovens, all the *Patupaiarehe* retired to their houses immediately they saw the clouds of vapour rising, and shut themselves up; they were afraid of the *mamaoa* —the steam."

Many are the tales which tell of how the Patupaiarehe seized upon beautiful Maori girls and bore them off to their fastnesses. In order to avoid such a fate Maori maidens smeared themselves with shark oil, a substance of loathing to the fair-haired outcasts of the heights. Some of the " Fairy " tribes made war on each other for the possession of Maori girls, fighting with burning spear-darts. But chiefly they fought to guard their sacred places of occult practice and their peculiar treasures—the red flax, red pigs and red eels in the streams.

Who were these white races of the Pacific ? Were they not the survivors of its sunken land-masses, its ruined civilization, were they not the last of the Lemurians ?

Taylor, in his work *Te Ika a Maui*, says, " they are supposed to have been of large size, and were regarded as giants, as in the story of Hatupatu, who was seized by a Patupaiarehe giantess called Kurangaituku. Yet they were seldom seen but in large numbers and only early in the morning; they held long councils, speaking and singing very loud, and they made raids and carried off women. They were not only white, but clothed themselves in white. The Maori thought that albinos had Patupaiarehe fathers; and one of their tribes was called *Ngati-Korako*, or ' the children of the albino.' "

Furthermore, they alleged in New Zealand and in the Cook group that their ancestors came from a land where for half the year the trees were without leaves, and the people could " walk upon water."

Hawaiian history relates that an early navigator brought back to his home two white men who married among his people. This event seems to have occurred about A.D. 800 and the probability is that it refers to the capture of individuals of the older and original race of Oceania.

Mr. James Cowan, in *The Journal of the Polynesian Society*, tells a story of this blond race " dating back untold centuries."

" A Patupaiarehe man called Miru, the chief and priest of his tribe, fell in love with Hinerangi, the *puhi* or virgin daughter of ' a man of this world,' and marrying her had two sons by her; but getting home-sick, he returned to his tribe, taking with him some companions, including his father-in-law and sister-in-law. As the *tohunga* (wizard) of his tribe he taught them in *Hui-te-rangiora* all the incantations and charms of his race, and various games, including the working of the wooden marionettes that were caused to imitate *haka* and other dances. The father-in-law of Miru in return bestowed on him the hand of his second daughter, and ' returned to this world ' and built a *Hui-te-rangiora* there and taught in it all the sacred wisdom and charms he had learned. ' That is how the people of this world came to possess the knowledge of these.' And the *Ngati-Maniopoto* continue to honour this name for a house of learning and council, *Hui-te-rangiora*.

" It is by no means a rash conclusion to draw from these indications that Miru was an honoured name in the Polynesian fatherland amongst a lighter-coloured race, who, though probably of higher culture, was driven into the wilds by the bolder sea-rovers that came later and ruled in Polynesia."

The great *marae* of Opoa in the island of Raiatea, near Tahiti, appears to have been one of the religious nuclei for the people of the surrounding archipelago. It was the shrine of Oro, the war-god of this area. But, says tradition, this had not always been so. In the ancient days it was the haunt of gods and other supernatural beings who practised shape-shifting, the resurrection of the dead and other marvels. That is, it was anciently the centre of a religion greatly more venerable than the Polynesian.

In many of the Polynesian groups there are traces of an older sun-worship prior to Polynesian times, in Tahiti, Rarotonga and Mangaia, for example, and that the divinities of that cult were displaced by later Polynesian gods is quite clear. A Samoan myth recounts that the ruling family in the islands was descended from beings who lived in the sky, and who built a palace known as " The Shining House."

" Whilst the ' sunken continent ' idea has no doubt much to support it," remarks Mr. S. Percy Smith in his *Hawaiki*, it seems to the writer " that everything proves the Polynesians to have arrived in the Pacific long after the existence of such a land." Of course he would admit that numerous insular areas in the Pacific region have been submerged or have actually reappeared since that epoch. But, substantially, his view is correct. We must certainly look for the presence of a much older race in Oceania than the Polynesian, who seem to have embraced the vestiges of its culture.

The New Zealand legend of the island of Ao-tea-oroa tells of numerous immigrations to its soil. First came the People of Maui, later the Tutu-mai-ao, who exterminated many of them and " assumed a superior knowledge " over them. Still later arrived a race called Turehu, " the sleepy, fairy-like people," who came from the other side of the ocean and attacked the Tutu-mai-ao and defeated them. Lastly came the Maori. There are thus indications that at least three races occupied New Zealand prior to the coming of the Maori. The Turehu, adds the tradition, are now represented by the Patupaiarehe, or wild white men, of whom we have already made mention.

The South Island of New Zealand, we are further informed, was first occupied by the Kahui-tipua, or " ogre band," giants who could stride from mountain-range to mountain-range (perhaps by the aid of aerial railways like those the remains of which are to be found in Easter Island) and transform themselves into any shape they chose. A myth concerning one of those beings is worthy of quotation.

"When the Te-rapu-wai, who dwelt at Matua, went in small parties of ten to hunt for *weka* they never returned. Tens and tens went out and never came back. Then every one felt sure something was consuming them, but what it was they could not tell. A long time passed, and then it was found how these people perished. It was learnt from a woman, the sole survivor of one of these hunting-parties. She said that on the hills they were met by a *tipua* (an ogre) accompanied by ten two-headed dogs. After killing all the men he carried her to his cave near the river, where she lived with him, and in time became covered all over with scales from the ogre's body. She was very miserable, and determined to escape; but this was not easy, as the ogre took care to fasten her by a cord, which he kept jerking whenever she was out of his sight. As the cave was close to the river, she crept to the entrance, where *raupo* grew thickly, and, having cut a quantity, tied it in bundles. The next day, when the monster slept, she crept out and formed the *raupo*-bundles into a *mokihi* (raft), and then tied the string to the rushes, which, being elastic, would prevent the immediate discovery of her flight when the cord was jerked. Getting on to the raft, she dropped down the river, the swift current bearing her rapidly towards its mouth, where her friends lived.

"The ogre did not wake for a long time. When he did he called out, ' Kai-a-mio, e ! (food of the dogs), where are you ? ' Not receiving an answer, he went to the entrance of the cave and searched. Not finding any footprints there he smelt the water, and at once discovered how she had escaped. Then in his rage he swallowed the river and dried it up from end to end, but not before Kai-a-mio was safely housed in her native village. After cleansing herself from the scales which covered her body, the woman told her people all she knew about the ogre, and they

NAVEL-STRING TOWER AT EASTER ISLAND
After Domeny de Rienzi.

resolved to put him to death. ' When does he sleep ? ' they asked. ' When the north-west wind blows,' was her reply, ' then he sleeps long and heavily.' So they waited for a north-wester, and then proceeded to the cave. Having collected a great quantity of fern, which they piled at the entrance, they fired it. When the heat awoke the monster, he could think of no way of escape except through a hole in the roof. While struggling to get out through this the people set upon him with clubs and beat him to death. Fortunately the ogre's dogs were away hunting, or else he never could have been killed."

There can scarcely be any doubt that this tradition has reference to an individual of a race which dwelt in New Zealand before the Maori. In nearly every country tales relating to ogres and giants are discovered, and folklore concludes that these represent an earlier stratum of population which only appeared monstrous to the newcomers by reason of their different appearance, habits and customs. The " scales " of the " ogre " mentioned in the above tale may well have been of the nature of scale-armour,[1] and the fact that he dwelt in a cave shows him to have resembled the Cyclops of Greek myth in his habits, a custom indicative of early or degenerate man.

The general circumstances of these traditions relate to the survivors of races which must have flourished in the Oceanic area at a period before catastrophe overtook its larger archipelagoes, and who entered Oceania long before the Polynesian immigration. Indeed the very names of some of the islands in Oceania are in themselves traditional or legendary of conditions of subsidence. Thus Mr. Smith points out that one of the names of Easter Island is Te Pito-te-henua, " which means either ' the navel of the land ' or ' the end of the land.' To those who favour the idea of a sunken continent," he says, " the tops of whose mountains are now represented over the Pacific, and especially in the Pau-motu group, of which Easter Island forms the S.E. extremity, this name—Te Pito-te-henua—' the end of the land,' may suggest a confirmation of the theory."

---

[1] This is alleged as regards the " Shelly-coat " men or demons of the east coast of Scotland, by Dr. Karl Blind.

Professor Macmillan Brown, alluding to the symptoms of decay manifest in Polynesian life, says: "We have not to search far in the central and eastern Pacific for a true cause. Submergence has been in process through all time and has by no means ceased in our era. It has been and is dominant in this area of the ocean in contrast to the area to the west, especially the south-west, where elevation has manifestly been going on, in our geological era at least, and is still dominant. The mythology everywhere in Polynesia bears record to submergence in early human times. And we have within the past century the disappearance of Tuanaki with all its people, and within the past two centuries the disappearance of Davis' Land. How chagrining it is to know that if only Davis had yielded to the desires of Lieutenant Wafer and his crew and visited that long archipelago which stretched away to the north-west over the horizon, we should have had some inkling of the culture and power of the people who used Easter Island as a mausoleum for their conspicuous dead! And it is similar submergences in the central Pacific that will account for the great voyagings of the Polynesians over the ocean and their sudden cessation."

We have now to examine those theories regarding the Lemurian race which have been set forth by Madam Blavatsky, Dr. Rudolf Steiner and others.

Madame Blavatsky, it would be merely foolish to deny, was a most distinguished student of the arcane, and everything she wrote was characterized, as a general rule, by logic and temperate statement. So much one is bound to admit in homage to a great mind.

In her *Isis Unveiled*, she has little to say about Lemuria. It is rather in her *Secret Doctrine*, a work often of surprising insight, that she deals with its problems.

Dealing with the four continents on which the four great races which she believed preceded the present, originated, she calls the third Lemuria. "The name," she says, "is an invention, or an idea, of Mr. P. L. Sclater, who asserted, between 1850 and 1860, on zoological grounds the actual existence, in prehistoric times, of a continent which he showed to have extended from Madagascar to Ceylon and Sumatra. It included some portions of what is now Africa ; but otherwise this gigantic continent, which stretched from the Indian Ocean to Australia, has now wholly disappeared beneath the waters of the Pacific, leaving here and there only some of its high-land tops which are now islands. Mr. A. R. Wallace, the naturalist, ' extends the Australia of the Tertiary Period to New Guinea and the Solomon Islands, and perhaps to Fiji ' ; and from its marsupial types he infers ' a connection with the Northern Continent during the Secondary Period.' "

The race which inhabited this continent, she states at a later stage, was bi-sexual, according to the *Secret Volume* from which she quotes, but how she comes to identify it with the Lemurians is by no means clear, at least to the writer. Lemurian man, she says, had an astral body only, and his continent was swept away before the third Eocene Age. She quotes Haeckel as saying that the Australians are direct descendants of the Lemurians, as are the Papuans and Hottentots.

In the *Theosophist* for August 1880, she wrote: " We have as evidences the most ancient traditions of various and wide-separated peoples—legends in India, in ancient Greece, Madagascar, Sumatra, Java, and all the principal isles of Polynesia, as well as the legends of both Americas. Among savages ; and in the traditions of the richest literature in the world—the Sanskrit literature of India—there is an agreement in saying, that, ages ago, there existed in the Pacific Ocean, a large Continent, which by a geological cataclysm was engulfed by the sea (Lemuria). And it is our firm belief . . . that most, if not all, of the islands from the Malayan archipelago to Polynesia, are fragments of that once immense submerged continent. Both Malacca and Polynesia, which lie at the two extremities of the ocean, and which, since the memory of man never had, and never could have any intercourse with, or even a knowledge of each other, have yet a tradition common to all the islands and islets, that their respective countries extended far, far into the Sea : that there were in the world but two immense continents, one inhabited by yellow, the other by dark men ; and that the Ocean, by command of the gods, and to punish them for their incessant quarrelling, swallowed them up. Notwithstanding the geographical proof that New Zealand, the Sandwich and Easter Islands, are at a distance from each other of between 800 and 1000 leagues, and that, according to every testimony, neither these nor any other intermediate islands, for instance, the Marquesan, Society, Fiji, Tahitian, Samoan, and other islands, could, since they became islands, ignorant as their people were of the compass, have communicated with each other before the arrival of Europeans; yet they one and all maintain that their respective countries extended far toward the west, on the Asian side. Moreover, with very small differences, they all speak dialects evidently of the same language; and understand each other with little difficulty; have the same religious beliefs and superstitions; and pretty much the same customs. And as few of the Polynesian islands were discovered earlier than a century ago, the Pacific Ocean itself being unknown to Europe till the days of Columbus, and as these islanders have never ceased repeating the same old traditions since the Europeans first set foot on their shores, it seems to us a logical inference that our theory is nearer to the truth than any other. 'Chance would have to change its name and meaning, were all this due but to chance alone.'"

"There are or were," she continues, "descendants of these half-animal tribes or races of remote Lemurian origin, Tasmanians, Australians, Andaman Islanders, etc. The Lemurians, in some cases, were gigantic and bestial and begat a species which later developed into 'mammalian apes.'

"Lemuria covered the whole area of space 'from the foot of the Himalayas which separated it from the inland sea rolling its waves over what is now Tibet, Mongolia' and the Gobi desert, 'from Chittagong westward to Hardwar, and eastward to Assam.'

"From thence, it stretched south across what is known to us as Southern India, Ceylon, and Sumatra; then embracing on its way, as we go south, Madagascar on its right hand and Australia and Tasmania on its left, it ran down to within a few degrees of the Antarctic Circle;

THE RACES OF LEMURIA

when, from Australia, an inland region on the Mother Continent in those ages, it extended far into the Pacific Ocean, not only beyond Rapa-nui (Teapy, or Easter Island) which now lies in latitude 26 S., and longitude 110 W. This statement seems corroborated by Science—even if only partially; as, when discussing continental trends, and showing the infra-Arctic masses trending generally with the meridian, several ancient continents are generally mentioned, though inferentially. Among such the 'Mascarene continent,' which included Madagascar, stretching north and south, is spoken of, and the existence of another *ancient* continent running ' from Spitzbergen to the Straits of Dover, while most of the other parts of Europe were sea bottom,' is taught. The latter corroborates, then, the Occult teaching which shows the (now) polar regions as the earliest of the seven cradles of Humanity, and as the tomb of the bulk of the mankind of that region during the Third Race, when the gigantic continent of Lemuria began separating into smaller continents. This is due, according to the explanation in the Commentary, to a decrease of velocity in the earth's rotation:

" ' When the Wheel runs at the usual rate, its extremities (the poles) agree with its middle circle (equator), when it runs slower and tilts in every direction, there is a great disturbance on the face of the Earth. The waters flow towards the two ends, and new lands arise in the middle belt (equatorial lands), while those at the ends are subject to pralayas by submersion . . .' "

And again : " ' Thus the wheel (the Earth) is subject to, and regulated by, the Spirit of the Moon, for the breath of its waters (tides). Toward the close of the age (Kalpa) of a great (root) race, the regents of the moon (the Pitar fathers, or Pitris) begin drawing harder, and thus flatten the wheel about its belt, when it goes down in some places and swells in others, and the swelling running toward the extremities (poles) new lands will arise and old ones be sucked in.' "

It is a little baffling to read that Scandinavia formed part of Lemuria and also of Atlantis " on the European side." Lemuria " perished about 799,000 years ago, before the beginning of the Tertiary Period." It has been " confused with Atlantis." The Lemurians " gravitated to the North Pole," or the Heaven of their progenitors (the Hyperborean continent), the Atlanteans to the South Pole. They mated with " animals," perhaps imperfectly developed men, and became degenerate. They possessed a " third eye," which conferred on them psychic vision.

It is to that part of Madame Blavatsky's argument, which is based solely upon the ancient Indian wisdom-writings, that exception must be taken and to the obviously allegorical and grotesquely fictional notions of a crude cosmology to which they refer. That most of them are allegorical in character is plain, and although allegory, like all tradition, has its uses, it stands in need of critical examination and selection before it can be employed as proof.

Rudolf Steiner's notions regarding Lemuria and its inhabitants are based to a great extent upon those of Madame Blavatsky. As given in his little book, *Atlantis and Lemuria*, they may be summarized as follows:

Lemuria was inhabited by " the third human Root-race," and lay to the south of Asia and extended from Ceylon to Madagascar. It also included parts of Southern Asia and Africa. The Theosophical accounts of it are derived from the " Akashic Records," but Dr. Steiner is of opinion that " nothing of a dogmatic nature should be assigned to these communications."

The memory of the Lemurian race was not as yet fully evolved, and they were without language, although they could communicate with each other by a species of thought transference. Lemurian man had " imbibed the physical and chemical forces inherent in lifeless things," and had but to look at objects to judge their weight-bearing capacity. Thus he could build and erect without recourse to the arts of engineering, and could lift enormous weights by the exercise of will-power alone. Will-power, was, indeed, the particular quality in which the Lemurians were transcendent.

They lived in caves and excavations, but remodelled

the hills as a labour of pleasure, but later they raised "erections," devoted to the service of "Divine Wisdom and Divine Art," which were not temples, but places of instruction in science and magic.

The knowledge acquired dealt with the natural forces in man, which they were taught to convert into will-power to enable them "to forestall the actions of Nature." It was "instinctive," or rather inspirational, and not due to thought or reason.

At this early period atmospheric conditions were denser than in later times, water was in a far more fluid state and the earth's crust in a less firm condition. Plant-life and the animal-world were "at the amphibious stage."

Lemurian man regarded himself as a servant of the world-forces, knowledge of which was cherished as a divine "secret." He was permitted to enjoy intercourse with the beings who are ever "building this world." From this intercourse the Mysteries were developed.

Man was still physically in a semi-material state, as was the earth-crust. In the middle of the Lemurian epoch he was also androgynous or bi-sexual. He needed no brain to think with, nor "any physical vehicle to attain connection with the spirit."

There is a great deal more of the same sort, but further summary or quotation seems needless. I do not care to dignify this description, the fruit of the pseudo-arcane schools, by refutation. The statements, indeed, refute themselves. One, if he believes such stuff, is compelled to accept the "Akashic Records," which seem for the most part to consist of the weakly effort of third-rate imaginations, wretched inventions which fall immeasurably beneath the avowed fictions of a Swift, an H. G. Wells, or an M. P. Shiel. The genuine mystic should shun this description of "science" as coming from intelligences which, if not mischievous, are certainly equivocal and dubious.

A review of the notions of Colonel Churchward as presented in his *The Lost Continent of Mu*, and *The Children of Mu* need not detain us long. This pair of handsome volumes, lavishly illustrated, purports to set forth in great detail the story of the sunken land of Mu, or Lemuria, the Atlantis of the Pacific, its archæology, its ethnology, and its colonial associations. Colonel Churchward tells us that he first discovered the clues of the submerged continent through the agency of a recluse in a monastery in India. But unfortunately he fails to specify the name or precise location of the monastery, nor does he supply anything approaching reasonable or sufficient description of the " Naacal " tablets, written in the language of Mu, which contained the information which sent him many thousands of miles in search of further proof of the former existence of the land of their origin.

Geology agrees with the hypothesis of the former existence of large land-masses in the Atlantic and Pacific Oceans. But the more definite and extended proof that they were actually occupied by civilized races is still so far to seek in its entirety, that comment or testimony regarding it should at present be based either on analogical assumption of the most rational kind, or on very definite historical, traditional, or archæological grounds. Otherwise untold mischief may be done to a study confessedly still in its early stages. With the best will in the world, one cannot find in Colonel Churchward's pages a scheme of such judicious demonstration as the nature of his subject demands.

Some of the author's acceptances are, indeed, already discredited, more especially those culled from the writings of the late Augustus Le Plongeon. Colonel Churchward states that, accepting the suggestions of Le Plongeon and Schliemann, he found evidences of the former existence of the continent of Mu in the Central American Maya Codex-Troano and Codex-Cortesianus, and in " an ancient Maya book written in Yucatan." But, as all Mayologists are aware, Le Plongeon's transliterations and " translations " of the Maya scripts were of the most fantastic description and manifestly imaginary. So far, the Maya script is only decipherable as regards its chronological system, and not at all in respect of any historic matter it may dubiously contain.

"Certain old symbols and customs, discovered in Egypt, Burma, India, Japan, and elsewhere, are," says the author, "so identical, it is certain they came from one source only—Mu," a continent which stretched far north of Hawaii, "down towards the south. . . . It was over 5000 miles from east to west, and over 3000 miles from north to south." In this early paradise, which existed 50,000 years ago, sixty-four millions of civilized human beings "reigned supreme." But a succession of volcanic cataclysms visited it, and in the last event some 12,000 years distant from our era it was engulfed wholesale. Only a handful escaped and these sank into the depths of savagery, a barbarism lightened only by the comparative civilization of the colonies which Mu had sent out to the ends of the more stable earth.

Colonel Churchward's statements, at least the more dogmatic of them, are scarcely worthy of refutation. In the mélange of his works mythology, symbolism, and tradition are not only hopelessly mingled, but so coloured and distorted by his own peculiar notions as to constitute an almost hopeless jumble from which the logical reader will turn in despair. Indeed, he may be said to follow his master Le Plongeon in general method, or, rather, the want of it.

The sequel book, *The Children of Mu*, which deals with the question of the colonies and settlements sent out by Mu before its submergence, is equally fantastic, and is chiefly interesting because of its chapter on Atlantis. " I found in an old Greek record," writes Colonel Churchward, " that when Atlantis disappeared there were 3000 Athenian soldiers on her, probably an army of occupation." If the statement that Athens 11,500 years ago could send " an army of occupation " from one end of the Mediterranean to another is true, the British School of Archæology at Athens is surely manned by persons of bromidic propensity. The crown of Poseidon, we read, had three points, and his sceptre was a trident, " showing Mu to be suzerain . . . later we find it as the sceptre of the Khmers of Cambodia."

Colonel Churchward actually gives credence to the

long-discredited writings of Dr. Paul Schliemann regarding Atlantis, and this in itself marks the quality of his critical faculty. But the pitch of absurdity seems to be reached when we find that the Maya of Central America are described in the Troano Codex as the first settlers in Atlantis, and that Orpheus is designated " a Greek philosopher." However, worse is to come, for we are assured that a Great Central Gas Belt ran beneath the earth, and that it was the explosion of this which submerged both Mu and Atlantis !

Works of this character, we repeat, however amusing, are capable of doing more damage to a serious quest even than " the credulity of incredulity " indulged in by some scientists, and all serious Atlantalogues should beware of their conclusions. It behoves Colonel Churchward to produce authenticated photographs of the " Naacal " tablets on which he bases his theory, and to indicate their find-spot in India.

We find much the same position as that of Steiner adopted by Mr. K. Browning in his pamphlet, *Lemuria and Atlantis*. He says : " The Story of Man, as discovered by occult investigation, can be briefly told. He is developed in seven clearly marked stages called Root-Races. The first three were occupied in the work of building a serviceable physical body and developing the senses of hearing, touch and sight. No physical traces will ever be found of the first two, for their bodies were made of such fine matter that no fossils could be left, and they did not build cities or temples. The third race has more in common with our own. It inhabited the continent of Lemuria in the Secondary Period, and it was therefore a contemporary of the gigantic saurians.

" We need not, therefore, be surprised to hear that the Lemurians were of great stature ; they could hardly have survived in their conflicts with the carnivorous reptiles of the primeval forests and swamps had they not been proportionally greater in size than ourselves, for the intellect of this early race was not sufficiently developed for them to have discovered effective weapons of defence. If the accounts are correct, we can truly agree with the Bible

THE RACES OF LEMURIA

that ' there were giants on the earth in those days.' In complexion, the Lemurians were very dark, and the ' black ' races may be considered the remnants of this ancient Race. There has been so much admixture of blood that probably only the very lowest types, such as the aborigines of South Australia, are direct descendants of the Lemurians.

" Lemuria was destroyed before the Eocene Period of the Tertiary, but colonies had been formed in adjacent lands, and in the cyclopean buildings of some of the South Pacific Islands, in the images of Easter Island, and in the lava cities of Madagascar, we find traces of their art and civilization.

" Before the final destruction of Lemuria, a colony had been established in a land to the North-west of Africa. The inhabitants were segregated from the remainder of their Race, and by careful selection a better type of humanity, with greater powers of mind and emotion, was evolved. They were also of lighter complexion, being red or yellow coloured. They migrated to the continent of Atlantis which thus became the home of the most advanced human beings. Here they lived and flourished exceedingly. At one time their civilization was so advanced that it is said that there was not a single person who was not well clad, well fed, well sheltered, with easy work and ample leisure for recreation. But that was in the childhood of the Race, when it was still under the guidance of the ' Divine Kings ' of whom we hear so much in the myths and traditions of various races. As humanity developed more intellect and will-power, it rebelled against these wise Rulers, and in the course of its experiments in self-rule it sank into the greatest depths of sensuality and vice. The intellect was not yet strong enough to control the emotions and the desires of the flesh.

" The direct descendants of the Atlanteans are still in the majority in the world. The Chinese, Japanese, Polynesians ; the Indians of the three Americas ; the tribes of Siberia and the regions round the North Pole, are Atlantean ; while many other races have been formed by the intermarriage of Atlanteans and Lemurians, though these are still very undeveloped. The Veddahs of Ceylon may be cited as an example.

"If we accept re-incarnation as the means for the evolution of the soul, there is an added interest in studying these records of the past. As Lemurians we traversed the gloomy forests of the Coal Period and fought with the monsters in the slime; as Atlanteans we learned more of the wonder and beauty of nature, developed the powers of emotion and observation; as Aryans we are striving to evolve the intellect and to apply it to both concrete and abstract problems."

I have quoted these writers at some length in order that the unsupported nature of their testimony may be recognized. May I add that it has been my lot to peruse in manuscript some hundreds of alleged records of Atlantis and Lemuria said to have been communicated through automatic writing in trance conditions or otherwise, and that not one of them has agreed in its general circumstances with another.

It is to be observed that such writers as Steiner and Churchward seldom or never make use of those scientific evidences which can be rationally employed to assist their hypotheses, and which lie naturally to their hands. They prefer rather to invent or repeat phantasies the most bizarre and grotesque which they are aware will satisfy or excite the feeble minds of those who crave for the pseudo-mysterious. Much as I abhor the " tape-measure " school of Archæologists, who have succeeded in destroying the romance once seemingly inherent in their science, I must confess to an even greater impatience with those who would transform it into a playground for the disordered and the ignorant, who are incapable of distinguishing fiction from fact, and who implicitly believe in the actuality of all they read. Moreover, Steiner and his school have rendered the ideas of Madame Blavatsky, evidently made in good faith, still more grotesque than before. It was her implicit faith in the writings of Indian antiquity which misled her into statements not at all consonant with an insight often inspired and an almost habitual shrewd common sense, and it is taking a wrong advantage of this absolute reliance on obviously elementary and exclusively archaic evidence to exaggerate her views as they have done.

Louis Jacolliot, in his *Histoire de Vierges : Les Peuples et les Continents disparus*, says : " One of the most ancient legends of India, preserved in the temples by oral and written tradition, relates that several hundred thousand years ago there existed in the Pacific Ocean an immense continent which was destroyed by geological upheaval, and the fragments of which must be sought in Madagascar, Ceylon, Sumatra, Java, Borneo, and the principal isles of Polynesia.

" The high plateaux of Hindustan and Asia, according to this hypothesis, would only have been represented in those distant epochs by great islands contiguous to the central continent. . . . According to Brahmans this country had attained a high civilization, and to the peninsula of Hindustan, enlarged by the displacement of the waters, at the time of the great cataclysm, has but continued the chain of the primitive traditions born in this place. These traditions give the name of *Rutas* to the peoples which inhabited this immense equinoctial continent, and from their speech was derived the Sanskrit.

" The Indo-Hellenic tradition, preserved by the most intelligent population which emigrated from the plains of India, equally relates the existence of a continent and a people to which it gives the names of Atlantis and Atlantides, and which it locates in the Atlantic in the northern portion of the Tropics.

" Apart from the fact that the supposition of an ancient continent in those latitudes, the vestiges of which may be found in the volcanic islands and mountainous surface of the Azores, the Canaries and Cape Verd, is not devoid of geographical probability, the Greeks, who, moreover, never dared to pass beyond the pillars of Hercules, on account of their dread of the mysterious ocean, appeared too late in antiquity for the stories preserved by Plato to be anything else than an echo of the Indian legend. Moreover, when we cast a look on a planisphere, at the sight of the islands and islets strewn from the Malayan Archipelago to

Polynesia, from the straits of Sund to Easter Island, it is impossible, upon the hypothesis of continents preceding those which we inhabit, not to place there the most important of all.

"A religious belief, common to Malacca and Polynesia, that is to say to the two opposite extremes of the Oceanic world, affirms 'that all these islands once formed two immense countries, inhabited by yellow men and black men, always at war ; and that the gods, wearied with their quarrels, having charged Ocean to pacify them, the latter swallowed up the two continents, and since then it had been impossible to make him give up his captives. Alone, the mountain-peaks and high plateaux escaped the flood, by the power of the gods, who perceived too late the mistake they had committed.'

"Whatever there may be in these traditions, and whatever may have been the place where a civilization more ancient than that of Rome, of Greece, of Egypt, and of India was developed, it is certain that this civilization did exist, and that it is highly important for science to recover its traces, however feeble and fugitive they may be.

"As to the Polynesian continent which disappeared at the time of the final geological cataclysms, its existence rests on such proofs that, to be logical, we can doubt no longer.

"The three summits of this continent, Sandwich Islands, New Zealand, Easter Island, are distant from each other from fifteen to eighteen hundred leagues, and the groups of intermediate islands, Fiji, Samoa, Tonga, Austral, Marquesas, Tahiti, Paumota, Gambier, are themselves distant from these extreme points from seven or eight hundred to one thousand leagues.

"All navigators agree in saying that the extreme and the central groups could never have communicated in view of their actual geographical position, and with the insufficient means they had at hand. It is physically impossible to cross such distances in a pirogue, without a compass, and travel months without provisions.

"On the other hand, the aborigines of the Sandwich Islands, of Fiji, of New Zealand, of the central groups, of

THE RACES OF LEMURIA

Samoa, Tahiti, etc., had never known each other, had never heard of each other before the arrival of the Europeans. And yet each of these people maintained that their island had at one time formed a part of an immense stretch of land which extended toward the West, on the side of Asia. And all, brought together, were found to speak the same language, to have the same usages, the same customs, the same religious belief. And all to the question, ' Where is the cradle of your race ? ' for sole response, extended their hand toward the setting sun."

Judging from the analogy of the present inhabitants of Oceania, it seems safe to say that the Lemurian races must have exhibited an equal degree of variety. It is impossible to believe that peoples dwelling at such extreme distances as those occupied by the several great land-masses which formerly covered the Pacific, could have displayed any very marked resemblance one to another. Yet it is equally probable that the civilization they enjoyed was homogeneous, and well-recognized laws make it certain that it must have originated in one definite area, whence it spread to the others. There remains, too, the fact that a people dwelling in a certain environment comes in time to produce the type native to that environment. It seems, therefore, reasonable to infer that in the continental masses of Oceania human types were produced which did not differ very greatly in physique or temperament from those presently occupying them. Of course anything approaching actual physical identity with present types is scarcely to be envisaged. But there seems to be sufficient evidence in practically every one of the Oceanic archipelagoes which we may regard as the vestiges of ancient continents, of the presence of a race preponderatingly white.

The concensus of opinion in present-day Ethnology is that this white race was originally derived from Indian sources. Says Mr. Smith : " If we allow that there is sufficient warrant for believing this contact with a white race, it is most likely to have occurred on the shores of India or the western parts of Indonesia." Fornander believed it to be derived from the Asiatic Archipelago and to have brought with it reminiscences of a previous national life in some other land, Cushite, Hindu, and Iranian, and a language fundamentally Aryan, but of course he applies such an origin to the Polynesians alone. He illustrates his theory with a wealth of material, archæological and philological.

But that the original Lemurian race emanated from Asia it seems unreasonable to believe, especially when we consider the great barrier of Negritic and Mongolian peoples which occupied the vast spaces betwixt them and the white races of Europe, and a colonization of white people from an early America is equally unthinkable. We are therefore thrown back on the hypothesis that the Lemurians were a white race having an extremely ancient development within the Oceanic area. Had they passed through darker Melanesia they would not have retained their fairness.

The theory that the Polynesians are a Caucasian race was entertained by Dr. A. H. Keane and is subscribed to by Professor Macmillan Brown. Keane supposed that they advanced from their original home in two streams, one through Europe, Northern Asia, and thence down through the Philippines to Indonesia, whilst another passed through Western Asia on to India. But the main stream, he believed, came by way of Korea and Japan and later amalgamated in Indonesia with the other branch. Professor Brown thinks that a branch of the race occupied the islands of the Pacific at a much earlier date, perhaps 100,000 years ago, when the Eastern Pacific was occupied by a continent. But there is no tangible evidence to lead us to the supposition that the Pacific was occupied by people of Polynesian stock at a period so remote. Tradition is all against it, and the Polynesian genealogies in particular do not support it. Moreover, the arguments in support of an Indian or Indonesian origin for the Polynesian race are no more remarkable than those which might give them a Lemurian origin, which we know they only partially could boast of.

As I have already remarked, the fact that the fairest denizens of the Oceanic area are to be found in its most easterly tracts supplies proof positive that they could not have passed from India and Java through Melanesia and other regions presently populated by races of dark and in many cases negro hue. That they did so before the advent of these dark races to their present seats is also more than improbable.

That the remnant of fair peoples of non-European origin in Oceania—no mere paltry handful, by the way—is of Lemurian origin, who can doubt ? Such an acceptance signifies that we must regard the ancient Lemurians, or at least their most advanced types, as a people of similar physical character to those of Northern Europe.

Were they originally of the same race ? We are left with no alternative hypothesis. It is an ethnological fact beyond dispute that similar races have a common seat of origin.

By what process the fair-haired races of Northern Europe and of Lemuria became separated from each other I cannot pretend to determine. The fact of fair races in Oceania is as yet too novel and the data regarding them too scanty to permit of anything approaching sound generalization or the statement of adequate theory.

If mere guessing be indulged in where all is presently so obscure, it appears as much more probable that the fair race colonized the north of Europe from Lemuria via Siberia than that it advanced from that latitude to Oceania.

The great civilizing races of the ancient world, Egyptian, Sumerian, and Babylonian, were dark rather than fair. There were, indeed, few " Caucasian " elements in their ethnological constitution, or, if there were any, these were remote and occasional.

It may be that the fair race of Lemuria, after the submergence of the main land-masses of that continent, seeking refuge from an area tormented by cataclysm, made their way northward and westward by slow degrees by Micronesia, to Japan, and thence to the Asiatic mainland, at a very early time when these were either not inhabited, or very sparsely so. Micronesia is still more pronouncedly " Caucasian " than anything else, the tint of the skin which prevails is little darker than that of the southern Italian, the features are Grecian. It is difficult to avoid the conclusion that long before the entrance of Japanese and Negrito elements to this area it was entered from the south by a Caucasian race driven there by submergence.

This fair race, coming from Lemuria, may have entered Japan and China at a very early period ere yet the Mongolian had left his centre of dispersal in Western Asia, and may have pressed onward, or have been driven by circumstances into Southern Siberia, which, it is generally agreed, is the point whence the fair peoples of the north of Europe commenced their migration to the countries they now occupy.

When all is said, such a theory is no more difficult of acceptance than that of those anthropologists who derive the Mongolian race from the Old Stone Age peoples of Europe, who, they believe, were pressed into Asia by the arrival of the people of the New Stone Age, nor than that other hypothesis which brings the Mediterranean race of Europe from Central Africa. But, I must repeat, any theory or surmise regarding the ethnic connections between Lemuria and Northern Europe must, because of its very novelty, abide the assize of time and of discussion.

Ernst Haeckel, the great German evolutionist, examined the racial associations of the inhabitants of Lemuria as well as its geological history. If his conclusions now seem a little out of date, it is well in this case to pursue our policy of embraciveness and insert his short essay on the subject.

"*Hypothetical Sketch of the Monophyletic Origin and the Diffusion of the Twelve Species of Men from Lemuria over the earth.* The *hypothesis* here geographically sketched of course only claims an entirely *provisional value*, as in the present imperfect state of our anthropological knowledge it is simply intended to show how the distribution of the human species, from a single primæval home, may be *approximately* indicated. The probable primæval home, or 'Paradise,' is here assumed to be *Lemuria*, a tropical continent at present lying below the level of the Indian Ocean, the former existence of which in the Tertiary Period seems very probable from numerous facts in animal and vegetable geography. But it is also very possible that the hypothetical 'cradle of the human race' lay further to the east (in Hindostan or Further India), or further to the west (in Eastern Africa). Future investigations, especially in comparative anthropology and palæontology, will, it is to be hoped, enable us to determine the probable position of the primæval home of man more definitely than it is possible to do at present.

"If opposition to our monophyletic hypothesis—which maintains the origin of the different human species from several different species of anthropoid ape—be preferred and adopted, then, from among the many possible hypotheses which arise, the one deserving most confidence seems to be that which assumed a double pithecoid root for the human race, namely, an Asiatic and an African root. For it is a very remarkable fact that the African man-like apes (gorilla and chimpanzee) are characterized by a distinctly long-headed, or dolichocephalous, form of skull, like the human species peculiar to Africa (Hottentots, Caffres, Negroes, Nubians). On the other hand, the Asiatic man-like apes (especially the small and large orang) by their distinct, short-headed, or brachycephalous form of skull agree with human species especially characteristic of Asia (Mongols and Malays). Hence, one might be tempted to derive the latter (the Asiatic man-like apes and primæval men) from a common form of brachycephalous ape, and the former (the African man-like apes and primæval men) form a common dolichocephalous form of ape.

"In any case, tropical Africa and Southern Asia (and between them Lemuria, which formerly connected them) are those portions of the earth which deserve the first consideration in the discussion as to the primeval home of the human race; America and Australia are, on the other hand, entirely excluded from it. Even Europe (which is in fact but a western peninsula of Asia) is scarcely of any importance in regard to the 'Paradise' question.

"The gradual transmutation of catarrhine apes into pithecoid men probably took place in the Tertiary Period in the hypothetical Lemuria, and the boundaries and forms of the present continents and oceans must then have been completely different from what they are now. Moreover, the mighty influence of the Ice Period is of great importance in the question of the migration and diffusion of the human species, although it as yet cannot be more accurately defined in detail. I here, therefore, as in my other hypotheses of development, expressly guard myself against any dogmatic interpretation; they are nothing but *first attempts*."

An amazing contribution to Lemurian lore comes from California, whence it was sent to me by a valued correspondent, Dr. Henry Hollen, author of *Clairaudient Transmission*, and the husband of Aura May Hollen, whose inspirational works have excited so deep an interest in America and in this country.

The contribution referred to is an article published in *The Los Angeles Times Sunday Magazine* of May 22nd, 1932, by Mr. Edward Lanser, whose permission I have to quote it in full. It deals with the presence in California to-day of a race said to be of Lemurian origin. Mr. Hollen accompanies the article with no comments as to its *bona fides*, and, personally, I can deal with it only on its face value. Indeed, in the circumstances, I can do no more than quote from it at some length in the hope that some of my readers in California who are aware of the local conditions will be able to cast some light upon the subject.

Mr. Lanser, who has kindly given me permission to quote this article, tells us that when *en route* for Portland on the Shasta Limited he went out to see the sunrise from the observation platform of the express and was captivated by the beauty of Mount Shasta in the morning glory.

" Gazing upon its splendour, I suddenly perceived that the whole southern side of the mountain was ablaze with a strange reddish green light. A flame of light that grew faint, then flared up with renewed brilliance.

" My first conjecture was a forest fire, but the total absence of smoke discounted that theory. The light resembled the glow of Roman candles.

" The rising sun dimmed the colour of the scene, and gradually, as the train crept north, the weird phenomenon was lost to view. The thing intrigued me; yet I felt

THE RACES OF LEMURIA

unable to discuss what I had seen with anyone. However, when I met my travelling-companion at breakfast, he asked me if I had seen the forest fire on Mt. Shasta.

" ' Did you see smoke ? ' was my quick question.

" ' No," he replied. ' Just a red glow.'

" Convinced that I had not been the victim of a mirage, I later asked the conductor about the mysterious pyrotechnics. His answer was short but enticing :

" ' Lemurians,' he said. ' They hold ceremonials up there.'

" Lemurians !

" The fact that a group of people conduct ceremonials on the side of a mountain is not of exceptional interest, but when these people are said to be Lemurians, that is startling, for the continent of Lemuria, like the lost Atlantis, disappeared beneath the ocean ages ago, and the Lemurians have long since been known as an extinct race.

" Just as soon as I had transacted my business in Portland I returned to the Mt. Shasta region, incredulous but consumed with curiosity. If there were survivors of the lost race I would find them, for I planned to equip myself for an expedition into the wilderness surrounding Shasta.

" I motored toward the point of my investigation, pausing at Weed, a town near Mt. Shasta, for the night. In Weed I discovered that the existence of a ' mystic village ' on Mt. Shasta was an accepted fact. Business men, amateur explorers, officials and ranchers in the country surrounding Shasta spoke freely of the Lemurian community, and all attested to the weird rituals that are performed on the mountain-side at sunset, midnight and sunrise. Also, they freely ridiculed my avowed trek into the sacred precincts, assuring me that an entrance was as difficult and forbidden as is an entrance into Tibet.

" It appeared that although the existence of these last descendants of the ancient Lemurians have been known to Northern Californians for more than fifty years, only four or five explorers have penetrated the invisible protective boundary of this Lemurian settlement ; but no one has ever succeeded in entering the village ; at least, no one has ever returned to tell the tale. It is of course quite possible that if anyone did manage to visit the Lemurians in their Mt. Shasta stronghold, such a person might have good and sufficient reasons to hold secret that which he may have seen.

" It is safe to say that fifty out of a hundred people living within a reasonable distance of Shasta have at some time or other tried to approach the Lemurians, yet many —who are known to have penetrated at least part of the mystery—will vehemently deny, perhaps out of some well-founded fear, having made such an investigation or having any knowledge concerning the Lemurians.

" It began to look as though the whole affair was a matter of well-seasoned legendry—and yet, I myself had seen the strange illumination on Mt. Shasta before I had heard any of the stories that are so common in the towns surrounding the mountain. And yet it seemed incredible that a colony of people could so successfully seclude themselves in the heart of our thoroughly explored State.

" Just then I learned that the existence of Lemurian descendants on Mt. Shasta was vouched for some years ago by no less an authority than the eminent scientist, Prof. Edgar Lucin Larkin, for many years director of the Mt. Lowe Observatory in Southern California.

" Prof. Larkin, with determined sagacity, penetrated the Shasta wilderness as far as he could—or dared—and then, cleverly, continued his investigations from a promontory with a powerful long-distance telescope.

" What the scientist saw, he reported, was a great temple in the heart of the mystic village—a marvellous work of carved marble and onyx, rivalling in beauty and architectural splendour the magnificence of the temples of Yucatan. He saw a village housing from 600 to 1000 people ; they appeared to be industriously engaged in the manufacture of articles necessary to their consumption, they were engaged in farming in the sunny slopes and glens surrounding the village—with miraculous results, judging from the astounding vegetation revealed to Prof. Larkin's spy-glass. He found them to be a peaceful community, evidently contented to live as their ancient forebears had lived before Lemuria was swallowed up by the sea.

THE RACES OF LEMURIA

"When Prof. Larkin concluded his investigation he had gathered enough proof to warrant him to say that in this village, in a secluded glen at the foot of Mt. Shasta's partially extinct volcano, far from the beaten paths that lead to our civilization, there live the last descendants of the first inhabitants of this earth, the Lemurians.

"Some scientists have long ago declared that certain of these early people migrated to other parts of the earth before the continents of Atlantis and Lemuria are supposed to have disappeared beneath the waters of the ocean and the Lemurians on Shasta are doubtless the descendants of those early survivors who trekked to the American continent, possibly South America, the succeeding generations finally moving north to California.

"That these Lemurians who live in California are cognizant of the disaster that befell their ancestors is revealed in the fact that each night, at midnight throughout the entire year, they perform a ritual of thanksgiving and adoration to 'Guatama,' which is the Lemurian name for America. The chief object of this midnight ceremony is to celebrate the escape of their forebears from the doomed Lemuria and their safe arrival in Guatama.

"In this midnight ceremony, as in the sunrise and sunset rituals, the weird but wonderful light that first attracted my attention when travelling on the Shasta Limited, is used. During my period of investigation I have seen the midnight ceremonials cause the entire southern side of Mt. Shasta to be illuminated in a most baffling way—a light that reaches up and covers the landscape for great distances. From a practical point of view alone, this mysterious village and its equally mysterious dwellers is of vital interest, for their display of light far excels our modern electrical achievements, and I for one am consumed with curiosity to know how these primitive people can produce such amazing light effects.

"The Lemurians have been seen on various occasions; they have been encountered in the Shasta forest, but only for a brief glimpse, for they possess the uncanny secret knowledge of the Tibetan masters and, if they desire, can blend themselves into their surroundings and vanish.

"At times they came into the neighbouring towns—tall, barefoot, noble-looking men, with close-cropped hair, dressed in spotless white robes that resemble in style the enveloping garment worn by the high-caste East Indian women to-day—to patronize certain stores.

"Indeed, the records reveal that at one time an official visit was made to the city of San Francisco by a white-robed patriarch from the mystic village. He came on foot, with an escort of younger men, to bring greetings and an assurance of goodwill upon the anniversary of the founding of their sacred retreat in California.

"The patriarch was met by an official committee at the Ferry Building and escorted to the City Hall. As soon as greetings had been exchanged, the visitors returned to their retreat.

"Various merchants in the vicinity of Shasta report that these white-robed men occasionally come to their stores. Their purchases are of a peculiar nature. They have bought enormous quantities of sulphur as well as a great deal of salt. They buy lard in bulk quantities, for which they bring their own containers, peculiar transparent bladders. The gay materials and novelties of our modern civilization do not attract these simple people at all.

"Their purchases are always paid for with gold nuggets, since of course they have no money, and the gold always far exceeds the value of the merchandise. The Lemurians are friendly in their contacts, though taciturn—searching through the shops until they find what they want, since they cannot speak our language—and they are certainly generous.

"To say that they must have a rich gold mine on Mt. Shasta is a foregone conclusion. Perhaps this—gold—is another reason why we are not made welcome in Lemurian territory.

"They have frequently donated their large gold nuggets to charity. During the World War, they came forward with generous gifts to the American Red Cross, and more recently they sent a bag of gold to the fund for sufferers of the Japanese earthquake . . .

THE RACES OF LEMURIA

"As an illustration of the true scientific knowledge possessed by these Lemurians, we can take the forest fires that raged in many parts of Northern California last year as an example. When a formidable fire crept up Mt. Shasta, threatening the mystic village, they caused a wall of invisible protection to rise between the village and the forest fires. As the flames reached that certain point, they were mysteriously arrested, snuffed out.

"One can see the very definite line where the fires ceased to this day.

"It is not incredible that the last sons of lost Lemuria are nestled at the foot of Mt. Shasta's volcano. The really incredible thing is that these staunch descendants of that vanished race have succeeded in secluding themselves in the midst of our teeming State and that they have managed through some marvellous sorcery to keep highways, hot-dog establishments, filling stations and the other ugly counterparts of our tourist system out of their sacred precincts."

Summarizing the ethnology of Lemuria and dismissing obviously irrelevant theories, we find that the races which presently occupy the greater part of Oceania cannot have done so for any prolonged period. Throughout the Pacific area the clearest traces of survival and traditions of a fair-haired race exist. Hawaii, the New Hebrides, New Zealand and Micronesia, all possess actual vestiges or tales of this race, who for the most part dwelt in secluded regions, and were frequently regarded as supernatural beings. Tradition also tells of a fair race who dwelt in the sea, and who cultivated weaving and woodcarving. Traces of them grow fainter toward the west of Oceania.

Former continental conditions in Oceania are revealed by the present dispersal within it of the Negrito race, which could not have negotiated sea-passages.

The fair races of the Pacific are regarded as wise men and enchanters, great builders, and as possessed of almost supernatural powers such as levitation.

In many Polynesian groups, Tahiti, Rarotonga and

Mangaia, there are traces of a pre-Polynesian sun-worship.

The Lemurians must have been of various race, though the ruling caste was certainly fair. It is unlikely that this caste came from Asia, and more probable that it was native to the Pacific.

CHAPTER VI

THE TESTIMONY OF CUSTOM

FROM what has gone before it will now be plain to the reader that the various types of social custom obtaining throughout the Oceanic expanse are not referable to a common basis. Thus in some areas we find a fairly well-marked tradition of father-right, in others a mother-right evidently of equally ancient sanction. It is not my intention to examine the entire customary practice of Oceania in an endeavour to discover the bases of these differences. My object is rather to find which of them, if any, point to a condition of things more venerable than the Polynesian or Melanesian. Throughout this work I have paid but scant attention to possible resemblances between Oceanic and Asiatic culture, for the reason that the bases of comparison appear to me as now much too vitiated by time and " overlay " on the Asiatic side to permit of reasonable analogy unless in certain well-marked instances. It " stands to reason " that any Lemurian influences upon such civilizations as those of China, Japan, or Cambodia must long ago have been overlaid by those coming from Egypt and India, while in the case of America there had been forthcoming, at the time of its discovery, no such influences. Fenellosa's theory, it seems to me, makes the most of credible associations between Asia and pre-Polynesian Oceania, and the cultural connections between the Asiatic continent and post-Polynesian Oceania will explain much.

Among the Polynesians the social tradition is based on the patriarchate, or father-right. The farther east one goes in Oceania he will find mother-right prevail, whilst on reaching the shores of Asia the patriarchate reassumes its sway. This is surely eloquent of an ancient mother-right in Oceania, derived from a system of great antiquity. In distant Yap, away to the north-west, mother-right obtains, whilst property is handed down from father to son, revealing that a patrilineal system has been superimposed on an older matrilineal one.

The culture of the Gilbert Islands, though on the whole Polynesian, exhibits other underlying elements associated by tradition with a submerged land. Its people have no forest timber, yet formerly used large canoes 60 feet in length, one of which is still kept by them as a curiosity, and they drink a fermented spirit instead of the universal kava of Polynesia. Their former god, Taburik, was a deity of thunder and storm, and is unknown to Polynesian myth, his name signifying an ancestral association. The land whence came the tree-trunks of which their canoes were built was known as Nabanaba, and lay toward the north-west, and was, perhaps, Ponape. Again, their heaven or paradise was called Mone, " a land below the sea."

Professor Macmillan Brown gives it as his opinion that the Polynesian system of taboo originated in the fatherland of the race, Hawaiki, " a large island or archipelago in the Central Pacific," now submerged, whence all Oceanic migration proceeded in the Polynesian sense. It was a substitute for law, but its cramping provisions prohibited freedom of action and development. Its chief prohibition was the liberty of woman, whom it regarded as a polluted being. She is, or was, the very fount of desecration in Polynesian eyes. This is surely a sign that in Oceania women belonged chiefly to a conquered race.

There is plenty of evidence that the institution of the family in Polynesia is of very ancient origin. Its arts, too, are specifically Palæolithic in character. " This," says Professor Brown, " takes it back ten or twelve thousand years, and that leaves plenty of time for the Palæolithic stepping-stones to have sunk in an ocean so mobile-bottomed as the Pacific and for numerous migrations of warriors and seamen to push into the isolated and unknown regions of the great ocean."

Quite, so long as these remarks do not refer to Poly-

THE TESTIMONY OF CUSTOM 118

nesians, for whose presence in the Pacific there is no actual proof more than eight hundred years old or thereabouts. Still, the Polynesians, coming from Asia, may well have conquered the wretched remnant of fair-haired Lemurians, some of whom still exist, and have intermarried with their womenkind. The majority of the immigrants would be men. But the odd thing is that the fair women were regarded as aristocrats, and that everything was done to make the bulk of the female population conform to their type. The Polynesian woman was subjected to a process of whitening or blanching by treatment of the hair with lime and by seclusion in a house which kept her out of the sun's rays.

What must we infer from this? We have also to bear in mind that the daughters of chiefs were not taboo, but received particular honours. All this seems to point to the conclusion that the vestigial white race of Lemuria which survived was regarded as sacrosanct in a measure and accepted by its conquerors at its own value. Yet we find blond-haired individuals in Hawaiian tradition treated as menials, and compelled to the making of earth-ovens and the drudgery of cookery. In all likelihood these were males. It seems as though the blonde women of the Lemurian remnant which survived in the islands until the coming of the Polynesians had been received into favour as the wives of chiefs and that their men-folk had been enslaved.

But the almost unnatural detestation of women as a sex which marked the Polynesian regime and which brought about taboo can only have arisen because of necessary unions with women of negroid type. The Polynesians on their entrance to the Pacific area as explorers and immigrants can have brought few women with them and the fair-haired Lemurian remnant would scarcely furnish wives for all. In order to continue the race, unions with females of negro origin would be essential. That Lemuria must have contained large numbers of people of dark hue we have seen, but it must have been with loathing that the intensely proud Polynesians took their womenkind to wife.

From this sense of loathing, then, arose the wellnigh

vindictive system of taboo which regarded woman as an unclean being almost of a different species from man. She must not share his canoe, and should she wish to approach a stranger ship, must swim for it. Her children cannot be born in his hut, she may not share his food. There was no exception to this rule throughout the entire Polynesian Pacific. It was universal. The flattening out of the nostrils of a Polynesian baby as soon as it is born shows that negroid features did not belong to the conquering Polynesians, but to the " native " women they married, who would strive to reproduce their own appearance in their children.

But although the various types of social custom obtaining throughout the Pacific are obviously not of common origin, in their own spheres, Polynesian, Melanesian and so forth, they are sufficiently homogeneous to demonstrate the fact that they are severally descended or borrowed from very ancient customary types, and this certainly assists the hypothesis that they were each developed in separate environments or continental masses by the forerunners of those who at present employ them. The low-caste negroid Lemurians would assuredly persevere in their ancient customary notions however the white conquering race, their neighbours, might strive to abolish these. There exist, however, sufficient traces of a general basis of customary principles to account for the insistence of a governing class upon partial acceptance of their system of taboo.

Leaving taboo aside, it is obvious that the examination of other customs will avail us little as providing evidence for the former presence of a highly civilized race in the Pacific. The descent into savagery, once the Lemurian land-masses had disintegrated and their remnants had been seized upon by new-comers, must have been rapid. In this connection I am happy to be able to concur with the theory of Colonel Churchward in his book *The Lost Continent of Mu*. This theory appeals to me as a real contribution to the Lemurian controversy, apart altogether from the somewhat rash conclusions he draws elsewhere in that volume —for it is unworthy not to accept and applaud sound reasoning, as it is appropriate to denounce its opposite. If I cannot approve of the argument by which Colonel Churchward seeks to show how civilization in Lemuria lapsed and disappeared, I can at least agree with his general conclusion. With a certain native power of description he provides us with a vivid picture of the destruction of Lemuria, or as he terms it " Mu," and the sequel to its obliteration.

" When the continent was rent asunder and went down, for geological reasons that will later be explained, ridges and points of land here and there remained above water. They made islands and groups of islands, but were jagged and broken up by the volcanic workings which had occurred beneath them.

" All these ridges and points were covered to their capacity with humanity escaped from the sinking land —their land, the Motherland of Man—which now formed the bed of seething, steaming muddy waters surrounding them.

" Having swallowed up the land with all thereon, the waters rested as if satisfied with their grim work, and these waters are the Pacific Ocean. Was ever a name more ironically applied ?

" On these islands, in the sight of a boiling sea, the remnants of Mu's population huddled, waiting for the terrific quakes to abate. They had seen their temples and palaces, their ships and their roads go crashing down, to be swallowed by the ocean. Nearly the entire population had been engulfed by the catastrophe. The few alive, all that were left of the Motherland of Man, discovered they were destitute. They had nothing—no tools, no clothing, no shelter ; little land, no food. Around them hissed and seethed the boiling waters that had rushed into the centre of the fiery pit ; above them dense clouds of steam, smoke, and ashes cut off the friendly light, making an impenetrable darkness. The despairing shrieks of their comrades who had perished in chaos still rang in their ears. It was a scene of horror for the survivors, who found themselves facing death by starvation and exposure. Few were able to survive the dreadful ordeal and most of them perished miserably.

"A portion of these unsubmerged fragments of the lost continent we know to-day as the South Sea Islands, and some of their inhabitants can claim, as remote ancestors, the people of Mu. . . .

"Under such circumstances it may easily be imagined what happened. Many, of course, were hopelessly insane, driven mad by sheer horror; others prayed for death to relieve them from a strain that was intolerable. To exist, one thing alone was left them: to go down into the lowest depths of savagery, and, for a time at least, live upon one another.

"Skins of animals, if any remained, and the leaves of coarse foliage must, in future, be their dress. Stones, spears, and arrows must be their weapons of defence and offence. Their cutting tools must be fashioned from flints and shells. But the primary thing was where to get food? No doubt many died from exposure, fright, and hunger, and as these died their bodies became the food of survivors. In this manner began the first cannibalism and savagery. Thus the survivors of the highest civilization descended to the lowest savagery, which has continued on through the ages.

"One may imagine the loathing and repugnance that these cultured beings must have had for such food, and we may believe that many died before they could force themselves to partake of it. Gradually, however, as generation followed generation through the long procession of years, the poor islanders sank lower and lower until even traditions of their past, which at first were religiously kept and handed down to posterity, became dim and at last forgotten. Their former greatness was erased from their minds as completely as the treacherous waters of the Pacific had wiped away Mu, but, forgotten though this past is by the islanders, marks have remained among them for future identification, thus carrying out an unvarying law."

Of course I cannot agree that the catastrophe took place so suddenly, so dramatically, or that it was not gradual. Yet the result would on the whole be such as Colonel Churchward has so vividly pictured. When the Polynesian and other immigrants in a much later day came in contact with the white remnant of Lemuria they must have discovered them in a relatively debased condition. The central founts and nuclei of civilization had broken down, although a certain degree of culture must have been preserved. We have seen that the white people of which Oceanic tradition speaks, and who indeed still survive in some localities, were in a measure almost as barbarous as their conquerors. They were living in caves and mountain fastnesses, and the food they consumed was the abomination of the naturally fastidious Maori. Even so they retained a mental and spiritual outlook which seems to have struck their conquerors with wonder. They refrained from daubing themselves with coloured earths as did the Maori, they carefully conserved and guarded their sacred places, they practised " magic " and their enemies believed that they possessed strange powers of transformation and invisibility, that they flew through the air by dint of levitation (not by the aid of airplanes !) and had a drama of their own. Indeed the Maori of New Zealand dubbed them *Iwiatua*, a god-like race, a people of supernatural powers. They still weaved and carved and taught the new-comers many arts.

It seems clear enough then that the degree of savagery to which they had sunk was a relative one, and scarcely so debased as Colonel Churchward would have us credit. It must in a relative sense have borne some resemblance to the condition of the Greeks in mediæval times compared with that they had enjoyed in the heyday of Athens and Corinth, or of the miserable condition of the Semitic peoples of Mesopotania in the present time compared with the imperial marvel of old Babylon at its most magnificent.

Little indeed but this can we glean from a consideration of the customary evidence. A comparison of the rites of marriage, burial, and barter as at present practised by the Oceanic races will not carry us far in arriving at a comprehension of Lemurian custom, for the simple reason that not only has barbarism blotted the record, but that a system of taboo which probably originated in times of stress and chaos cannot altogether supply us with a just view of Lemurian practice—and with this observation for the present we must remain content.

Summarizing, we find the several types of social custom obtaining in the Pacific are not referable to a common basis. Toward the East mother-right prevails, to the West father-right, a condition eloquent of an ancient matriarchate in Oceania.

The culture of the Gilbert Islands exhibits elements associated by tradition with a submerged land. Their people have now no timber, yet once used canoes, one of which they retain as a curiosity. Their heaven is a land beneath the sea.

Professor Macmillan Brown believes that the Polynesian system of taboo originated in Hawaiki, the legendary fatherland, now submerged. The fact that it regarded woman as " polluted " shows that in Oceania woman, on the whole, belonged to a conquered race. Yet fair women were regarded as aristocrats, and everything was done to make the bulk of the female population conform to their type. That is, the surviving remnants of the Lemurian race was regarded as sacrosanct. The tabooed women were probably of Negroid race.

Although the several types of social custom obtaining in the Pacific are not of common origin, they are still sufficiently homogeneous to show that they were borrowed from very ancient customary types, each developed in separate environments or continental masses by the forerunners of those who employ them.

But the descent into savagery or barbarism must have been fairly rapid after the final disintegration of the continental land-masses, as tradition avers, although a certain standard of culture was sporadically maintained.

CHAPTER VII

THE PROOF FROM ART

PROFESSOR FENELLOSA in his *Epochs of Chinese and Japanese Art* lays stress on the influence of Pacific art on early Chinese culture. For him Pacific art is that particular school which revealed a unity of art-form caused by actual dispersion throughout the vast basin of the Pacific, including Peru, Central America, Mexico and Alaska, Hawaii, Micronesia, Macronesia, Formosa, China, and Japan.

" It is," he says, " quite sharply differentiated from the schools of all other parts of the world, never penetrating far to the west of a longitudinal line drawn from Central China to Borneo. Most of these Pacific arts (in Polynesia) are fixed and traditional. But it is of the utmost importance to find that the very oldest forms of Chinese design, preserved to us in bronze, are in the majority of cases nearly identical with the bulk of the island decorations." This implies an antiquity, he thinks, of at least 5000 years from the present era.

" Prominent everywhere," he writes, " we find the suggestion of faces more or less human, with two staring eyes and eyeballs in the centre. Upon the lintels and rafter-ends of New Zealand huts, and upon the totem poles (that is, the carved posts) at their entrance, for all the world like those in the far-away regions of Alaska, we find these faces carved ; and it is a striking feature that almost universally we find these staring eyes slanted at a decided angle, similar to but much more pronounced than the national eye-slant of Mongolian races. Where, upon handles of utensils or in full relief statues, these faces form logical parts of heads, we can see that many of the pattern marks represent tattooing." " The specimens of similar tattooed heads that have come from the Philippines show eyes of less angle perhaps, but with a more consciously demoniac expression, as if the spirit represented lent evil force to the use of the dagger whose handle it decorates. This eye-form, too, appears modelled upon the sides of Aztec pottery, and sometimes with lines and bosses that suggest derivation from tattooing. This pair of eyes is the most conspicuous feature of Alaskan art, worked as patterns on blankets and carved or painted on the prows of boats, as we still can see in China to-day." " Now it is a most striking fact that a practically identical use of the face-forms, the slanting almond eyes in pairs, the relics of marks of tattooing, and the bosses, appear as the most salient features upon the majority of ancient Chinese bronzes." " In old Chinese tradition " this face is that of " a glutton with a cannibalistic appetite." " This very tradition, probably one out of many from forgotten remote ages of Pacific relationship, only confirms the theory of connection."

"Another Pacific feature in the decoration of these bronzes is the fish, or marine monster, the ancestor of the Chinese dragon, which is identical with forms found from South Pacific Islands to North-eastern America. This sea creature has a head unlike a fish, with curved snout, opened nostrils, sometimes with tusks and a curving tail, also unlike a fish. Yet it is often found in connection with forms that are clearly fish-like. It occurs in New Zealand and Micronesian art, carved on the handles of utensils, on gourd bottles, and woven in stuffs, and it reappears in almost identical form in Alaskan patterns. Its shape, identical on the early Chinese bronzes, is probably their dragon, only we see here that a ' dragon ' means no lizard monster of Western tradition, but a semi-fishlike or possibly seal-form—evidently a spirit symbol connected with water. This figure is carved or moulded on all parts of the oldest Chinese vases. In later forms appear the tusks, which are more like those of the Aztec stone dragon."

" The Polynesian and Malay masks have the slanting eyes, the tattooed faces, and the ogre-like features of the totem poles. In New Guinea, Borneo, and the Philippines we find these masks. Now, although we have no primitive Chinese masks preserved, we do find among the earliest Japanese masks, used in the Shinto sacred dances, identical, though more beautifully carved forms, with the long nose, the bird-like beak, and the slanting eyes. In Alaskan ritual art these figures become accentuated in the enormously projecting beak of the bird mask. Among Aztec and Hawiian masks we find sockets, in which movable pieces, such as the jaw or the eyelid, were set, just as in some of the Japanese Shinto dragon-spirit masks. This dragon world underneath the sea is part of primitive Chinese myth."[1] " Still another more special form of parallelism in ornament is the frigate-bird pattern, so conspicuous in the finest æsthetic carving of New Guinea. There, through centuries, it has become conventionalized into lovely spiral bands, which we find identically reproduced on some of the ancient Chinese bronzes."

All this, of course, implies the existence of a very early culture and art in the Pacific basin before the coming of the Polynesians. If Professor Fenellosa's words mean anything at all, they imply an ancient land-connection between the Oceanic area and Asia, or at least the existence at one time of an insular chain which connected Asia and America. He labels the art-forms engendered in the area " Pacific," which reveals that he believed them to have been developed in the oceanic region in remote ages. The frigate-bird motif, of which he writes as being common to New Guinea and China, is also to be found as a character in the undecipherable script of Easter Island.

Professor Fenellosa's theory includes the presence of the art of tattooing in the Pacific area at a very remote period. Let us examine the origins of tattooing, its " reasons " and technique at some length, as it certainly has a bearing upon the problem of Lemuria.

Primitive man's main reason for tattooing himself is capable of being sub-divided into a number of intentions. For him it has a very real significance beyond making him a mere perambulatory picture-gallery which may attract

---

[1] It is also part of Central American myth. See the allusions to " the serpents covered with green feathers " which lay in the depths of the ocean in the First Book of the Popol Vuoh."

attention and gain him fame as a local beau, although that is certainly a part of his desire. The real and underlying meanings of tattooing are either religious, magical, or social. Thus the Naga of Assam believe that tattoo marks are useful as an identification in the spirit world, a means by which not only will the gods know their chosen people, but husband and wife will recognize each other in the hereafter.

Some Polynesians used to have the figures of their patron gods tattooed on their bodies, and Ainu women still mark themselves to look like the goddess Aioina.

These are, of course, strictly religious " signatures," but similar designs are employed for magical purposes. Some people have talismans or charms tattooed on various parts of the body to keep away pain, the Malays paint themselves black, white, and red to avert cholera, and body-marking to bring good luck is fairly common, children often being painted with symbols of happy omen soon after birth. Again, body-markings for tribal or social purposes are widely spread. They identify the person as a member of the community, and without them he would be an outcast and of no account in the clan, either in this world or the next.

Before pursuing this part of the subject farther, let us glance at the evolution of the art itself. That it developed from face or body-painting we cannot doubt. Prehistoric man, judging from his remains, painted the bones of his dead a brilliant red to give them the colour of life and induce the vitality needed for a future existence. That he painted his face and body in a similar way is probable, and the habits of primitive people to-day support this view. The North American Indian, for example, even though he tattooes freely among certain tribes, has never lost the art of face-painting, which may therefore be regarded as the basis of tattooing.

Patterns, evidently of an elementary character, are to be found among the Andaman Islanders, a people long separated from others. But gradually a symmetrical system appears to have been developed among more advanced communities. These pass from a mere haphazard collection of dots and lines, as found among the Australian blacks, to the more intricate patterns of the African Bushongo, which reveal spirals and swastika shapes, the quite elaborate markings of the people of Borneo, and lastly the very involved patterns of the Maoris of New Zealand and the delicate and artistic coloured tattooing of Japan, in which the art reaches its apogee.

With the Borneans we arrive at a phase in which a beautiful symmetrical arrangement of scroll-work, intermingled with straight lines, reveals the actual beginnings of artistic impulse. The Polynesians, and especially the Maoris, exhibit a further proficiency in dealing with geometrical figures and a finer balance in the designs with which the cheeks are marked, especially in the wonderful *moko* system of the latter, in which the spiral is employed as a basis on which to build up complex ornament. The tattoer first traced the designs in black, then went over them with a small adze-shaped needle dipped in red ochre. Some of the patterns employed would be difficult to effect even with perfect mathematical instruments, and the *moko* system frequently resulted in giving the Maori women the appearance of wearing a close-fitting chintz dress, so fine and close was its intricate tracery.

The Samoan tattooing, still extensively practised, is a symmetrical arrangement of lines, dots, arrowheads, and stars, the combinations of which are almost inexhaustible. It was really effected on the inner side of the thigh, but often follows the curves of the whole body, and may be regarded as the development of an independent school of the art. A common pattern is like the crown of a palm tree, springing from the centre of the back and curving round both sides.

Natural objects are frequently shown in tattooing, animals, birds and fishes, and perhaps the best examples of such a system are those current among the Haida Indians of the Queen Charlotte Islands, off the coast of North-west Canada. Often these are highly conventionalized, but bears, frogs and squids are the favourite designs, doubtless the emblems of tribal totems or patrons. The people of the Torres Straits and the Tamil of Ceylon also employ naturalistic body-markings.

Quite as interesting as the art itself are the ideas which underlie it. We have already seen that tattooing has not only a religious but a magical and social significance. The North American Indian believed that after death he would be halted on the way by guardian spirits and searched for his tattoo marks to discover if he were in communion with his tribal or patron deity. Some women in the South of India think that their tutelary god will beat them should they die without his symbol on their bodies, and the Ainu woman dreads that the process will be carried out in the Otherworld should she neglect it here.

Among the Red Men of North America the ceremonial use of body-paint was taught by gods and culture-heroes, and Pawnee babies are still dedicated to the sky-god by painting their little bodies. The Polynesians and Samoans preserve legends of the divine origin of tattooing, and in Formosa, and formerly among the Maoris, it was a necessary adjunct to priesthood.

That tattooing has a totemic significance and that it is associated with the tribal sacred animal there is plenty of proof, especially in North America and Australia.

Very important is the significance of tattooing with reference to the puberty, marriage and fertility of women. Among the hill tribes of Fiji a girl was compelled to fast for twelve hours, to search all night for prawns (perhaps symbolical of the sharp spines used in the process) and to secure three lemon thorns for the tattooing instrument employed by the wise women. Among some South American tribes the ritual is most elaborate. In most African tribes girls must be scarified or cicatrized on the back and loins before marriage. The chin tattooing of women has a very wide range, and probably has a sex significance.

From the social point of view, tattooing is employed as a distinctive tribal or clan mark. The theory has been advanced that man, seeing certain animals marked alike by stripes or spots, adopted similar stigmata. Whether the hypothesis be correct or otherwise, the fact remains that among many tribes to-day a man is not considered a member of the community unless he be marked with its particular symbols or tokens, and with certain primitive peoples it is even a "class affair," the rank or caste of an individual being indicated by his or her body-markings. Savage man also tattoos, gashes and paints himself as a sign of mourning, or to placate the angry spirits of the dead.

But tattooing has also a curative or medicinal and protective significance for primitive peoples. It is used as a charm against the evil eye, as a cure for defective eyesight, for rheumatism, and as a defence against the weapons of enemies.

In what manner did tattooing have its origin in the Pacific? I believe it to be a custom of most ancient development, with a wide ritual and social significance, and that it originated in one specific area is surely clear enough. But where?

That it was regarded as coming from a distance in some parts of the Pacific is plain from the fact that in certain islands, as in Yap, in the Carolines, it is practised only by the upper classes (a complete suit of it being the mark of high aristocracy), is said to have "come from the east," and that in order to be tattooed the people of Yap must go to Mukmuk, an island ninety miles to the east. The slaves are never tattooed.

As regards the origin of tattooing in the Pacific area, Maori myth has it that Mataora learned the art from a fair people of the Underworld. This at once links the art and practice of tattooing with a vanished or vanquished race. We have already seen that the Lemurians were probably of fair stock, and this tradition reveals them as the inventors of tattooing.

It is also manifest that the people who invented tattooing are much more likely to have been a fair rather than a coloured race. The skin of the white man constitutes a natural parchment. The black races more usually gash or cicatrize themselves. The inventors of tattooing employed it as a species of record or iconography as well as a mere personal or tribal marking. It must have had affiliations with a very early system of writing or hieroglyphics.

The most common tattoo-mark among the men in the Solomon Islands is a conventionalized figure of the frigate-bird. It must have come from the north-east, as in that area it is the sacred bird. Cicatrized on the palm of the hand, it implies a frank or entrance-mark to the world of the departed, the submarine world. Clear across the Pacific, thousands of miles away, we find the frigate-bird as a sacred figure in the script of Easter Island. It is also found in the script of Oleai, one of the most westerly of the Caroline Islands, vastly distant from both the Solomons or Easter Island.

From this data it seems clear enough that tattooing originated with a fair people, whose land was believed to have been submerged, and that it was probably developed from a most ancient script similar to those still in use in Easter Island and Oleai. If, then, we find tattooing in China to the west and in Central America to the east, we may surely infer that large spaces now submerged must once have existed betwixt them. The problem, in this regard, is practically the same as in the case of Atlantis, where we find tattooing in Western Europe and Eastern America, and their adjacent islands, with a blank space in between, and, in the case of Europe at least, no central continental tattooing at all.

So far as the architectural relics of the older Oceania are concerned, it has already been pointed out that they bear no relationship whatsoever to those of the Polynesians or Melanesians. Skilled observers have given it as their opinion that the native races which at present inhabit the Pacific could never have even approached their construction, and it is plain that their general technique is at once much more ancient than and entirely alien to anything of Polynesian or Melanesian construction. The objection of Polynesian architecture to walls makes it positive that the race which entertained it can have had no part in the construction of Metalanim, or the Easter Island enclosures.

We see then, from the foregoing, that Professor Fenellosa

believed in a particular school of Pacific Art which revealed a unity of art-form caused by actual dispersion throughout the whole basin of the Pacific and its adjoining coasts, fixed and traditional, and implying an antiquity of at least 5000 years from the present era.

This, of course, posits not only the existence of a very early culture and art in the Pacific basin before the coming of the Polynesians, but an ancient land-connection between the Oceanic area and Asia.

It seems as if tattooing may have had its origin in the Pacific from Lemurian sources, as the Maori myth of its invention in an underworld sphere would seem to imply. In any case, its place of origin seems to have been in the north-east, as that is the habitat of the frigate-bird, which is so often employed as a motif in tattooing. The Pacific problem, as regards tattooing, is the same as that associated with the practice in Atlantis, and infers submerged land connections.

CHAPTER VIII

THE GEOLOGY OF LEMURIA

I MUST preface this chapter by declaring that I do not believe the former existence of a Lemurian continent can be proved or disproved by the findings of Geology alone. In view of an amazing amount of favourable proof of another kind, traditional, archæological and ethnological, I hold that it is unwise to rely solely upon geological opinion for an answer to a question of such moment to the consideration and comprehension of the past. I am inclined to stress this conviction, because of the striking diversity of opinion as regards the Lemurian question on the part of geologists themselves. Nearly all agree that a great continent or continents formerly occupied the major portion of the Pacific basin, but as regards the area or areas occupied, and the period of its disappearance, authorities of the highest standing are so much at variance that any logical inquirer is justified in accepting their main conclusion regarding the bare fact of the existence of large land-masses in the Pacific, and in discarding their discordant inferences concerning the area and date of submergence of these continental lands.

There has also been a tendency to consider the problem too closely in connection with such questions as the permanence of ocean basins and the growth and structure of coral reefs and atolls, instead of on its own merits, important as are these phases of the question. In the following pages I have summarized the available evidence for and against the former existence of a Lemurian continent, and have supplied a careful precis of such evidence, to which I have appended a critical view of the whole. As in the case of Atlantis, there is a consensus of opinion in favour of the existence of a Lemurian continent or conti-

THE GEOLOGY OF LEMURIA

nents, but as in the Atlantean study, authorities are sharply divided as regards the era at which this continent flourished.

In order that the non-scientific reader may better be able to follow the evidence placed before him in this chapter, I have prefaced its consideration by a brief and simple outline of geological time. The two great epochs of the earth's physical history which are connected with mankind are the Tertiary and the Quaternary. The first of these is divided into Early and Late Tertiary. The Early Tertiary Period is again subdivided into Palæocene, Eocene, and Oligocene, the last of which is contemporary with the appearance of the anthropoid apes. The Late Tertiary is subdivided into Miocene and Pliocene, during the latter of which true man first makes his appearance.

The great Quaternary epoch is divided into the Pleistocene or Ice Age, and the Holocene or recent. The whole may be tabulated as follows:

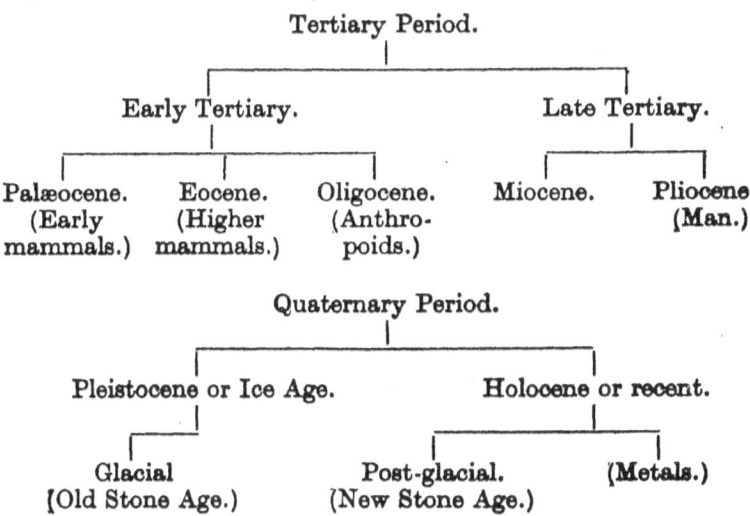

The problem before us is, then, with what stage of the earth's and man's history does the esistence of such an island-continent as that which has come to be known as Lemuria coincide? That is the crux of the whole matter from the geological point of view. Is it capable of proof that such a continent or region existed at such a period as would permit of its being peopled by the human species?

It will be obvious from the foregoing that the only part of the above human-geological table which concerns us is that which deals with the Quaternary epoch as a whole.

As has been said, the belief that a great land-mass once occupied the basin of the Pacific is accepted by the majority of modern geologists, even the most conservative agreeing that from the Primary to the Secondary geological period an immense continent, ringed round with an ocean which communicated with the Arctic, occupied the greater part of the present Pacific area. At the end of the Primary Period this ocean flowed over what is now the region of the Andes and the present Rocky Mountains on the east, and above New Zealand, Melanesia and Papuasia, the Philippines and Japan on the west. By the end of the Secondary Period the Pacific continent had begun to founder, and the west coast of South America to rise correspondingly. So much is generally conceded. It is only regarding the approximate period of the ultimate disappearance of the last vestiges of this continent that debate formerly arose, and if it ever did so it is because the data in favour of the quite recent existence of numerous large island-groups in the Pacific has only recently been collected and published.

The problems associated with the elevation and depression of land are expressed with neatness and lucidity by Mr. A. J. Jukes-Browne of the Geological Survey of England and Wales in his *Handbook of Physical Geology*, published in 1892. Large areas of the earth's crust, he says, have been affected by changes in the level of the land similar to the action of earthquakes, but taking place gradually and imperceptibly. Certain facts are accepted as sufficient evidence of subsidence and elevation.

As satisfactory proofs of elevation we may trustworthily accept such evidence as the testimony of human erections, such as the appearance of ancient moles and harbours being raised above the sea-level, the appearance of raised rocks and islands where these were before unknown, the presence of marine shells and raised beaches, and of old sea-caves.

The proofs of depression or submergence are the presence of the ruins of ancient towns and buildings sometimes visible beneath the sea, as at the eastern extremity of Crete, the testimony of submerged forests, and of fjords. It is particularly to be remarked that in the " general conclusions " which complete the chapter on these phenomena Jukes-Brown arrived at a belief in the absolute instability of the earth's surface. He writes: " We arrive at the conclusion that the earth's crust, instead of being a rigid, immovable mass, as was formerly supposed, is, and always has been, utterly unstable. It is probable, indeed, that no part of the land remains stationary for any long period of time, geologically speaking; but is eventually either slowly depressed, or as slowly upraised to a still higher elevation above the sea. It is certain, at any rate, that the form of the great continents has been continually altered, parts being elevated, and parts depressed, so that every portion has in its turn been brought beneath the level of the sea. It is certain, also, that every country is now dry land only because it has been upraised from beneath the neighbouring sea."

Writing in *Nature*, November 4th, 1880, Professor Huxley gave it as his opinion that, " there is nothing, so far as I am aware, in the biological or geological evidence at present accessible, to render untenable the hypothesis that an area of the mid-Atlantic or Pacific sea-bed as big as Europe should have been uplifted as high as Mont Blanc, and have subsided again any time since the Palæzoic epoch, if there were any grounds for entertaining it." This appeals to me as an almost unrivalled example of the kind of statement which might mean anything or nothing.

The hypothesis of a great Pacific continent was first mooted by Dr. Augustus Gould in 1854 in a striking paper, " Remarks on Mollusks and Shells," published in *The Edinburgh New Philosophical Journal*. Charles Darwin in his *Journal of Researches* (1889) demonstrated that the formation of coral reefs and atolls demanded a long-continued subsidence of the Pacific region, and, acting on his suggestion, Professors Sollas and David undertook the boring of the atoll of Funafuti to a depth of 1114 feet, where cores were obtained which showed that the whole mass of rock was composed of pure coral. As the organisms which form coral reefs cannot live at a depth of more than

150 feet, it was manifest that the ocean floor must slowly and continuously have subsided.

In 1884 Hutton, in his *Origin of Flora and Fauna of New Zealand*, advanced the theory that New Zealand, Eastern Australia, and India formed one biological region in the Secondary Period, and that in Lower Cretaceous times a large Pacific continent extended from Lower Guinea to Chile. Later on, he thought, New Zealand became separated and this continent broke up.

Von Ihering believed the Pacific land-mass to have gradually subsided during the Secondary Period, and Dr. Pilsbry was of opinion that it was finally separated from other lands as early as the middle of that period, and that the northern portion became disconnected when the remainder was still joined to the mainland. A careful review of some of the lesser fauna, especially of ants and lizards, led Professor Baur to formulate the theory of a former Indo-Pacific continent extending from Malaysia to the west coast of America. He looked upon the Pacific islands as the last remnants of this continent, which still existed, he thought, until the commencement of the Miocene Period in Tertiary times.

Mr. Speight, in his *Petrological Notes from the Kermadec Islands*, presents geological evidence of the former extension of continental conditions over a large area of the mid-Pacific region. Many volcanic islands, he remarks, now classified as oceanic, will ultimately have to be regarded as having been built up out of the remnants of a continental area. He believes that a continent covered the greater part of the Pacific Ocean in Primary and early Secondary times, and that a subsidence occurred during later Secondary and Tertiary times with more recent local elevations.

The well-known parallelism of the several groups of the Pacific Islands has been advanced as an argument in favour of a formerly existing Pacific continent. It seems possible to explain this "lay of the land" by the supposition that these islands are the remains of a series of mountain-chains, as has been suggested by Herr T. Arldt.

Professor Francis Scharff in his *Origin of Life in America* remarks: "If a Pacific continent existed, and I quite concur with those who are of that opinion, it must have largely subsided before the Tertiary era. It seems to me as if the central part of it had broken down gradually, the margins slowly following suit, both on the Eastern and Western Pacific, only leaving here and there a few remnants which either remain as isolated pillars far out in the ocean, or have become joined to more recent land-masses. I imagine that the latest pre-Pliocene land connection between North America and Asia was not the Pacific continent but merely its margin, which persisted probably until Oligocene or Miocene times. . . . I suggest that in Tertiary times a belt of land, possibly representing the margin of the more ancient Pacific continent, extended from the south-west coast to North America in a great curve to Japan and further south."

There is, however, Professor Scharff admits, an extraordinary amount of evidence that an ancient land occupied that portion of the Pacific contiguous to the west coast of Guatemala. The present Central America is, he thinks, "partly formed of the remnants of that land having eventually become moulded together by geologically recent volcanic deposits." Mr. O. H. Hershey is of opinon that this ancient land lay mainly south of the present isthmus of Panama, and that it was a land-mass of considerable extent is indicated by the heavy beds of conglomerate formed from it.

There seems to be good reason for the inference that this Pacific land persisted until comparatively recent geological times. Agassiz found that not a single station between Acapulco on the west coast of Mexico and the Galapagos Islands could be characterized as strictly oceanic. The trawl brought up a sticky mud containing logs of wood, branches, twigs and decayed vegetable matter.

Dr. Burckhardt argued from the enormously thick deposits of porphyrite conglomerates in Western Chile that these were laid down on the ancient shore-line of a vast western land-mass of which the existing coast cordillera of Chile is the last remnant. Says Scharff, dealing with

Burckhardt's theory: "He advocates, in fact, nothing short of what we might call a Pacific continent which lay mainly to the westward of Chile. That land formerly extended in that direction I have endeavoured to demonstrate from purely faunistic evidence, but I believe that it stretched mainly northward, communicating from time to time with Central America and the Antilles, and also with Mexico and Western California, and then eventually bending across to Eastern Asia in a great loop and thus joining New Guinea, Australia and New Zealand."

A more recent protagonist of the theory of a great Pacific continent from the fragments of which Polynesian civilization emerged is Professor H. Macmillan Brown of Christchurch, New Zealand, who, in his recent remarkable work, *The Riddle of the Pacific*, has reviewed the whole subject with impartiality and a marked capacity for dealing with a problem of such complexity in a simple manner. In a passage which will certainly become memorable in the annals of the controversy which has raged so long around the subject of sunken land-areas, he says, "Whether we assume a continental area in the central region of the Pacific or not, there must have been enormously more land than there is now, if not some land connection between the Hawaiian Archipelago and the south-west of Polynesia; for the American scientists, working from the former, find a close affinity between its flora and fauna and those of the latter."

The extraordinary evidence of subsidence and later emergence afforded by the phosphate islands must not be ignored. These are to be found only in isolated regions of the Pacific and in those, moreover, which are subject to elevation and depression. Phosphates are not formed from guano unless the island sinks below the surface of the ocean and rises again more than once. The sea-water must separate the phosphate from the bird-manure and coagulate it under pressure.

Malden Island well exemplifies this condition. Remote from all other insular localities in the Pacific it still retains numerous temples and altars, showing that it was a sacred isle and that the neighbouring localities from which its devotees came must have sunk. The guano with which it is covered goes down two feet or more below the surface of the sea, showing that it is presently in process of ubsidence.

Nauru and Ocean Island have sunk and risen repeatedly. They have been isolated probably for thousands of years, and the formation of their beaches and terraces reveal that they have been submerged and have risen again on at least two occasions.

Man must have landed on Ocean Island at an early period, for fire-marked stones have been found there. Its people employ a language which differs from the Polynesian in the use of many archaic and unknown words.

The entire history, human and geological, of the Pacific is eloquent of disappearing and reappearing islands. Tuanaki, in the Cook Islands, disappeared about the middle of last century. It lay to the south-east of Rarotonga, between that island and Mangaia, and more than one of its inhabitants who had landed on Rarotonga died within the present century. The Rev. William Gill in his *Gems of the Coral Islands*, published in 1865, tells us that in 1844 a small schooner came from Rurutu in search of Tuanaki, " said to consist of three low islands . . . and thickly inhabited. Two native sailors had seen the island at different times when on board whaling vessels," and had had intercourse with the people, who resembled the Mangaians in dress, manners and customs. " They had heard of the overthrow of idolatry on Rarotonga and Mangaia, and they were waiting with expectation some foreign teachers to visit them."

In the *Rarotongan Records* of the Rev. W. Wyatt Gill, published in 1916 by the Polynesian Society, the report of a sailor of Aitutaki on the islands is quoted. He says:

" Two years have passed since I saw that island. We went thither by way of Rurutu Island, and, when we found it, our captain searched for the entrance and then lowered a boat, into which he descended—there were seven of us. No one was on the beach. I was sent inland and saw the house of the *Ariki* or high chief full of men; I told the chief I came from Araura " (an old name of

Aitutaki). "There were no women inside, as they had a separate house. 'We do not kill men; we only know how to dance and sing; we know nothing of war,' said the chief." "The captain afterwards went inland, and we slept there that night, taking some food—fowls, pigs, yams, and bananas. We were six days ashore there." When asked what the people were like, he said: "They are exactly like us. Their water is scraped up in a bowl or in a leaf of the giant taro. Their dialect is that of Mangaia, and they wear the *tiputa* (or poncho), and use the same kind of fans as at Mangaia." "It takes one night (and day) to reach Tuanaki from Mangaia."

This island must have been submerged soon afterwards with all its inhabitants. Some degrees nearer the Equator Captain Williams of the auxiliary schooner *Awarua* reports that two reef islands to the south-east of Manihiki have completely disappeared and that Victoria Land, two or three degrees north of Manihiki, has also been submerged.

Ernst Haeckel, in his *History of Creation*, states the case succinctly for the Lemurian theory as it was understood by its protagonists in 1876.

" The history of the earth's development shows us that the distribution of land and water on its surface is ever and continually changing. In consequence of geological changes of the earth's crust, *elevations* and *depressions* of the ground take place everywhere, sometimes more strongly marked in one place, sometimes in another. Even if they happen so slowly that in the course of centuries the seashore rises or sinks only a few inches, or even only a few lines, still they nevertheless effect great results in the course of long periods of time. And long—immeasurably long—periods of time have not been wanting in the earth's history. During the course of many millions of years, ever since organic life existed on the earth, land and water have perpetually struggled for supremacy. Continents and islands have sunk into the sea, and new ones have arisen out of its bosom. Lakes and seas have been slowly raised and dried up, and new water basins have arisen by the sinking of the ground. Peninsulas have

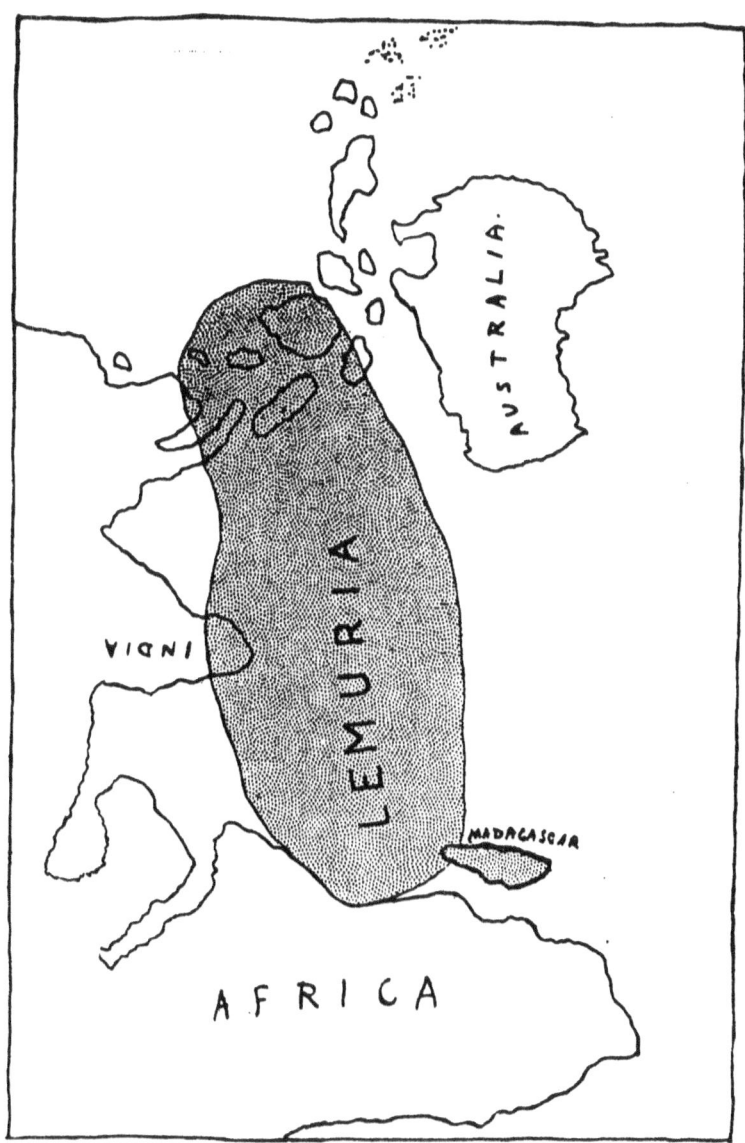

HAECKEL'S SUGGESTED SITE FOR LEMURIA IN THE INDIAN OCEAN

The shaded space indicates the limits of the now submerged continent.

become islands by the narrow neck of land which connected them with the mainland sinking into the water. The islands of an archipelago have become the peaks of a continuous chain of mountains by the whole floor of their sea being considerably raised.

" Thus the Mediterranean at one time was an inland sea, when, in the place of the Straits of Gibraltar, an isthmus connected Africa with Spain. England even during the more recent history of the earth, when man already existed, has repeatedly been connected with the European continent and been repeatedly separated from it. Nay, even Europe and North America have been directly connected. The South Sea at one time formed a large Pacific continent, and the numerous little islands which now lie scattered in it were simply the highest peaks of the mountains covering that continent. The Indian Ocean formed a continent which extended from the Sunda Islands along the southern coast of Asia to the east coast of Africa. This large continent of former times Sclater, an Englishman, has called *Lemuria*, from the monkey-like animals which inhabited it, and it is at the same time of great importance from being the probable cradle of the human race, which in all likelihood here first developed out of anthropoid apes. The important proof which Alfred Wallace has furnished, by the help of chorological[1] facts, that the present Malayan Archipelago consists in reality of two completely different divisions, is particularly interesting. The western division, the Indo-Malayan Archipelago, comprising the large islands of Borneo, Java and Sumatra, was formerly connected by Malacca with the Asiatic continent, and probably also with the Lemurian continent just mentioned. The eastern division, on the other hand, the Austro-Malayan Archipelago, comprising Celebes, the Moluccas, New Guinea, Solomon Islands, etc., was formerly directly connected with Australia. Both divisions were formerly two continents separated by a strait, but they have now for the most part sunk below the level of the sea. Wallace, solely on the ground of his accurate chorological observations, has been able in the most accurate manner to

[1] Chorology = the science of geographical distribution.

determine the position of this former strait, the south end of which passes between Balij and Lombok."

Elsewhere Haeckel wrote : " Of the five now existing continents, neither Australia nor America nor Europe can have been this primeval home (of man), or the so-called ' Paradise,' the ' cradle of the human race.' Most circumstances indicate Southern Asia as the locality in question. Besides Southern Asia, the only other of the now exisiting continents which might be viewed in this light is Africa. But there are a number of circumstances (especially chorological facts) which suggest that the primeval home of man was a continent now sunk below the surface of the Indian Ocean, which extended along the south of Asia, as it is at present (and probably in direct connection with it), towards the east, as far as Further India and the Sunda Islands; towards the west, as far as Madagascar and the south-eastern shores of Africa. We have already mentioned that many facts in animal and vegetable geography render the former existence of such a South Indian continent very probable. Sclater has given this continent the name of Lemuria, from the semi-apes which were characteristic of it. By assuming this Lemuria to have been man's primeval home, we greatly facilitate the explanation of the geographical distribution of the human species by migration."

The late Mr. Alfred Russel Wallace in his work, *The Geographical Distribution of Animals*, published in the same year as Haeckel's, alluded to the Lemurian hypothesis as " a legitimate and highly probable suggestion." " We have already had occasion," he writes, " to refer to an ancient connection between this sub-region (the Ethiopian) and Madagascar, in order to explain the distribution of the Lemurine type, and some other curious affinities between the two countries. This view is supported by the geology of India, which shows us Ceylon and South India consisting mainly of granite and old-metamorphic rocks, while the greater part of the peninsula is of tertiary formation, with a few isolated patches of secondary rocks. It is evident, therefore, that during much of the Tertiary Period, Ceylon and South India were bounded on the north by a considerable extent of sea, and probably formed part of an extensive Southern Continent or great island. The very numerous and remarkable cases of affinity with Malaya require, however, some closer approximation with these islands, which probably occurred at a later period. When, still later, the great plains and tablelands of Hindostan were formed, and a permanent land communication effected with the rich and highly developed Himalo-Chinese fauna, a rapid immigration of new types took place, and many of the less specialized forms of mammalia and birds became extinct. Among reptiles and insects the competition was less severe, or the older forms were too well adapted to local conditions to be expelled; so that it is among these groups alone that we find any considerable number of what are probably the remains of the ancient fauna of a now submerged Southern Continent.

" In the Southern Hemisphere there appear to have been three considerable and very ancient land-masses, varying in extent from time to time, but always keeping distinct from each other, and represented more or less completely by Australia, South Africa, and South America of our time. Into these flowed successive waves of life as they each in turn became temporarily united with some part of the Northern land."

But in his *Island Life*, published in 1880, Wallace rather abruptly resiled from his former position regarding the Lemurian theory. Criticizing Dr. Hartlaub's work on the *Birds of Madagascar*, in which that writer had insisted on the former existence of Lemuria because of the presence of Indian bird-types in Madagascar, he gave it as his considered opinion that the Lemurian continent must have existed, if at all, " at so remote a period that the higher animals did not then inhabit either Africa or Southern Asia, and it must have become partially or wholly submerged before they reached those countries." This would imply the disappearance of Lemuria about the earlier part of the Miocene epoch. The Indian birds at that epoch, if they then existed, must have had a widely different distribution from what they now have, and probably entered

Madagascar at a much later period, via recently submerged islands which formerly existed between that island and Africa.

Proceeding, Wallace alluded to the Lemurian theory as "essentially a provisional hypothesis, very useful in calling attention to a remarkable series of problems in geographical distribution."

Wallace was, of course, driven to these conclusions by his adoption of the theory of the general permanence of continents and oceans. He believed that the sedimentary deposits which in the ultimate are composed of landmasses through countless ages have been formed under water, but in lakes and inland seas, or near the coasts of continents or great islands, and even then in limited areas, and not at great oceanic depths, and he thought that the enormous depths and great extent of the oceans is eloquent of their permanence, as is the fact that they "have not preserved any fragments of the supposed ancient continents nor of the deposits which must have resulted from their denudation during the whole period of their existence."

Dr. Hartlaub, who had criticized Wallace's conclusions, summarized his belief in an ancient Lemuria as follows : "Five and thirty years ago, Isidore Geoffroy St. Hilaire remarked that, if one had to classify the Island of Madagascar exclusively on zoological considerations, and without reference to its geographical situation, it could be shown to be neither Asiatic nor African, but quite different from either, and almost a fourth continent. And this fourth continent could be further proved to be, as regards its fauna, much more different from Africa, which lies so near to it, than from India which is so far away. With these words the correctness and pregnancy of which later investigations tend to bring into their full light, the French naturalist first stated the interesting problem for the solution of which an hypothesis based on scientific knowledge has recently been propounded, for this fourth continent of Isidore Geoffroy is Sclater's 'Lemuria'—that sunken land which, containing parts of Africa, must have extended far eastwards over Southern India and Ceylon, and the highest points of which we recognize in the volcanic peaks of Bourbon and Mauritius, and in the central range of Madagascar itself—the last resort of the almost extinct Lemurine race which formerly peopled it."

In an article containing a criticism of Mr. A. R. Wallace's *Island Life*—a work devoted largely to the question of the distribution of animals—Mr. Starkie Gardiner writes ("Subsidence and Elevation," *Geological Magazine*, June, 1881):

"By a process of reasoning supported by a large array of facts of different kinds, he arrives at the conclusion that the distribution of life upon the land as we now see it, has been accomplished without the aid of important changes in the relative positions of continents and seas. Yet if we accept his views we must believe that Asia and Africa, Madagascar and Africa, New Zealand and Australia, Europe and America, have been united at some period not remote geologically, and that seas to the depth of 1000 fathoms have been bridged over; but we must treat as utterly gratuitous and entirely opposed to all the evidences at our command, the supposition that temperate Europe and temperate America, Australia, and South America, have ever been connected except by way of the Arctic or Antarctic circles and that lands now separated by seas of more than 1000 fathoms depth have ever been united. Mr. Wallace, it must be admitted, has succeeded in explaining the chief features of existing life distribution, without bridging the Atlantic or Pacific, except towards the Poles, yet I cannot help thinking that some of the facts might perhaps be more easily explained by admitting the former existence of the connection between the coast of Chile and Polynesia and Great Britain and Florida, shadowed by the submarine banks which stretch between them. Nothing is urged that renders the more direct connection impossible, and no physical reason is advanced why the floor of the ocean should not be upheaved from any depth. The route by which" (according to the anti-Atlantean and Lemurian hypothesis of Wallace) "the floras of South America and Australia are supposed to have mingled, is beset by almost insurmountable obstacles, and the apparently sudden arrival of a number of sub-tropical American plants in our Eocene flora, necessitates a connection more to the south than the present 1000 fathom line . . . forces are unceasingly acting, and there is no reason why an elevating force once set in action in the centre of an ocean should cease to act until a continent is formed. They have acted and lifted out from the sea, in comparatively recent geological times, the loftiest mountains on earth. Mr. Wallace himself admits repeatedly that sea-beds have been elevated 1000 fathoms and islands have risen up from the depths of 8000 fathoms—and to suppose that the upheaving forces are limited in power is, it seems to me, ' utterly gratuitous and entirely opposed to all the evidences at our command.' "

Mr. H. F. Blandford, in 1875, in an essay on " The plant-bearing series of India and the former existence of an Indo-Oceanic Continent," summarized his reasons for his belief in the former existence of Lemuria as follows :

" 1st. The plant-bearing series of India ranges from early Permian to the latest Jurassic times, indicating (except in a few cases and locally) the uninterrupted continuity of land and fresh-water conditions. These may have prevailed from much earlier times.

" 2nd. In the early Permian, as in the Postpliocene age, a cold climate prevailed down to low latitudes, and I am inclined to believe in both hemispheres simultaneously. With the decrease of cold the flora and reptilian fauna of Permian times were diffused to Africa, India, and possibly Australia ; or the flora may have existed in Australia somewhat earlier, and have been diffused thence.

" 3rd. India, South Africa and Australia were connected by an Indo-Oceanic Continent in the Permian epoch ; and the two former countries remained connected (with at the utmost only short interruptions) up to the end of the Miocene Period. During the latter part of the time this land was also connected with Malayana.

" 4th. In common with some previous writers, I consider that the position of this land was defined by the range of coral reefs and banks that now exist between the Arabian Sea and East Africa.

" 5th. Up to the end of the Nummulitic epoch no direct

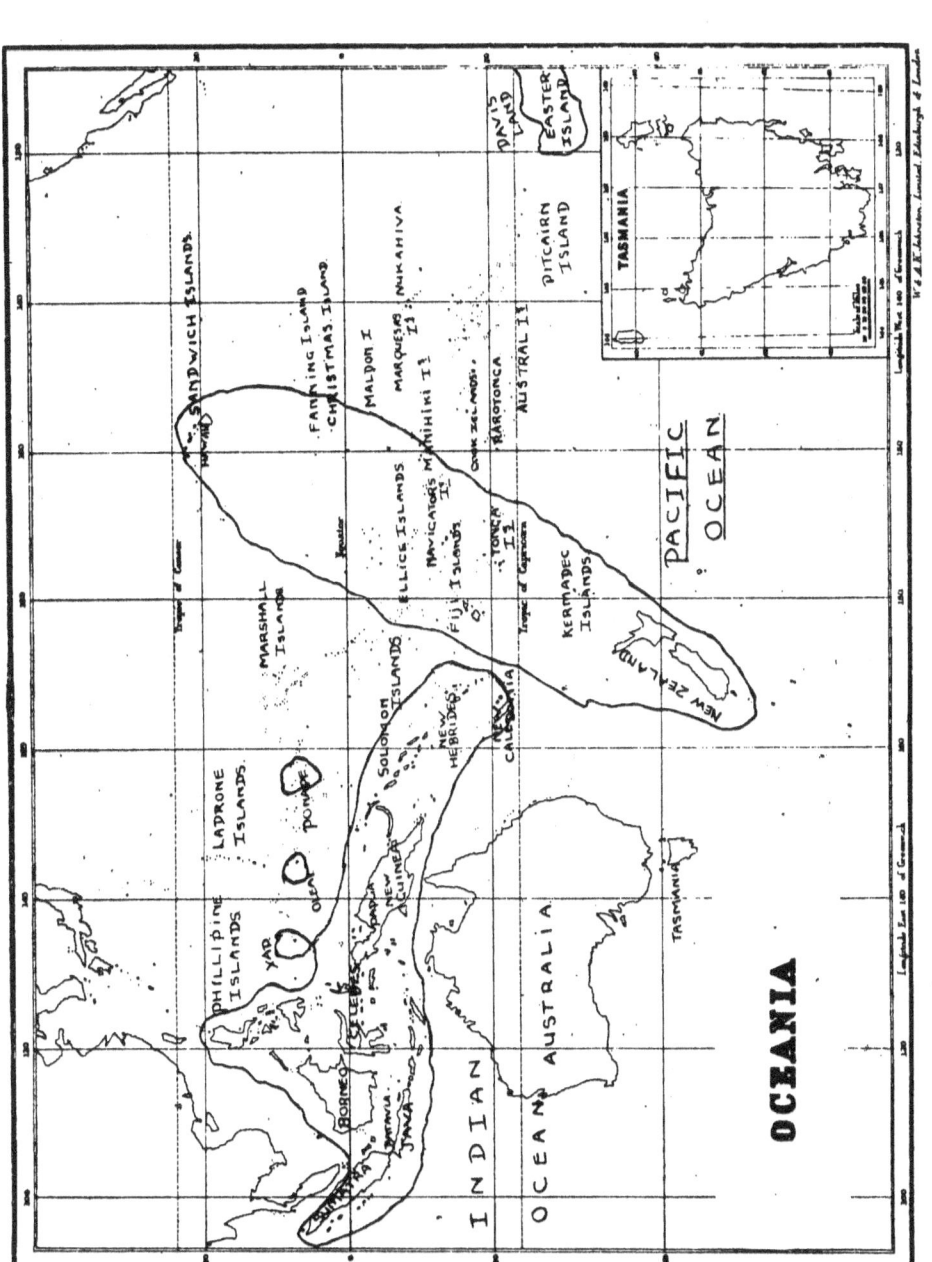

THE LEMURIAN CONTINENTAL LAND-MASSES, ACCORDING TO THE AUTHOR

THE GEOLOGY OF LEMURIA

connection (except possibly for short periods) existed between India and Western Asia."

Sir Archibald Geikie, describing the submarine outlines of the Pacific Ocean, writes : " The general contour of the bottom of the Pacific Ocean is indicated by the distribution of the islands, and has been further elucidated by recent soundings. The bottom of this vast basin lies generally more than 2000 fathoms below the surface. But across its centre, between Japan and the coast of Chili, it is varied by a series of ridges separated by deep hollows which have a general trend from north-west to south-east. On these ridges numerous islands and archipelagoes rise to the surface and form the most characteristic feature of this ocean. The ridge which culminates in New Zealand runs at a right angle to the prevalent direction of the sub-oceanic ridges, but it is really a branch of one of these. We see that in the North Island the land turns round towards the north-west, and this direction is maintained by the continuation of the ridge under the sea. The New Hebrides, Solomon Islands, and New Guinea mark the unsubmerged peaks of another great ridge, which is prolonged westward by Celebes and Borneo, and sends a branch northward through the chain of the Philippine Islands. A strongly defined ridge strikes southward from Japan, and is marked at the surface by the Bonin and Marianne groups of islands. The Caroline, Marshall, Gilbert, Ellice, Fiji, Friendly, and Hervey Islands show the positions of other elevated portions of the ocean-floor. It is worthy of notice that while the large islands on the prolongation of the Asiatic and Australian plateau (New Caledonia, New Zealand, and others) are composed mainly of non-volcanic rocks, such as those of which the continents chiefly consist, the scattered oceanic islands, where they present any other material than coral-rock, reveal a volcanic origin. They have probably been formed by the piling up of volcanic rocks from submarine eruptions. In the case of Hawaii the volcanic peaks rise 18,760 feet above the sea-level.

" As in the Atlantic basin, the hollows between the ridges sink into deep troughs, some of which have been distinguished by special names generally taken from the names of the investigators or the vessels engaged in deep-sea research. Thus in the northern Pacific, between the chain of the Aleutian Islands and the great submarine bank from which the Sandwich Islands rise, a vast hollow stretches from the coast of Japan towards that of North America. This depression has been called the Tuscarora Deep, after the United States surveying ship of that name. It sinks westward along the east side of Japan into a long, narrow abysmal trough in which, in the year 1874, the *Tuscarora* took a sounding of 4655 fathoms or 27,980 feet. For some years this remained the deepest known abyss on the floor of any part of the ocean. The *Challenger* had already recorded a depth of 4475 fathoms in the Caroline Archipelago. But the British surveying ship, *Penguin*, has since obtained still deeper soundings to the south of the Tonga or Friendly Islands. In 1895, in lat. 23° 40′ S., long. 175° 10′ W., the sounding-tube had reached a depth of 4900 fathoms when, unfortunately, the wire broke. The investigation was resumed later by the same ship with success. In lat. 30° 28′ S., long. 176° 39′ W., a depth was obtained of no less than 5155 fathoms or 30,930 feet—the greatest depth anywhere yet known. It will be seen from the map that this profound abyss lies to the south of the Kermadec Islands and about 800 miles north-east from the East Cape of New Zealand. *It is a remarkable fact that the deepest parts of the oceans, as revealed by actual soundings, do not lie in or near the centres of their basins, but in every case have been met with not far from land.*[1] While the greatest depths have been observed between the Tonga Islands and New Zealand, profound abysses have been found close to the borders of the Pacific. Besides the Tuscarora Deep, parallel with the trend of Japan, another trough, upwards of 4000 fathoms deep, has been met with lying parallel with the giant chain of the Andes at a distance of only 50 miles from the coast of Peru."

Sir Archibald summarized accounts of the submarine eruptions which have taken place in the Pacific Ocean as follows : " In recent years various submarine eruptions

[1] Italics mine. L.S.

have taken place in the Pacific Ocean. The history of one of these in the Friendly or Tonga group of islands has been given by Admiral Sir William Wharton. In the year 1867 a shoal was reported 30 miles west of Nomuka Island in that group. In 1877 smoke was observed to be rising from the sea at the spot. In 1885 a volcanic island which was named Falcon Island rose from the sea during a submarine eruption on 14th October; it was reported by a passing steamer to be two miles long and about 250 feet high. Next, year its length was estimated at rather less than a mile and a half, and it height at 165 feet, with a crater from which dense columns of smoke were rising. In 1889 it was carefully surveyed by Commander Oldham, R.N., of H.M.S. *Egeria*, who found it to be $1\frac{1}{10}$th mile long and nine-tenths of a mile wide, and to slope upwards from a plain a little above the sea-level on the north side to a height of 153 feet, plunging thence in a line of cliff into the sea. Apparently composed of nothing but fragmentary materials, it was rapidly attacked by the waves, and while the survey was in progress continual landslips were taking place from the face of the sea-washed precipice. A little steam issuing from cracks in the cliffs was the only sign of volcanic activity. In the autumn of 1892 it was found by a passing French war-vessel to be only 25 feet high. The place was again examined by an English surveying vessel in 1898, and the island was found to have disappeared, leaving only a shoal over which the waves were breaking.

"Another example from the same region is supplied by the history of Metis Island, about 75 miles N.N.E. from Falcon Island. This volcanic islet was first noticed in 1875, when it was 25 feet high, which elevation was increased by subsequent eruptions to 150 feet, but in twenty-four years it had been washed away, leaving only a submerged bank in its place. In these instances the erupted materials consisted only of ashes and blocks, with no inner plug of lava which would have longer resisted the power of the waves.

"Among the numerous volcanic groups of islands in the Pacific Ocean no rocks of continental types have been found, though upraised coral-reefs are not infrequent round their coasts, and marine limestones. Some of these volcanic cones have been quiescent since their discovery while others have been in eruption or have been constantly active. A chain of volcanic vents may be traced from the Santa Cruz Islands to the southern end of the New Hebrides group, a distance of 600 miles. The island of Ambrym in the New Hebrides rises to a height of 4380 feet, but has originally been twice as high. By repeated eruptions volcanic material may be heaped up to a height of many thousand feet, as in Hawaii, where it has risen some 14,000 feet above the sea.

"The numerous volcanoes which dot the Pacific Ocean," thought Sir Archibald Geikie, " began their career as submarine vents, their eventual appearance as subaerial cones being mainly due to the accumulation of erupted material, but also partially, in at least their later stages, to actual upheaval of the sea-bottom. These features are impressively displayed among the Fiji Islands."

Volcanic vents are indeed most abundantly distributed in the region of the Pacific Ocean. " On the western side of this vast basin it has been estimated that there are 102 active vents, but the true number is probably much higher. On the eastern side the number is given as 118. The linear grouping of these volcanoes along the border of the Asiatic mainland extends through Kamtschatka, the Kurile Isles and Japan, southwards to the Malay Archipelago. In Sumatra, Java and the adjoining islands no fewer than fifty vents are placed, and the series is prolonged through New Guinea into New Zealand."

Where are the principal earthquake centres in the Pacific ? Sir Archibald Geikie believed them to reside on its coastal fringes rather than in its basin.

CHAPTER IX

THE GEOLOGY OF LEMURIA
(*continued*)

IN his famous work *On the Structure and Distribution of Coral Reefs*, published in 1842, Charles Darwin dealt at considerable length with areas of subsidence in the Pacific in relation to his theory of the origin of coral reefs and atolls. Before Darwin wrote it was universally believed that coral atolls were formed by the coral polypes growing upon submerged volcanic craters. Darwin argued that as the coral polypes could not exist at a greater depth than 100 feet, and are killed by exposure to sunshine and air, depression must have taken place, that, in fact, wherever a coral atoll or island existed submergence of the land on which it stood must have occurred gradually.

An attempt even to summarize in this place Darwin's theory relative to coral islands would occupy many pages, and it is merely the testimony of subsidences which it provides with which we are here actually concerned. In a striking passage the famous evolutionist wrote:

" The existence in many parts of the world of high tableland, proves that large surfaces have been upraised in mass to considerable heights above the level of the ocean: although the highest points in almost every country consist of upturned strata, or erupted matter: and from the immense spaces scattered with atolls which indicate that land originally existed there, although not one pinnacle now remains above the level of the sea, we may conclude that wide areas have subsided to an amount sufficient to bury not only any formerly existing tableland, but even the heights formed by fractured strata, and erupted matter. The effects produced on the land by the later elevatory movements, namely, successively rising cliffs, lines of erosion, and beds of littoral shells and pebbles, all requiring time for their production, prove that these movements have been very slow; we can, however, infer this with safety only with respect to the few last hundred feet of rise. But with reference to the whole vast amount of subsidence necessary to have produced the many atolls widely scattered over immense spaces, it has already been shown (and it is, perhaps, the most interesting conclusion in this volume) that the movements must either have been uniform and exceedingly slow, or have been effected by small steps, separated from each other by long intervals of time, during which the reef-constructing polypifers were able to bring up their solid frameworks to the surface. We have little means of judging whether many considerable oscillations of level have generally occurred during the elevation of large tracts, but we know, from clear geological evidence, that this has frequently taken place; and we have seen on our map that some of the same islands have both subsided and been upraised. I conclude, however, that most of the large blue spaces[1] have subsided without many and great elevatory oscillations, because only a few upraised atolls have been observed: the supposition that such elevations have taken place, but that the upraised parts have been worn down by the surf, and thus have escaped observation, is overruled by the very considerable depth of the lagoons of all the larger atolls; for this could not have been the case if they had suffered repeated elevations and abrasion. From the comparative observations made in these latter pages, we may finally conclude that the subterranean changes which have caused some large areas to rise, and others to subside, have acted in a very similar manner."

Elsewhere he says: "The central spaces of the great Indian and Pacific Oceans are mostly subsiding; between them, north of Australia, lies the most broken land on the globe, and there the rising parts are surrounded and penetrated by areas of subsidence, so that the prevailing movements now in progress seem to accord with the actual states

[1] Darwin alludes here to those spaces on his map which were coloured blue to indicate the presence of coral atoll formations.

of surface of the great divisions of the world. The areas which subsided during the formation of the great north and south lines of atolls in the Indian Ocean—of the east and west line of the Caroline atolls—and of the north-west and south-east line of the barrier-reefs of New Caledonia and Louisiade, must have originally been elongated, or if not so, they must have since been made elongated by elevations which we know to belong to a recent period.

"We cannot tell whether the Caroline and Marshall Archipelagoes, two groups of atolls running in different directions and meeting each other, have been formed by the subsidence of two areas, or of one large area, including two distinct lines of mountains. We have, however, in the southern prolongation of the Mariana Islands, probable evidence of a line of recent elevation having intersected one of recent subsidence."

Darwin also showed how subsidence could be proved by such instances as falling trees and a ruined storehouse, as in the case of Keeling Island, which sinks as Sumatra, 600 miles away, rises, Keeling Island thus acting as an index of the movement of the bottom of the Indian Ocean. The Pacific, he believed, could also be divided into two symmetrical areas, one sinking, as deduced from the presence of barrier reefs and lagoon islands, and the other rising, as known from uplifted shells and corals and skirting reefs. The absence of lagoon islands in parts of the Pacific are thus explained, as proofs of elevation are there abundant.

In several of his notes Darwin supplies interesting evidence of subsidence. For instance in the Island of Pouynipete, in the Carolines, at a place called Tamen, there are the ruins of a town, now only accessible by boats, the waves reaching the steps of the houses. Thus the island must have partially subsided since these houses were built. Several writers, he adds, found shells and corals high up on the mountains of the Society Islands. At Tahiti, Mr. Stutchbury found on the peak of one of the highest mountains, between 5000 and 7000 feet above the level of the sea, a distinct and regular stratum of semi-fossil coral.

Active volcanoes, Darwin believed, were absent in the area of subsidence and frequent in those of elevation, a circumstance which strangely enough agrees with the testimony of native tradition as evinced in myth and legend.

Lastly, Darwin could not credit the existence of submarine chains of mountains of almost the same height extending over areas of many thousands of miles in the Pacific on the peaks of which the coral atolls had been raised. " There is," he says, " but one alternative," namely the prolonged subsidence of the foundations on which the atolls were primarily based."

Darwin's theory found no more acute critic than Sir Archibald Geikie, who wrote that it " led up to the impressive conclusion that a vast area of the Pacific Ocean, fully 6000 geographical miles from east to west, has undergone a recent subsidence and may be slowly sinking still." Darwin's views, he said, were generally accepted by geologists, coral islands having been regarded as furnishing proof of vast oceanic subsidence. But the German geologist, Semper, pointed to some cases of atolls which he said could not be explained by Darwin's theory and he thought they were accounted for rather by elevation than by subsidence. Sir John Murray, too, who examined many coral reefs in the course of the *Challenger* expedition, remarked that barrier-reefs do not necessarily prove subsidence, as they may grow outward from the land upon an accumulation of their own debris broken down by the waves, and may thus appear to consist of solid coral which had grown upward from the bottom during depression, while only the upper layer in reality shows such solidity.

Professor A. Agassiz arrived at similar conclusions. He believed that barrier-reefs and atolls have arisen without the aid of subsidence upon a platform prepared for them by the upward growth of submarine banks. He shows that in the Pacific upheaval has extended over the whole of the Fiji group, where it has exceeded 1000 feet in amount, and that in the Tonga, Society, and Cook groups recent corals have played no part in the formation of the land. He also proved that atolls do not always rise from profound depths, but, as in the case of the Fiji Islands, may be formed on the top of eminences rising from a submarine platform not much more than 800 fathoms beneath sea-level. He found proofs of elevation along the coast of Queensland, where it is said to exceed 2500 feet, and in the New Hebrides and the Solomon Islands coral reefs which had been upraised at least 1500 feet above sea-level. It would thus appear that widespread traces of upheaval have been met with all over the Pacific basin, which, as Geikie remarks, " has been claimed as especially a region of subsidence.

" At the same time," Geikie admits, " it may be granted that the necessary conditions for the formation of barrier-reefs and atolls might sometimes be brought about by subsidence. So long as a suitable bottom is provided for coral growth it is probably immaterial whether this is done by the submergence of land or by the ascent of the sea-floor. That subsidence has in some cases taken place may be indicated by the depths of some atoll-lagoons."

In his admirable volume, *The Riddle of the Pacific*, which deals with the history, archæology and folklore of Easter Island, Professor J. Macmillan Brown of Christchurch, New Zealand, offers cogent geological and other reasons for the former existence of a great continent in the Pacific basin. Summarizing the geological evidence, he writes :

" Most geologists who study the whole surface and crust of the earth assume a hypothetical Pacific continent from the latter part of the Primary Period to the end of the Secondary, ringed round by an ocean that communicates to the north with the ancient Arctic Ocean and on its east and west with the narrow and shallow Mesogean Sea, the Tethys of Suess. At the end of the Primary Period this ocean flows over what is now the region of the Andes and the Rocky Mountains on the east and over the long sinuous strip on the west in which New Zealand and Melanesia, Papuasia, and Eastern Indonesia, the Philippines and Japan now rise above the sea. By the end of the Secondary Period the Pacific continent is in process of foundering ; and the west coast of America, with its great range of mountains, is in process of elevation, whilst the islands to the west are preparing to appear. And Polynesian cosmology is not without consciousness of such great areas of land ; for example, in the Tahitian, Ru, the god of the winds, broke up the fenua nui, or single continent, into the existing islands."

As regards Darwin's theory of coral atolls, he says : " It is growing more and more clear from the reports on the boring on Funafuti in the Ellice group, bringing out the shallow-water formation of every part of the core, that Darwin's and Dana's theory of the formation of atolls and reefs is in accordance with facts.[1] In the Pacific Ocean at least, wherever there is a coral island there has been subsidence, even if followed by elevation. For the volcanic activity that raised the high land primevally becomes not suddenly but slowly quiescent. In some coral groups there are volcanic islands, as in the Tongan, Samoan, Society, and Marquesan groups ; and raised coral islands, like Niue and Rimatara, are not infrequent. In fact, there is clear evidence of alternate subsidences and elevations ; the phosphate islands, Makatea in the north-west of the Paumotus, and Ocean Island and Nauru in the west of the Gilberts, have gone down to leach out the nitrates of their blanket of bird manure and come up to have a new blanket several times.

" And away in the south-east of the Pacific the rise of the two cordilleras of the Andes along the coast of South America must have had full compensation in subsidence ; and this is apparent in the long stretch of the Paumotus and the almost islandless seas to the south of them."

On the subject of the former existence of a great Pacific mountain-range, he writes : " As we recede north-westwards from the deep that fringes the South American coast we have less and less of the wide landless expanse of waters that is so characteristic of the south-east Pacific. The surface of the ocean is stippled with islands, chiefly coral. And, if the subsidence theory of these far-sprent

---

[1] Darwin's theory that reefs were built on submerged or sinking land was tested on Funafuti, an island of the Ellice group. Borings were made there in 1896, and later, to a depth of 1114 feet and no trace of any rock but limestone was found. As the coral insect cannot build under 150 feet of tropical water, the result had an obvious significance.

coral islets is accepted, we may take them as buoying the highest peaks of a great mountain range that once ran across the hypothetical Pacific continent in an arc from the Ladrones to Easter Island.

" That this range has not gone down suddenly we may take for granted if we believe in the slow processes of Nature taken as a whole. Through the Tertiary Period and the Pleistocene and right up to our own day the process must have been going on, in one part slow, in another rapid, with occasional compensatory elevations and volcanic spurts. Not infrequently the same point would reverse the process several times; examples are the phosphate islands, Makatea, Ocean Island, and Nauru. And in the case of Ocean Island at least, Polynesians perched on the island before one of its submersions; for deep down in the phosphatic rock there were found fire-marked volcanic stones such as are used in the earth-oven; and such stones are not to be found nearer than Kusaie, six hundred miles away."

Professor Wegener is of the opinion that the Old and New Worlds have actually drifted more or less slowly apart, and still continue to do so. The student of geology will recognize in this argument an old theory the recent consideration of which has had surprising developments as regards the internal constitution and condition of our globe. The earth, as most of us know, is 8000 miles thick, so that the nature of its inner constituents must naturally remain matter of conjecture. But its weight shows that it is at least twice as heavy as it ought to be if it consisted throughout of matter of the same ponderability as the rocks of its outer crust. The nucleus must, therefore, be of much weightier matter than the crust, and good reasons exist for the belief that it consists of nickel and iron.

Many scientists believe that the earth is composed of three concentric zones—the nucleus of nickel and iron alluded to, and called, from the chemical symbols of these two elements (Fe and Ni), the Nife. Regarding this nucleus little can be posited, and whether it is solid, liquid, or gaseous is unknown. The stratum superimposed upon it is, however, in a liquid condition, and is thought to be composed of silica and magnesia, the symbols of which confer upon it the artificial name, Sima. Above all is the outer crust, which is made up of silica and aluminium, and is consequently named the Sial.

The more conservative school of geologists believe the sial to be a true crust, but unequal in thickness. In those places where it is thick continents exist, while in the thinner parts we have ocean basins. But more daring speculators believe that beneath the ocean spaces no solid sial exists at all, and that the continental masses float in the liquid Sima much as icebergs in the ocean. If, for any reason, a fissure develops in these floating masses, the break may grow until at last two separate bodies appear, which will naturally drift away from each other by degrees. Such a condition, it is thought, accounts for the separation of the American Continent from the Old World. To commence with, the degree of separation may have been comparatively rapid, but careful observations made during the past forty years show that, after all possible errors in longitude have been eliminated, the mass of Greenland is farther from Europe by 2500 yards than it was at the beginning of that period.

Wegener, dealing with the subject of Lemuria, says that it is regarded as certain by the majority of geologists that a Lemurian land-bridge existed between Madagascar and India, and that this broke down at the beginning of the Tertiary Period. His own map reveals a Lemurian or Pacific Continent breaking off from the original general world-mass in the Eocene Period, and quite independent of it in the Older Quaternary, but lying much farther south than is generally accepted.

As regards the manner in which Lemuria disappeared, Professor Wegener has a decidedly original theory to offer. He says: " The enormous folds of the Himalayan mountain system, formed essentially in the Tertiary, denote a compression of a considerable portion of the earth's crust, by the reconstruction of which the outlines of Asia become very much altered. The whole of Eastern Asia from Tibet and Mongolia to Lake Baikal, and possibly even to the Bering Straits, probably took part in the compression.

Recent work has shown that the processes of folding were by no means confined only to the Himalayas, but, for example, Eocene beds have been folded up to an altitude of 5600 m. above sea-level in Peter the Great Mountains, and great overthrusts have been produced in the Tienshan System. But even where such folding phenomena are absent, the recent elevation of undisturbed country is in just as close connection with this process of folding. The huge masses of sial, which become depressed to great depths by the folds, must be melted there and spread out beneath the adjacent parts of the blocks, which therefore become elevated. If in this connection we confine ourselves to the highest region of the Asiatic block, lying on an average 4000 m. above the level of the sea, measuring 1000 km. in the direction of thrust, and if, in spite of the much greater elevation, we take only a similar shortening to that of the Alps (namely, to a fourth of its original length), we obtain a displacement of India of about 3000 km. India must therefore have lain near Madagascar before the thrusting began. No room remains for a submerged Lemuria, in the older sense."

In his interesting book, *Observations of a Naturalist in the Pacific*, Mr. H. B. Guppy states that, according to Wichmann, the Fiji Islands were in a continental condition until the later Tertiary Age, and that submergence and subsequent emergence during that period are facts that cannot be gainsaid. He is, however, not in favour of the continental theory, for which he finds no evidence in the deposits of the islands. The Fiji Islands emerged during the Tertiary Period to an extent in some places of over 2000 feet above the sea. He believes this movement of emergence to be still proceeding, but thinks it is confined to the southern portion of the tropical Pacific. Volcanic outbreaks, too, have taken place since the last upheaval.

Dealing with the geology of the island of Vanua Levu, Mr. Guppy writes : " The hypothesis of a Pacific continent, whether it takes a trans-Oceanic form, as advocated by Von Ihering, Hutton, Baur and others, or whether it is represented by an island-continent isolated in Mesozoic times as suggested by Pilsbry, receives no support from the geological characters of Vanua Levu. . . . There is no evidence that the various islands of the Fiji group were ever amalgamated, and no indication of a geological nature that they were ever joined to the Solomon group. . . . The dilemma into which such discussions lead us is amply stated by Dr. Pilsbry. If we do not accept the hypothesis of a Pacific continent we have to explain the cessation of the means of transportal in later geological times, since this is implied in the isolation necessary for the development of peculiar characters in a fauna or a flora." Dr. Guppy then goes on to say that birds have been active agents in dispersing seeds and fruits over these archipelagoes and this accounts for the differentiation in the island plants.

I shall now proceed to summarize the above views before subjecting them to criticism in order that the reader may receive a more definite impression of the theories advanced.

We find, then, that Haeckel, who by the way was more a biologist than a geologist, was definitely in favour of the Lemurian hypothesis. He believed that " the Indian Ocean formed a continent which extended from the Sunda Islands along the southern coast of Asia to the east coast of Africa." He also thought that the Austro-Malayan archipelago, comprising the Celebes, New Guinea, the Moluccas, Solomon Islands, etc., was formerly directly connected with Australia, and that both divisions were formerly two continents separated by a strait. He further considered that the Western Lemurian continent was the earliest home of the human race.

Alfred Russell Wallace at first credited the existence of a Lemurian continent, but later held the opinion that if it ever existed at all it must have done so at such a date as implied its disappearance about the earlier part of the Miocene epoch. Still later he discerned against the whole hypothesis on the grounds that he believed in the permanence of ocean basins. His counter-theory was in great measure refuted by Starkie Gardiner.

Geoffroy St. Hilaire made the first statement concerning

THE GEOLOGY OF LEMURIA

the continental character of the zoology of Madagascar, from which emerged the hypothesis of Sclater's Lemuria.

Sclater, for his part, believed that Lemuria contained parts of Africa and extended far eastward over India and Ceylon, embracing also the volcanic peaks of Bourbon and Mauritius.

Blandford thought that India, South Africa and Australia were connected by an Indo-Oceanic continent in the Permian epoch, and that the two former countries remained connected up to the end of the Miocene Period. During the latter part of the time this land was also connected with Malaya. He considered that the position of the continent was defined from the range of coral reefs and banks which now exist between the Arabian Sea and East Africa.

Sir Archibald Geikie contented himself, for the most part, with summarizing the submarine geography of the Pacific Ocean without much comment as to whether its floor had sunk or risen, excepting in the latter case certain submarine eruptions. He stresses, however, the volcanic nature of its bed.

Charles Darwin was concerned with areas of subsidence in the Pacific only in relation to his theory of the origin of coral reefs and atolls. He believed that large masses had been upraised to considerable heights above the level of the ocean and that from " the immense spaces scattered with atolls which indicate that land originally existed there, although not one pinnacle now remains above the level of the sea, we may conclude that wide areas have subsided." He also concluded that many large tracts had subsided because only a few upraised atolls had been observed in the areas concerned, and that the central spaces of the great Indian and Pacific Oceans are still mostly subsiding. Furthermore he states his belief that the areas which subsided during the formation of the great North and South lines of atolls in the Indian Ocean must have originally been elongated by elevations taking place at a recent period. He is in doubt whether the Caroline and Marshall archipelagoes have been formed by the subsidence of one or two large areas. Criticizing this view, Sir Archibald Geikie pointed out that Semper and Sir John Murray indicated that the presence of atolls and barrier-reefs do not necessarily prove subsidence.

Professor A. Agassiz believed that the Pacific area exhibited many more signs of elevation than subsidence, but, in summing up, Geikie admitted that there was room for the belief both in elevation and subsidence in the Pacific.

Professor J. Macmillan Brown gives it as his opinion that wherever there is a coral island there has been subsidence and that the boring of Funafuti, in the Ellice group, by Sollas, has proved that Darwin's theory on the formation of atolls is in accordance with facts. There is, he thinks, clear evidence of alternate subsidences and elevations, and, if this theory be accepted, the coral islands of the Pacific mark the highest peaks of a great mountain range which once crossed the Pacific continent from the Ladrones to Easter Island. This range, he thinks, has been slowly subsiding from the Tertiary Period until our own day, with occasional elevations and volcanic spurts.

Wegener shows that it is regarded as certain by the majority of geologists that a Lemurian land-bridge existed between Madagascar and India and even provides a chart to prove this. This land-bridge, he thinks, broke down at the beginning of the Tertiary Period, but he believes that no room remains for a submerged Lemuria in the older sense and, appealing to his theory of continental movements, believes it to have been heaped upon the Indian sub-continent.

Wichmann was of the opinion that the Fiji Islands were in a continental condition until the later Tertiary Age.

Mr. H. B. Guppy finds no evidence in favour of the continental theory in the deposits of the Fiji Islands.

As regards the views of others Hutton advanced the theory that New Zealand, Eastern Australia and India formed one biological region in the Secondary Period and that in lower Cretaceous times a large Pacific continent extended from Lower Guinea to Chile. Later on, he thought, New Zealand became separated and this continent broke up.

Von Ihering believed the Pacific land-mass to have

THE GEOLOGY OF LEMURIA

gradually subsided during the Secondary Period and Dr. Pilsbry was of opinion that it was finally separated from other lands as early as the middle of that period and that the northern portion became disconnected while the remainder was still joined to the mainland. Baur formulated the theory of an Indo-Pacific continent extending from Malaya to the west coast of America and Speight believed that a continent covered the greater part of the Pacific in Primary and early Secondary times, and that a subsidence occurred during the later Secondary and Tertiary times.

T. Arldt explained the parallelism of the several groups of the Pacific Islands as the remains of a series of mountain chains on a sunken continent and Scharff, stating his belief in the former existence of such a continent, gives it as his opinion that it must largely have subsided before the Tertiary era. Burckhardt argued in favour of a Pacific continent lying to the westward of Chile.

We find then that Haeckel, Sclater, Blandford, Darwin, Macmillan Brown, Wichmann, Hutton, Von Ihering, Pilsbry, Baur, Arldt, Scharff and Burckhardt give credence to the hypothesis of a Lemurian continent having occupied some part of the Pacific basin at one period or another, that Wallace first accepted and latterly denied the justice of this theory, that Geikie felt there was room for the belief of subsidence in the Pacific and that Guppy is averse from the theory.

The balance of authority is thus assuredly on the side of the former existence of Lemuria.

Haeckel believed in two Lemurian continental masses, a Sunda-Asiatic-African, and an Austro-Malayan, the first of which was the earliest home of the human race. Sclater's Lemuria practically coincides with the first of these, while Blandford believed in a like extension of the Lemurian mass, only that it had unity and was not divided.

Darwin, apart from his theory regarding coral islands, contented himself by stating his belief that the Caroline and Marshall archipelagoes were formed by the subsidence of one or two large areas, and Macmillan Brown thinks that the Lemurian continent spread from the Ladrones to

Easter Island. Wegener shows that most geologists agree that a Lemurian land-bridge existed from Madagascar to India. Hutton pins his faith to a New Zealand–East Australia–India continent, and Baur in a Malaya–American land-mass.

As regards the period at which Lemuria sank, we find that most geologists agree that it had begun to founder about the end of the Secondary Period. It is only regarding the approximate period of its ultimate disappearance that debate arises.

But I should like to stress a consideration as yet neglected and which I think places the whole question on a basis of more certainty. It is obvious to me, as an anthropologist, that the positions of the several races of Oceania coincide with its geographical divisions. Thus Micronesia is occupied by the Indonesian race, the Sandwich Islands group, Polynesia and the New Zealand group by people of Polynesian race, all lying well to the east of the other groups, while the Solomon Island group, including Fiji, is inhabited by people of Melanesian stock.

This induces a belief that these separate races, the Polynesian and Indonesian-Melanesian, may have effected at an early period a settlement on several great Pacific land-masses while as yet they were still in a continental or semi-continental condition, and before they had assumed an insular one. The sharp division of race seems to point to the existence of several land-masses divided by water, at a comparatively late date.

This would infer the former existence of at least a great Pacific continent or land-mass stretching from the Sandwich Islands to New Zealand, and from Samoa to the Society Islands, and a second narrower land-mass reaching from the neighbourhood of New Caledonia to Sumatra. These would be separated by a narrow strait only.

These boundaries, I may point out, also agree in an archæological sense. The archæology of the Polynesian area differs considerably from that of Indonesia or Melanesia. Indeed the latter race seems to me either a degenerate Indonesian or, and this more probably, the relic of an earlier and more primeval savagery.

THE PACIFIC OCEAN WITH PROBABLE ARCHIPELAGIC LAND-BRIDGES DOWN TO HUMAN TIMES

THE GEOLOGY OF LEMURIA

The traditions of these two areas, moreover, speak of ancient continental conditions as existing prior to their present insular state.

There is, however, a consensus of opinion that Lemuria foundered in the Secondary Period. But I prefer to adopt the commonsense attitude of Macmillan Brown that " whether we assume a continental area in the central region of the Pacific or not, there must have been enormously more land than there is now." I have already quoted his reasons for so thinking, but the quality of the above statement suffices me more than all the complicated theoretical arguments of Suess, which appear to me much too elaborate to be convincing.

We must bear in mind that such geological opinion as we possess on the subject of Lemuria is now somewhat out of date. In any case, there are points of view other than the geological which demand consideration, and the general evidence which I have placed before the reader in the foregoing chapters practically infers the presence in the Pacific within the historic period of a great continent or continents. At the same time it is necessary to remember that such geological evidence as we possess is by no means unfriendly to the Lemurian hypothesis save as regards its belief in a period when it was inhabited by human beings, and, even so, Haeckel, Sclater, and Macmillan Brown, authorities weighty enough to be sure, agree in the statement that the great Pacific continent was the home of man, Haeckel, indeed, stressing his belief that it was the birthplace of the human species.

I therefore—with some boldness perhaps—accept from the geological and traditional proof the belief in at least two great Lemurian land-masses having areas and dimensions as outlined above, and separated by a narrow strait alone. To such a hypothesis I am compelled by archæological and ethnological reasons, and I think I have been able to show that there is also traditional and archæological proof to uphold the justice of this view.

I have transcribed the following paragraphs from *The Sunday Times,* of July 31st, 1932, as affording some evidence of the manner in which islands in the Pacific area are wont to disappear from geographical ken :

"Where is the island of Sarah Ann ? Astronomers want to know, because there is to be a total eclipse of the sun on June 8, 1937.

"The island of Sarah Ann was once marked on the charts of the Pacific Ocean just north of the Equator. In recent years the name of Sarah Ann has disappeared from the map, as it is a lost island.

"'When Professor James Robertson, Director of the Nautical Almanac of the U.S. Naval Observatory, plotted the path of totality of the 1937 sun's eclipse, he found that it will lie about 9 deg. north of the Equator across landless Pacific waters,' says *Science To-day*.

"Sarah Ann Island seemed to be the only possibility of finding dry land for the instruments of astronomers who are eager to journey around the world for the opportunity of seeing the moon hide the sun for a few minutes. The U.S. Navy's Pacific Fleet has been asked to search for this island that has disappeared. Probably the Germans will also try to locate it, for the U.S. Naval Observatory has made special computations for the 1937 eclipse at the request of the Germans.

"The 1937 eclipse will have the longest period of totality in recent years, lasting for 7 minutes 3·5 seconds. The longest duration possible is 7 minutes 30 seconds, but the total phase of the eclipse of next month, which will attract thousands to Northern New England, lasts only about $1\frac{1}{2}$ minutes.

"The next total solar eclipse after that in August will be in 1934, visible from the Pacific Ocean, and exceptionally favourable for another check of the Einstein theory of relativity. In 1936 there will be an eclipse in Japan."

CHAPTER X

THE EVIDENCE FROM BIOLOGY

THE biological evidence in favour of the existence of a former Lemurian continent is extensive, and may, indeed, be regarded as the original cause of the hypothesis in its favour.

In 1884 Hutton, in his *Origin of the Flora and Fauna of New Zealand*, advanced the theory that New Zealand, Eastern Australia and India formed one biological region in the Secondary Period. To this conclusion he was driven by the resemblances betwixt the general life of these regions in ancient times. A careful review of lesser fauna, especially of ants and lizards, led Professor Baur to formulate the theory of a former Indo-Pacific continent extending from Malaysia to the west coast of America.

This, in effect, is also the belief of Professor Macmillan Brown, who thinks that the view that much more land must have at one time been present in the central Pacific is strengthened by the researches of the American naturalists, who have discovered an affinity between the flora and fauna of the Hawaiian Archipelago and those of the south-west of Polynesia. They have, on the other hand, discovered no resemblances of a biological connection with the American continent. " In the flora," he says, " the only great genera of the south-west that are absent in the north-east are the aroids, ficoids and pines. The affinity of the land-shells is even more convincing."

But the earliest notable contribution to the discussion was, as has been said in the chapters on Geology, that of Alfred Russel Wallace in his great work, *The Geographical Distribution of Animals*, published in 1876. Dealing with the Oriental zoological region, he wrote :

" Before leaving this region a few words may be said about Lemuria, a name proposed by Mr. Sclater for the site of a supposed submerged continent extending from Madagascar to Ceylon and Sumatra, in which the Lemuroid type of animals was developed. This is undoubtedly a legitimate and highly probable supposition, and it is an example of the way in which a study of the geographical distribution of animals may enable us to reconstruct the geography of a bygone age. But we must not, as Mr. Blyth proposed, make this hypothetical land one of our actual zoological regions. It represents what was probably a primary zoological region in some past geological epoch; but what that epoch was and what were the limits of the region in question we are quite unable to say. If we are to suppose that it comprised the whole area now inhabited by Lemuroid animals we must make it extend from West Africa to Burmah, South China, and Celebes, an area which it possibly did once occupy but which cannot be formed into a modern zoological region without violating much more important affinities. If, on the other hand, we leave out all those areas which undoubtedly belong to other regions, we reduce Lemuria to Madagascar and its adjacent islands, which, for reasons already stated, it is not advisable to treat as a primary zoological region."

But it is in the chapter which deals with the Australian zoological region that Wallace chiefly discussed the theory that certain animals and birds must have originated in a Pacific continent. Defining the Australian zoological region, he says: " The Australian is the great insular region of the earth. As a whole it is one of the best marked, and has even been considered to be equal in zoological value to all the rest of the globe; but its separate portions are very heterogeneous, and their limits sometimes ill-defined. Its central and most important masses consist of Australia and New Guinea, in which the main features of the region are fully developed. To the north-west it extends to Celebes, in which a large proportion of the Australian characters have disappeared, while Oriental types are mingled with them to such an extent that it is rather difficult to determine where to locate it. To the south-east it includes New Zealand, which is in some respects so peculiar that it has even been proposed to constitute it a

THE EVIDENCE FROM BIOLOGY

distinct region. On the east it embraces the whole of Oceania to the Marquesas and Sandwich Islands, whose very scanty and often peculiar fauna must be affiliated to the general Australian type."

Now it will be observed that Wallace admits that this region is " one of the best marked " of all, and that it has been considered by some to be " equal in zoological value to all the rest of the globe." His admission, too, that it embraces the whole oceanic tract (for that is its extent) is important for the student of Lemurian archæology. He also affirms that the scanty fauna of Oceania " must be affiliated to the general Australian type.

Yet in the Celebes it naturally takes on an Oriental character. Now does not the fact that the remainder of Oceania exhibits no " Oriental character " show plainly enough that it has a well-defined type of its own, a type once much more clearly defined, but whose larger congeners must have been destroyed by cataclysm ?

The subdivisions of the " Australian region " are the Austro-Malayan, including the islands from Celebes and Lombock on the west to the Solomon Islands on the east, the Australian, consisting of Australia and Tasmania, the Polynesian, and that of New Zealand. The peculiarities of New Zealand zoology are due, says Wallace, " to its great isolation and to its being the remains of a more extensive land."

It is pretty clear, then, that it is virtually impossible in such an inquiry to leave out the consideration of extensive submerged localities. Wallace admits this himself. Yet with amazing inconsistency, he is constantly arguing against the existence of such submerged areas the moment he escapes from their biological implications, where, indeed, he cannot avoid them ! Tasmania, he also admits, is " a detached portion " of the Australian continent. Yet he insists elsewhere that continents can have detached no portions, that their outlines are constant and have existed almost since time began.

As regards the Austro-Malay sub-region (New Guinea and the surrounding lands) its islands " possess one of its most characteristic groups, the birds of paradise, and have no doubt only recently (in a geological sense) been separated from it." The large island of Celebes is surrounded by deep seas and volcanic islets indicating former elevations and subsidences, yet its fauna presents " the most puzzling relations, showing affinities to Java, the Philippines, to the Moluccas, to New Guinea, to Continental India, and even to Africa." Are not these " relations " " puzzling " simply because the fact of the subsidences and elevations here admitted geologically is not admitted biologically, just as elsewhere Wallace would not admit as proof biological facts as resolving geological difficulties ? How obstinate and illogical Victorian science could be is surely well illustrated in this particular connection.

We now arrive at Wallace's treatment of the Polynesian area. He says : " The next sub-region consists of the extensive series of islands scattered over the Pacific, the principal groups being the Sandwich Islands, the Marquesas and Society Islands, the Navigators', Friendly, and Fiji Islands. New Caledonia and the New Hebrides have rather an uncertain position, and it is difficult to decide whether to class them with the Austro-Malay Islands, the Pacific Islands, or Australia. The islands of the West Pacific, north of the Equator, also probably come into this region, although the Ladrone Islands may belong to the Philippines ; but as the fauna of all these small islets is very scanty, and very little known, they are not at present of much importance."

They were " not of importance," so we cannot discuss the probability that their fauna had a connection with that of the surrounding countries. At least not yet. It is when we come to the question of a hypothetical land connection between Australia and South America that we discover some strange admissions. The passage in which this land connection is discussed should, when its importance to our whole inquiry is considered, be quoted at some length.

" We may now consider how far the different classes and orders of vertebrates afford indications that during the past ages there has been some closer connections between Australia and South America than that which now exists.

" Among Mammalia we have the remarkable fact of a

group of marsupials inhabiting South America, and extending even into the temperate regions of North America, while they are found in no other part of the globe beyond the limits of the Australian region ; and this has often been held to be evidence of a former connection between the two countries. A preliminary objection to this view is that the opossums seem to be rather a tropical group, only one species reaching as far as 42° south latitude on the west coast of South America ; but whatever evidence we have which seems to require a former union of these countries show that it took place, if at all, towards their cold southern limits, the tropical faunas on the whole showing no similarity. This is not a very strong objection since climates may have changed in the south to as great an extent as we know they have in the north. Perhaps a more important consideration is that *Didelphys* is a family type unknown in Australia ; and this implies that the point of common origin is very remote in geological times. But the most conclusive fact is that in the Eocene and Miocene Periods this very family, Didelphidæ, existed in Europe, while it only appeared in America in the post-Pliocene or perhaps the Pliocene Period ; so that it is really an Old-World group, which, though long since extinct in its birthplace, has survived in America, to which country it is a comparatively recent emigrant. Primeval forms of marsupials we know abounded in Europe during much of the secondary epoch, and no doubt supplied Australia with the ancestors of the present fauna. It is clear, therefore, that in this case there is not a particle of evidence for any former union between Australia and South America ; while it is almost demonstrated that both derived their marsupials from a common source in the northern hemisphere."

Numerous instances of the lack of connection between the continents is afforded by birds, we are told. Where evidence is forthcoming of similar origin it must be due " to the survival of an ancient and once widespread type." The affinities, in fact, are usually most remote. The penguins alone have passed from one continent to another, " but no actual land connection is required for birds which can cross considerable areas of the sea."

Yet among reptiles, lizards of exactly similar type are found both in Australia and South America, but not in the Oriental region. Among amphibians, too, the tree-frogs are confined to the two regions alone, and another family, Discoglossidæ, is found both in Australia and Chili, and there alone.

Summing up Wallace wrote: " It is important here to notice that the heat-loving Reptilia afford hardly any indications of close affinity between the two regions, while the cold-enduring amphibia and fresh-water fish offer them in abundance. Taking this fact in connection with the absence of all indications of close affinity among the mammalia and terrestrial birds, the conclusion seems inevitable that there has been no land connection between the two regions within the period of existing species, genera, or families. Yet some interchange of amphibia and fresh-water fishes, as of plants and insects, has undoubtedly occurred, but this has been effected by other means. If we look at a globe we see at once how this interchange may have taken place. Immediately south of Cape Horn we have the South Shetland Islands and Graham's Land, which is not improbably continuous, or nearly so, with South Victoria land immediately to the south of New Zealand. The intervening space is partly occupied by the Auckland, Campbell, and Macquaries' Islands, which, there is reason to believe, are the relics of a great southern extension of New Zealand. At all events they form points which would aid the transmission of many organisms; and the farthest of the Macquaries' group, Emerald Island, is only 600 miles from the outlying islets of Victoria land."

To buttress his theory Wallace asks us particularly to notice that so far as the intercommunication of fishes is concerned, " it has continued down to the epoch of existing species," for Dr. Gunther finds the same species of fresh-water fish (*Galaxias attenuatus*) inhabiting Tasmania, New Zealand, the Falkland Islands, and temperate South America, while another species is common to New Zealand and the Auckland Islands. We cannot believe that a land connection has existed between all these remote lands within the period of existence of this one species of fish, not only on account of what we know of the permanence of continents and deep oceans, but because such a connection must have led to much more numerous and important cases of similarity of natural productions than we actually find. And if within the life of *species* such interchange may have taken place across seas of greater or less extent, still more easy is it to understand how, within the life of *genera* and *families*, a number of such interchanges may have occurred; yet always limited to those groups whose conditions of life render transmission possible. Had an actual land connection existed within the temperate zone, or during a period of warmth in the Antarctic regions, there would have been no such strict limitations to the intermigration of animals. It may be held to support the view that floating ice has had *some* share in the transmission of fish and amphibia, when we find that in the case of the narrow tropical sea dividing Borneo from Celebes and the Moluccas no proportionate amount of transmission has taken place, but numerous species, genera, and whole families terminate abruptly at what we have other reasons for believing to be the furtherest limits of an ancient continent. We can hardly suppose, however, that this mode of transmission would have sufficed for such groups as tree-frogs, which are inhabitants of the more temperate or even warm portions of the two southern lands. Some of these cases may perhaps be explained by the supposition of a considerable extent of land in the South Temperate and Antarctic regions now submerged, and by a warm or temperate climate analogous to that which prevailed in the Arctic regions during some part of the Miocene epoch; while others may be due to the cases of survival in the two areas of once widespread groups, a view supported in the case of the Amphibia by the erratic manner in which many of the groups are spread over the globe.

"From an examination of the facts presented by the various classes of vertebrates we are, then, led to the conclusion that there is no evidence of a former land connection between the Australian and Neotropical regions; but that the various scattered resemblances in their natural productions that undoubtedly occur are probably due to three distinct causes.

"First, we have the American Didelphyidæ, among Mammals, and the Cracidæ, among birds, allied respectively to the Marsupials and the Megapodiidæ of Australia. This is probably more a coincidence than an affinity, due to the preservation of ancient widespread types in two remote areas, each cut off from the great northern continental masses, in which higher forms were evolved leading to the extinction of the lower types. In each of these southern isolated lands the original type would undergo a special development; in the one case suited to an arboreal existence, in the other to a life among arid plains.

"The second case is that of the tree-frogs, and the genus *Osteoglossum* among fishes, and is most likely due to the extension and approximation of the two southern continents and the existence of some intermediate lands, during a warm period when facilities would be afforded for the transmission of a few organisms by the causes which have led to the exceptional diffusion of fresh-water productions in all parts of the world. As, however, *Osteoglossum* occurs also in the Sunda Islands this may be a case of survival of a once widespread group.

"The third case is that of the same genera and even species of fish, and perhaps of frogs, in the two countries, which may be due to transmission from island to island by the aid of floating ice, with or without the assistance of more intervening lands than now exist."

Regarding the ornithology of New Guinea, Wallace thought that it is "pre-eminently Australian in character and possesses many peculiar developments of Australian types, it has also—as might be expected from its geographical position, its climate, and its vegetation—received an infusion of Malayan forms. But while one group of these is spread over the whole Archipelago, and occasionally beyond it, there is another group which presents the unusual and interesting feature of discontinuous distribution, jumping over a thousand miles of island-studded sea from Java and Borneo to New Guinea itself. It is a parallel case to that of Java in the Oriental region, which we have already discussed, but the suggested explanation in that case is more difficult to apply here. The recent soundings by the *Challenger* show us that although the several islands of the Moluccas are surrounded by water from 1200 to 2800 fathoms deep, yet these seas form inclosed basins with rims not more than from 400 to 900 fathoms deep, suggesting the idea of great lakes or inland seas which have sunk down bodily with the surrounding land, or that enormous local and restricted elevations and subsidences have here occurred. We have also the numerous small islands and coral banks south of Celebes and eastward towards Timor-Laut and the Aru Islands, indicating great subsidence; and it is possible that there was an extension of Papua to the west, approaching sufficiently near to Java to receive occasional straggling birds of Indo-Malay type, altogether independent of the Moluccas to the north."

Of the animals of the Timor group between Java and Australia, Wallace says: " On looking at our map, we find that a shallow submerged bank extends from Australia to within about twenty miles of the coast of Timor; and this is probably an indication that the two countries were once only so far apart. This would have allowed the purely Australian types to enter, as they are not numerous; there being about 6 Australian species, and 10 or 12 representatives of Australian species in Timor. All the rest may have been derived from the Moluccas or New Guinea, being most widespread genera of the Australian region; and the extension of Papua in a south-west direction towards Java (which was suggested as a means of providing New Guinea with peculiar Indo-Malay types not found in any other part of the region) may have probably served to supply Timor and Flores with the mass of their Austro-Malayan genera across a narrow strait or arm of the sea. Lombok, Blay, and Sumbawa were probably not then in existence, or nothing more than small volcanic cones rising out of the sea, thus leaving a distance of 800 miles between Flores and Java. Subsequently they grew into islands, which offered an easy passage for a number of Indo-Malay genera into such scantily stocked territories as Flores and Timor. The north coast of

Australia then sank, cutting off the supply from that country; and this left the Timorese group in the position it now occupies."

The Celebes also presents a curious problem. "We seem," says Wallace, " to have indications of two distinct periods, one very ancient, when the ancestors of the then peculiar genera roamed over some unknown continent of which Celebes formed, perhaps, an outlying portion." Further on, when considering what past changes of physical geography are indicated by the zoological facts he has made use of, Wallace says :

"We have evidently, in Celebes, a remnant of an exceedingly ancient land, which has undergone many and varied revolutions; and the stock of ancient forms which it contains must be taken account of, when we speculate on the causes that have so curiously limited more recent immigrations. When we have before us such singular phenomena as are presented by the fauna of the island of Celebes, we can hardly help endeavouring to picture to our imaginations by what past changes of land and sea (in themselves not improbable) the actual condition of things may have been brought about."

Dealing with the Polynesian sub-region, Wallace states that for 5000 miles, from the Ladrones on the west to the Marquesas on the east, the same genera of birds prevail, while mammals are absent and reptiles very scarce. The Sandwich Islands are the only exception to this uniformity, and might, indeed, form a separate sub-region. As regards the former continental condition of the Sandwich Islands, he writes :

" The existence of these peculiar groups of birds and land-shells in so remote a group of volcanic islands, clearly indicates that they are but the relics of a more extensive land; and the reefs and islets that stretch for more than 1000 miles in a west-north-west direction, may be the remains of a country once sufficiently extensive to develop these and many other, now extinct, forms of life.

" Some light may perhaps be thrown on the past history of the Sandwich Islands, by the peculiar plants which are found on their mountains. The Peak of Teneriffe produces

THE EVIDENCE FROM BIOLOGY

no Alpine plants of European type, and this has been considered to prove that it has been always isolated; whereas the occurrence of North Temperate forms on the mountains of Java, accords with other evidence of this island having once formed part of the Asiatic continent. Now on the higher summits of the Sandwich Islands, nearly 30 genera of Arctic and North Temperate flowering plants have been found. Many of these occur also in the South Temperate zone, in Australia or New Zealand; but there are others which seem plainly to point to a former connection with some North Temperate land, probably California, as a number of islets are scattered in the ocean between the two countries.

" None of these are found in Australia or New Zealand; and their presence in the Sandwich Islands seems clearly to indicate a former approximation to North Temperate America, although the absence of any American forms of vertebrata renders it certain that no actual land connection ever took place."

" We have already discussed in some detail the various modes in which the dispersal of animals in the southern hemisphere has been effected; and in accordance with the principles there established, we conclude that the New Zealand fauna, living and extinct, demonstrates the existence of an extensive tract of land in the vicinity of Australia, Polynesia, and the Antarctic continent, without having been once actually connected with either of these countries, since the period when mammalia had peopled all the great continents. That event certainly dates back to Secondary, if not to Palæozoic, times, because so dominant a group must soon have spread over the whole continuous land-area of the globe."

Summing up, he declares that " It was probably far back in the Secondary Period, that some portion of the Australian region was in actual connection with the northern continent, and became stocked with ancestral forms of Marsupials; but from that time till now there seems to have been no further land connection, and the Australian lands have thenceforward gone on developing the Marsupial and Monotremate types, into the various living and extinct races we now find there. During some portion of the Tertiary epoch Australia probably comprised much of its existing area, together with Papua and the Solomon Islands, and perhaps extended as far east as the Fiji Islands; while it might also have had a considerable extension to the south and west. . . . The whole of these remains demonstrate that, as in the northern so in the southern hemisphere, a much warmer climate prevailed in the Eocene and Miocene Periods than at the present time. This is a most important result, and one which strongly supports Mr. Belt's view, before referred to, that the warmer climates in past geological epochs, and especially that of the Miocene as compared with our own, was caused by a diminution of the obliquity of the ecliptic, leading to a much greater uniformity of the seasons for a considerable distance from the Equator, and greatly reducing the polar area within which the sun would ever disappear during an entire rotation of the earth. During such a' period, tropical forms of marine animals would have been able to spread north and south, into what are now cool latitudes; and the southern shores of the old Palæarctic continent, from Britain to the Bay of Bengal, and southward along the Malayan coasts to Australia."

Wallace then arrived at the conclusion that Darwin's researches on the subject of coral islands proved that large areas in the Pacific had recently been subsiding. He adds that " the peculiar forms of life which they present, no less clearly indicate the former existence of some extensive lands." The total absence of Mammalia, however, prove that these lands never formed part of the Australian or Papuan continents, or, if they did, the degree of subsidence which they had suffered must have exterminated most of their higher forms of terrestrial life—a conclusion, it will be recalled, in which the writer agrees.

The islands of New Zealand, Wallace believed to be " completely oceanic," but he admits that had they been joined to the lesser islands which lie not far distant, Norfolk, Lord Howe's island, the Kermadecs and Auckland, etc. " They would have formed an island-continent not much inferior in extent to Australia itself." New Zealand, he states, possesses a wonderful amount of zoological speciality so far as birds are concerned, " yet the affinity of the fauna, whenever they can be traced, are with Australia or Polynesia." But he falters very badly in explaining the amazing presence of the wingless kiwi in New Zealand, as will be seen a little further on. The more modern theory that the birds of insular localities tend to lose the power of flight may be well illustrated in a few instances, but it fails when generally applied to insular avian forms. One class of birds cannot well lose its wing-power and another retain it even though the former be of more ancient provenance, for many thousands of years would be required to bring about such a physical change and no intermediary forms are visible, as would be the case were the process still in being, as it needs must be in any insular locality.

Nearly every page of Wallace's long chapter on the Australian zoological region shows that he was haunted by the conception of the former existence of a great continent or continents in the Pacific, and that in later embracing the opposite belief he was doing violence to his own earlier findings and conclusions, as indeed Mr. Starkie Gardiner proved conclusively. Dealing with the origin of the fauna of New Zealand Wallace wrote :

" As the outlying Norfolk, Chatham, and Lord Howe's Islands, are all inhabited (or have recently been so) by birds of New Zealand type or even identical species, almost incapable of flight, we may infer that these islands show us the former minimum extent of the land-area in which the peculiar forms which characterize the sub-region were developed. If we include the Auckland and Macquarie Islands to the south, we shall have a territory of not much less extent than Australia, and separated from it by perhaps several hundred miles of ocean. Some such ancient land must have existed to allow of the development and specialization of so many peculiar forms of birds, and it probably remained with but slight modifications for a considerable geological period. During all this time it would interchange many of its forms of life with Australia, and there would arise that amount of identity of genera between the two countries which we find to exist.

Its extension southwards, perhaps considerably beyond the Macquaries, would bring it within the range of floating ice during colder epochs, and within easy reach of the Antarctic continent during the warm periods ; and thus would arise that interchange of genera and species with South America, which forms one of the characteristic features of the natural history of New Zealand."

The manner in which he begs the question of an ancient Southern Pacific continent while still advocating it, is perhaps typical of the science of his day, and the general results of his researches appear as much too confused to invite acceptance. He has been quoted at such length in these pages because he is usually indicated as the chief protagonist of the belief that Lemuria never existed, and it is hoped that the present revelation of his inconsistencies may bring about a reconsideration of the whole question of the biological affinities of the several Pacific areas.

"As bearing on the question of the isolation and antiquity of the Pacific Islands," writes Guppy, "the following approximate results for the Hawaiian, Fijian, and Tongan floras may be here quoted. These data are liable to correction ; but they are near enough to the truth to be very suggestive. Of peculiar genera of flowering plants and ferns the Hawaiian Islands possess about forty, the Fiji group about sixteen and the Tongan Islands none. Of endemic species of flowering plants there are about 80 per cent in Hawaii, about 50 per cent in Fiji, and 3 or 4 per cent in Tonga. Granting that there is much to be done yet in the investigation of these floras, it would be underrating the brilliant results of the labours of Hillebrand and Seemann to characterize their work as sampling. Let us suppose, however, that the floras of Hawaii, Fiji, and Tonga have been only sampled, the data above given would be still reliable. It is quite possible to obtain a botanical equivalent corresponding to the geological estimates of the relative ages of these islands ; and taking the proportion of endemic plants as our guide, the Lau stage, as represented by the Tongan Islands, would have a value of 3 or 4, the Pre-Lau stage now exhibited in the earliest stage of emergence of Vanua Levu would have a value of 50, and the Hawaiian stage older than all would have a value of 80. These results are intended as suggestive and I hope to work out this subject in the second volume. They make the problem of the relative antiquity of these islands more mysterious than it even appeared before.

"With regard to the vexed question of the light thrown on the past condition of these islands by the present state of their floras and faunas, it may be at once observed that my belief in the general principle that islands have always been islands has not been shaken by the results of the examination of the geological structure of Vanua Levu."

Professor Angelo Heilprin of Philadelphia, in his book, *The Geographical and Geological Distribution of Animals*, published in 1887, adopted a non-committal attitude. "The presence of lemurs on the Island of Madagascar, the continent of Africa, and Southern India (with Ceylon)," he wrote, "has led some naturalists to the conclusion that at one time direct land connection existed between the several regions, an assumption that is by some naturalists considered to be further borne out by other equally well-marked faunal characteristics. To this supposed formerly-existing land-mass of the Indian Ocean, which, if it ever existed, may or may not be represented in part by the sunken 'Chagos Banks,' and the outlying islands, such as the Seychelles, Laccadives, and Maldives, the name of 'Lemuria' has been given."

Writing on the same subject farther on, he remarks: "The most aberrant form of lemur is the Madagascan aye-aye (*Chiromys Madagascariensis*), an animal of about the size of a cat, with a rodent-like dentition, and singularly elongated fingers furnished with pointed claws. For a long time the position of this remarkable animal was misunderstood, it having been placed alternately with the lemurs, insectivores, and rodents. It constitutes the type of a distinct family, Chiromyidae.

"The somewhat anomalous distribution of this group of animals, taken as a whole—their headquarters in Madagascar, with a thinning out towards the west on the African continent, and their reappearance in Ceylon and the mainland of Asia—has suggested to some naturalists the notion that at a former, and fairly ancient, period of the earth's history direct land connection existed between these various points, bridging over the chasms that now separate them in the way of water, and permitting of ready migration from one region to another. For this hypothetically assumed, now sunken, continent, Mr. Sclater has proposed the name 'Lemuria.' In how far such a connecting landmass may have existed in fact, or in how far, if it actually existed, it was directly concerned with the present distribution of the lemurs, still remains to be determined."

W. Lutley Sclater, son of the zoologist who proposed the name "Lemuria," writing on the past history of the mammalia of the Austral sub-region, says :

"None of the remains hitherto found in Australia throw much light on the origin of its remarkable fauna. But quite recently evidence of an extensive mammalian fauna has been discovered in certain beds, of probably Upper Eocene age, in Santa Cruz, Patagonia. In addition to a number of other forms, this series contains the remains of many Marsupials, and though the most prominent of them belong to the *Didelphyidæ*—the Marsupial family now confined to America, and apparently distributed over the whole northern hemisphere during Tertiary times, but not found in Australia—a certain number of them show an Australian stamp. Some of them have even been relegated by Ameghino, to whose researches our knowledge of the Santa Cruzian fauna is mainly due, to the existing Australian family, *Dasyuridæ*.

"If, on further investigation, these references shall be found to be correct, the inference would seem to be that in very remote times—probably in the early Tertiary or the late Secondary Period—there has been some sort of land-connection between South America and Australia. In such case there would be no necessity to suppose that Australia was ever directly connected with the rest of the Old World at all, none of the peculiar forms of Australian Marsupials having yet been detected in any other part of the globe.

"Besides the common possession of Marsupials, many

THE EVIDENCE FROM BIOLOGY

other resemblances between the faunas of Australia and South America have been pointed out to occur among the Birds and Amphibians, and especially among the Fishes. Two families of freshwater fishes (Galaxidæ and Haplochitonidæ) are found exclusively in these two regions, and are not known to occur elsewhere.

"Apart from speculation, however, there is no question that Australia has been isolated from all the other continents since the end of the Secondary, or at least since the beginning of the Tertiary Period of geological time."

Mr. Sclater believes that, as New Zealand is disconnected by about 1400 miles of ocean from the nearest mainland, that it has never been joined directly by land with Australia in recent times, even in the geological sense. He does not hold that the Polynesian sub-region was ever directly connected with any of the great land-masses of the globe.

Dealing with marine mammals, he says that the sea-mammals of the south must have encountered a barrier which kept them out of the Atlantic. That barrier, he thinks, must have been a land uniting South America and Africa.

We find, then, from the biological evidence, that Hutton believed that New Zealand, Eastern Australia and India formed one biological region, that Macmillan Brown supports the view that the flora and fauna of Hawaii and south-western Polynesia have a close affinity, that Wallace regarded Lemuria first as a probability, secondly as hypothetical, lastly as mythical. Yet he admits that it is impossible in such a controversy to escape from the consideration of submerged localities. While he is engaged in most strenuously denying the existence of Lemuria, he is constantly agreeing that such submerged localities must have existed, as, for example, between Timor and Australia and a possible continent of which the Celebes are the remains. He also credited the former existence in the Secondary Period of " an extensive tract of land in the vicinity of Australia, Polynesia and the Antarctic continent which had not been connected with any of these lands, and he agreed with Darwin's theory of subsidence in the Pacific.

Indeed he was haunted by the conception of the former existence of a great continent.

Guppy believed that the Hawaiian group had always been insular, Heilprin was dubious, and the younger Sclater non-committal.

Others have of course taken up the argument, but have added little or nothing of actual moment to it. Indeed the whole body of biological proof regarding Lemuria is, so far, much too contradictory to allow the layman to arrive at any conclusion, and it is included in this volume simply for the sake of completeness. We must rely on data of another kind to prove or disprove the existence of a Lemurian land.

CHAPTER XI

THE CATASTROPHE AND ITS RESULTS

THE question as to whether Lemuria disappeared wholly or partially it is almost unnecessary to pose when so many insular evidences of its former existence remain. Indeed, I have some difficulty in comprehending the kind of mentality which can view a map of Oceania, fulfilled as it is with insular groups, without almost at once agreeing with the hypothesis of the former existence of great land-masses in an area so vast. Seriously, are we to suppose that of all the earth's regions this alone, with the exception of the Atlantic, was destitute of continental land, especially when we behold the evidence of the mountain-peaks of that land still littering a space occupying so many thousands of miles? Surely to do so is the credulity of incredulity, and I must admit to a feeling of considerable impatience with the lack of vision which insists upon demurring to what to my manner of thought is baldly self-evident.

But aware as I am how many dangers lurk in the acceptance of the seemingly self-evident, I have no desire to scoff at the views of those who have made a life-study of the geological conditions of the Pacific, and whose ideas are fortified by long experience and technical accomplishment. Even so, the weight of opinion is favourable to the theory I uphold. But when experience is under review, one may at least be permitted a humorous and good-natured jibe that unless it is accompanied by vision it is much in the same position as is the empiricism which lacks technique. In a word, doctors who lack vision are quite as dangerous as visionaries who lack technical knowledge, even more so, perhaps, for the simple reason that they are so much the more numerous.

For every falsely inspired charlatan we have a hundred

scientific dullards, who, acting on the assumptions and acceptances of stupid convention, actually believe that the mere collection of data suffices for the foundation of a theory. But how frequently have we seen these admired pyramids of journeyman labour opposed and overshadowed by others, still greater in mass, builded by equally blind toilers even more industrious. The gift of clairvoyance, using the term in sense of clear vision, might have obviated many years of needless work to generations of scientists afflicted with inspirational myopia.

The day is passing when mere weight of evidence alone, unsupported by considerations which result from inspiration and insight, can be accepted of the world, which, indeed, is weary of the blundering processes of that species of thought which refuses to avail itself of those intuitional gifts without which real knowledge and progress can never be accomplished.

The Lemurian position, as I have said, differs somewhat from the Atlantean, but the difference is all in favour of the former hypothesis. The former existence of Atlantis can scarcely be posited from the incidence of its vestigial islands alone. These are few, and gathered almost in one restricted area, whereas the insular remains of Lemuria are legion and scattered across thousands of miles of ocean. We have already settled the question—at least to our own satisfaction—of the continental character of Lemuria. It now remains to see whether the disappearance of its *oikoumenoi* or sub-continents was total or partial.

Such an examination need not long detain us. As I think I have proved in the chapters on Geology, several large land-masses existed, and practically none of these but left insular vestiges of its former existence.

What were the causes of the submergence of these masses ? We must here examine a novel theory concerning this point which has at least the merit of interest. In *The Bulletin de la Société des Sciences naturelles de l'Ouest de la France* for April 80th, 1981, is to be found a long article of 127 pages by General Jourdy, past-president of the Société Geologique de France, under the title " Les epaves du pays du diamant."

This enchanting caption deals with the geology of Lemuria, or Gondwana Land, as some geologists call it, and with the causes of its disappearance. In the primary epoch, General Jourdy thinks, America, Africa, Hindustan and Australia formed a single great Continent. The remains of this continent permit of the restoration of its process of development.

Dynamic action in that period favoured the appearance of the diamond in the southern hemisphere, and it is thus to be found chiefly in Australia, in the Belgian Congo, in Brazil, and South Africa. An immense submarine layer of diamentiferous deposit appears to connect the strata of Kimberley in South Africa and Minas Geräes in Brazil. The wreck of the ancient continent holds exclusively the diamonds of the globe, and the space where they appear is inhabited by the survivors of a primitive black race.

Electro-magnetism, thinks General Jourdy, explains the presence of heavy metals near the North Pole, such as ferroplatinum, and of the lighter metalloids (phosphorus, sulphur, and carbon) at the South Pole, the law of electrolysis directing the metal by the cathode and the metalloids by the anode. The disappearance of a part of the primitive continent was due, he thinks, to the concentration in the southern hemisphere of hydrocarburates of a light and inflammable character. Escaping from the fissures of the soil, they were set alight by the formidable fires of the Pliocene epoch coming from the " circle of fire " in the Pacific Ocean, the volcanic area. The escape of the masses of gas thus produced under the burning earth hastened the sinking process, and transformed the greater part of the southern hemisphere into an immense ocean.

The black races arrived in this area before Europeans, and about the art of chipped stone-working they were ignorant. To them is due the cave-paintings of Rhodesia.

Colonel James Churchward, in his book *The Lost Continent of Mu*, puts forward a theory of similar character. Granite, " the primary rock in the formation of the earth's crust," he writes, " appears to have been honeycombed with huge chambers and cavities, and these were filled with highly explosive gases. When these chambers were emptied of their gases, the supporting roofs caved in, and the submersion of the land alone logically followed."

We know that volcanic explosion has sufficed to destroy certain insular areas or nearly so. It is, however, unlikely that it could be the predisposing cause of the destruction of a large continent. It seems much more probable that slow disintegration occurred through vast periods of time, and that at last the fragmentary remaining portions of the Lemurian land-masses were still further demolished and broken up by volcanic agency. The general causes of such disintegration are, indeed, to be discovered in the history of Oceanic geology as narrated in the chapters thereon, however unavailing the conclusions drawn from it by its protagonists.

We must now ask ourselves how the gradual submergence of their fatherlands affected emigration on the part of the Lemurian races. That there was, unless in particular and exiguous cases, any definite folk-movement on a large scale and extending over a great distance seems unlikely. It is more probable that the Lemurian peoples gradually abandoned regions and islands which were either in danger of submergence or which, if they were insular, were notoriously volcanic. That wholesale destruction of life occurred in certain areas we cannot doubt, having regard to the quite recent geological history of Japan, where earthquake has accounted for hundreds of square miles, and horrified beholders on vessels at sea have witnessed the lapse and engulfment into ocean of entire countrysides with their houses, farms, animals and population complete.

Though occurrences of this kind must have been far from common, the normal course of submergence must have been that due to slow " geological " sinking aided by volcanic and seismic action. It follows that gradual emigration would be compelled upon the population and that by degrees they would be driven from area to area until at length no alternative was left them but to betake themselves either to islands still existing or to the coasts of the adjoining continents. In few cases would those nearest the said continents have very far to betake themselves, unless, perhaps in the case of America, and that they possessed the

THE CATASTROPHE AND ITS RESULTS

nautical means of doing so it seems reasonable to infer, judging from the legend of Easter Island and the data yet to be advanced.

Not only from the theory so ably put forward by Professor Fenellosa may the dispersal of a great school of art from the Pacific area to Asia and America be posited, but by evidence equally cogent. If it be granted that an art of a specific character reached these continents from Oceania at an epoch which he delimits as to its latest influences as 5000 years ago, other elements of culture may as readily have been borne to either Pacific coast, and their resemblance to each other, though separated by thousands of miles of ocean, will plead eloquently for their dispersal from a common centre.

Thus the calendars, solar and occasional, of China and Central America display an intimate resemblance which has never been accounted for, and, as shown by Payne in his *History of the New World called America*, the Chinese and Central American count-systems are egregious from all others, yet common. Chinese tradition, architecture, and many other aspects of Asiatic life bear a distinct resemblance to their American counterparts, as we shall see at a later stage.

This is altogether apart from the fact that people of Chinese race actually visited and perhaps settled on the coasts of America. Such visitations must have occurred at a much later date, and, indeed, seem to have happened about the eighth century of our era, if numismatic evidence be regarded as entirely satisfactory, Chinese coins of that century having been discovered on American soil, and the Kuro Siva, or tropical current from Japan, has been bringing the junks of that country which have lost their bearings for generations to the American coast.

The Indians of the north-west coast of America, like the Polynesians, never made pottery, which seems to show that Asia contributed little to the ponderable culture of either. Both draw their alimentary supply from tubers and not from cereals, and both use the earth-oven for cooking. The carving of the Haida Indians of the north-west coast is surprisingly like that of the Maori. Now we know that the Maori art is derived from some older Oceanic art, and it would appear as scarcely a rash inference that Haida art may have originated from the same source. Also, although the Haida are more isolated from Europeans than perhaps any other Indians, they are certainly more Caucasian in their general appearance than any other indigenous American people.

The old, fascinating theory of an Asiatic settlement in America previous to its discovery by Europeans has existed more or less since the days of Las Casas, and although some fifteen years ago official antiquarianism on both sides of the Atlantic assured us that it had at last been finally laid, it has reappeared in even more vigorous and portentous guise than before. As one who, from the first, has been intrigued by its possibilities, the writer may be permitted briefly to remark on these. But he does so without prejudice, for, although he has a special bias to the prodigious, he admits an equal terror of its atmosphere.

After more than four centuries we are still much in the dark concerning the wonderful civilization of the Maya Indian tribes of Guatemala, Chiapas, and Yucatan. The United States Bureau of Ethnology has heroically striven to achieve results in American archæology comparable with those arrived at by workers in the lore of the ancient East. But although the effort has been admirably organized, it has been to some extent devoid of imagination, and the gaps in our knowledge of the Maya and Mexican past are still so great as to arouse the feeling that as yet we are only at the beginning of a quest of extraordinary difficulty and complexity. For example, although the symbols employed in Maya arithmetical computation and dating have been unriddled, the hieroglyphs accompanying them, which probably relate to the details of religious festivals, still baffle the ingenuity of investigators. Again, the several epochs in the history of the Maya people can only be estimated broadly by a comparative study of the development of art-forms. But one arresting fact emerges from the welter of evidence and theory. The earliest known forms of Maya art and carven inscription differ so slightly from the latest known examples as to induce the belief that this civilization did not have its origin on American soil. Authorities are at variance regarding the best method of collating Maya chronology, as expressed in the dates sculptured on the temples of Central America, with our own. But there is a general agreement that the earliest of these nearly coincide with the beginning of the Christian era. If this be granted, and we lean towards the notion of an Asiatic origin, for an art and architecture which first appear on American soil as almost fully developed, we must look for signs of their introduction at some time shortly before the beginning of our present chronological era—in a word, at a period when Buddhist missionary enterprise was in its heyday.

As is well known, evidence of a kind is not wanting that Buddhist monks from Kabul in Afghanistan reached America at some time in the fifth century A.D. This is contained in certain Chinese annals. Regarding this evidence the present writer is of the opinion that the theory that these missionaries reached America is " not proven." The most satisfactory proof of the early Asiatic penetration of America must surely be sought for on American soil.

It is in the worship of the god known in Mexico as Quetzalcoatl, and in Central America as Gucumatz and Kukulkan (all of which mean " Feathered Snake "), that perhaps the strongest psychological proof of contact with Asia is to be found. At the period of the Conquest he had developed into a god of the trade wind, but in an earlier day he possessed a very different significance. There are several versions of his legend, some of which state that he came from the East, whilst others give the impression that he entered the country by way of the west coast. However that may be, he is decidedly Buddhistic in his aspect and insignia, as well as in the traditions which relate to him. His was a religion of pious contemplation and penance. His priests rose several times in the watches of the night to indulge in prayer and penance, they drew blood from their ears, noses, and thighs by means of thorns, they bathed in the early watches of the dawn. They had their religious adepts and arahats precisely as among the

Buddhist fraternities, and the personal piety of Quetzalcoatl himself and his strenuous "passive resistance" to the horrid rites of human sacrifice of which the lower Aztec religion was so prolific, lend colour to the theory of his Buddhist origin.

Nor is this weakened by the sculptured and other representations of Quetzalcoatl which have come down to us. In these, in the regions of Guatemala and Yucatan, at least, he is shown, not as squatting with knees drawn up to the chin, as in the native manner, but as sitting cross-legged, often in a shrine, in the most approved manner of the Buddhist saint, wearing necklaces of beads and other hierophantic insignia, and a head-dress which recalls those of numerous Buddhist personages. But there are other and still more disconcerting evidences of contact with Asia. At Copan is a stela of considerable proportions which exhibits two strange supporters oddly resembling elephants. These animals have coiled and elongated trunks, but are without tusks. The authorities of the United States Bureau of Ethnology are of the opinion that these are exaggerated representations of the macaw bird. But Professor Elliot Smith, of London University, who has extensive experience in mythology and symbolism as well as in comparative anatomy, assures us that the sculptures are those of "undoubted elephants," a statement which he clinches by saying that the auditory meatus observable is not that of the macaw, but of the elephant.

The architecture of Central America resembles that of old Cambodia more than any other. Leagues of ocean separate the two countries. But they are in the same latitude and, I believe, may have had direct communication, accidental or otherwise, at a much later period than that we are dealing with. I have traced many peculiarly Maya customs to Cambodia and Siam, and I should say that, making allowances for a new environment and admixture with a separate but not very dissimilar race, we find in the American isthmus the dim, western reflection of a Cambodian Buddhist or proto-Buddhist state, whose civilization, agriculture, religion, and handicraft strongly resemble those of the south-eastern corner of Asia. In the

THE HOUSE OF THE VIRGINS OF THE SUN, CUZCO, PERU. ILLUSTRATING RESEMBLANCE BETWEEN INCAN PERUVIAN STONE-MASONRY AND THAT OF EASTER ISLAND

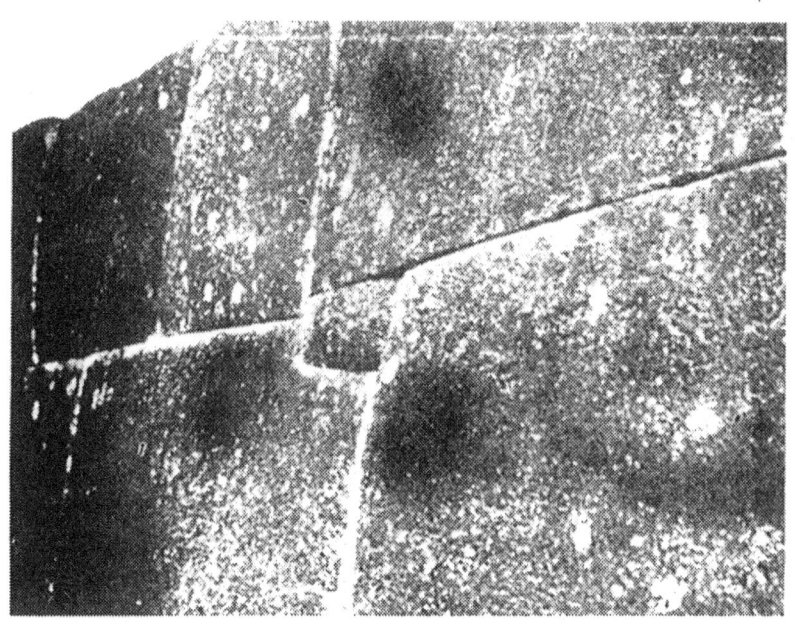

SECTION OF WALL ON PLATFORM AT VINAPU, EASTER ISLAND

more egregious culture of Mexico, with its savage orgies of ceremonial cannibalism, we may, perhaps, see the enlightening efforts of the Maya kingdoms, as expressed in the culture and faith of Quetzalcoatl, superimposed upon a condition of things which strongly recalls the social structure of the Polynesian peoples, who also seem to have reached America.

Much, of course, very much, has been written in this vein. That early America drew sap, sinew, and inspiration from Asia can hardly be doubted. But that American civilization owed its inception to Polynesian immigration is a theory which recommends itself to a growing number of adherents. Perhaps its most direct advocate is Professor J. Macmillan Brown, who sees in the architectural and other manifestations of the Incan culture of Peru a close resemblance to the megalithic culture of Easter Island, and this again he connects with Polynesia, seeing in the hermit isle of the Pacific a stepping-stone by way of which Polynesian arts and beliefs were introduced to American soil. He indicates that the Cyclopean work of some of the burial platforms in Easter Island is precisely the same in character as that to be found at Cuzco in Peru. On the brick-building civilization of the early Andeans, Professor Brown believes, a stone-building structure borrowed from the Pacific was superimposed by the Incas, who improved and refined it. Professor Brown shows that certain plants which had been acclimatized in Polynesia, the banana and the plantain, the leaves of which are found in Peruvian graves, flourished in South America, and from the presence of the sweet potato he assumes Polynesian influence on the Pacific coast of South America, where the tuber flourished exceedingly.

In certain South American customs and forms of artistic endeavour, too, Professor Brown discerns evidences of Polynesian influence. The *tiputa* or *poncho*, the mantle with a single hole for the head, which is so generally worn from Mexico to the Argentine, he believes to be of western insular origin. The salivary ferments common to both areas, *chicha* and *kava*, he compares as having a unity of origin in Polynesian practice, and the chewing of the

Andean coca with lime he likens to the practice of masticating the areca nut, which is also chewed with lime in the Pacific. Moreover, the Peruvian *quipos* or system of knotted cords, the purpose of which was to serve as a mnemonic register for facts and numbers and even to supply the first words of songs and chants, he likens to the mnemonic sticks used in Tahiti and among the Maori, who also possessed knotted cords somewhat resembling those in use in Peru. The *umu* or earth-oven of the Pacific also penetrated South America by way of the west coast, and the stone axe or adze of the western insular area was also adopted in the Pacific regions of South America.

Lastly, he infers the arrival of a considerable body of Polynesians on South American soil. Assisted by the Humboldt current, these adventurers landed on the coast near the site of Truxillo, and founded the now ruined city of Grand Chimu, where still stand three double-walled enclosures, each covering more than a hundred acres. Within that nearest to the coast are the foundations of many large edifices in front of small cubicles, entered only from the roof. These, he believes, were barracks for the soldiery of the conquering intruders, who reserved them as a fortified retreat in the last resort. From the gateway there stretches into the sea about a mile off a weir containing in the middle a dock large enough to accommodate an ocean-going craft, by the aid of which the garrison could if necessary make its escape! But the evidence from which he chiefly identifies the invaders as of Polynesian race is to be found in the cemetery outside the northern wall, in which not a single shard of pottery has been found—for of all the Pacific peoples the Polynesians alone made no pottery, while the native Peruvians lavishly furnished the graves of their dead with ceramic mementoes. A tradition from Lambayeque, an ancient city farther to the north, has it that across the sea came a band of naked warriors who worshipped a god of green stone and who ruled for a time in the neighbourhood and later disappeared.

From what part of Polynesia did these conquering immigrants come? Professor Brown believes that the settlers in Grand Chimu were no mere haphazard adventurers, but came to Peru as the result of a definite quest for a new home. Searching for other land more or less known, they got into the track of the trades, and were unavoidably blown on to the Pacific coast of South America. He thinks it not improbable that these voyagers came from the Marquesas, where alone in the Pacific area is to be found the combination of megalithic work and statuary reproduced in Incan Peru.

The argument that America was not only peopled from Polynesia but also drew the seeds of her culture from that region is ably summarized by Mr. Clark Wissler, who says: " Repeated efforts have been made to show that all the higher culture-complexes of the New World were brought over from the Old, particularly from China or the Pacific Islands. Most of these writings are merely speculative or may be ignored, but some of the facts we have cited for correspondences to Pacific Island culture have not been satisfactorily explained. Dixon has carefully reviewed this subject, asserting in general that among such traits as blow-guns, plank canoes, lime-chewing, head-hunting cults, the man's house and certain masked dances common to the New World and the Pacific Islands, there appears a tendency to mass upon the Pacific side of the New World. This gives these traits a semblance of continuous distribution with the Island culture. Yet it should be noted that these traits, as enumerated above, have in reality a sporadic distribution in the New World, and that there are exceptions. On the other hand, there is no great *a priori* improbability that some of these traits did reach the New World from the Pacific Islands."

Good evidence exists that the races of the west coast of South America possessed their own traditions of a great flood, and this assists the theory that the region in which they dwelt had been at one time settled or invaded by people of Lemurian race who had brought with them the memory of cataclysmic happenings.

Like other races, the Peruvians had their own version of the Flood. A certain man took his llama to a good feeding-place, but the beast moaned and would not eat, and on its master questioning it, assured him that in five days the sea would rise and engulf the earth. The man, alarmed, asked if there was no way of escape, and the animal advised him to climb to the top of a high mountain, taking with him food sufficient for five days. The Flood came as predicted, and after another five days the water fell, leaving only this one man alive.

This cataclysm was followed by a peculiar incident. On a high mountain-top appeared five eggs, from one of which a demi-god Paricaca emerged. Now, as all students of symbolism know, the egg is the same as the fertility pot, which in turn is the equivalent of the Ark in which the universal Noah embarks during the season of world-flood. I believe these Peruvian " eggs " to symbolize the great arks or ships of the Lemurians washed up by the Flood upon some mountain-top in Peru. From the ark of the Flood humanity is, as it were, rehatched and born anew. All races appear to have regarded the Flood as a rebirth.

The Peruvians had at least one tale referring to a sunken island. The water-goddess, who presided over Lake Titicaca, became angry with Huaina Ccapac, the eleventh Inca, who had determined to build on an island in the lake a shrine to the god Yatiri or Pachacamac. He accordingly raised a temple on the island of Titicaca itself. But the deity in whose honour it had been built refused to vouchsafe any reply to his worshippers or priests. Huaina then commanded that the shrine should be transferred to the island of Apiuguela. But still there was no response. He then inaugurated a temple on the island of Paopiti, and lavished upon it many sacrifices. But the offended tutelary goddess of the lake, irritated beyond endurance by this continued invasion of her domain, lashed the waters into such a frenzy of storm that the island and the shrine which covered it disappeared beneath the waves, and were never thereafter beheld by mortal eye.

But the worship of the Peruvians shows very clearly that at one time they must have dwelt in an oceanic area. It is significant that the inland tribes looked upon the sea as a menacing deity, whilst the people of the coast

THE CATASTROPHE AND ITS RESULTS

reverenced it as a benevolent spirit, calling it Mama-cocha, or "Mother-sea," since it yielded them a prolific harvest of fish. They worshipped the whale, fairly common on that coast, and even the lesser fish were adored by them. It was believed that the prototype of each species of fish dwelt in the upper world and sent his servants into the deep for the use of man.

In the legends of Viracocha, a great culture-hero and rain-god, who is similar to the Mexican Quetzalcoatl, we read that again and again he sent terrible storms and cataclysms upon mankind, for their sins against him. He finally forgave them, and taught them the arts of life, and in the end disappeared into the ocean, like Quetzalcoatl, and, like him, was thought of as coming from the region of the dawn.

The Canaris Indians of Canaribamba in Quito had a myth of deluge and destruction closely resembling those of Central America and Mexico. They told how, when a great flood overtook them, twin brothers fled to a very high mountain called Huacaquan, and as the waters rose the hill ascended simultaneously, so that they escaped drowning. When the flood had abated, they built a small house in a valley and lived on herbs. Eventually they married "bird-women"—that is, women dressed in the plumage of birds.

Thonapa, a divine personage, was so badly treated by the people of Yamquisapa in the province of Alla-suyu that he laid a curse upon them, and caused a lake to appear where their town stood. The people of this locality worshipped an idol in the form of a woman on the top of a high hill, Cachapucara. This idol Thonapa detested, so he burnt it and destroyed the hill on which it stood. He changed an entire concourse of Indians into stones because they refused to hearken to his preaching. The people of Tuja-manacu were so bent upon pleasure that he treated them in a similar fashion. Like Quetzalcoatl he disappeared into the sea.

We have further good evidence, I believe, that people of Lemurian stock settled in Peru in the ruins of Titicaca, built, say archæologists, by the prehistoric "Andeans," who developed their civilization long before the days of the Incan dynasties. On this plateau was situated the " city " of Tiahuanaco, on the southern side of the lake, built at a level 13,000 feet above the sea, occupying nearly half an acre in extent, and constructed of enormous megalithic blocks of trachytic rock. The great doorway, carved out of a single block of rock, is 7 feet in height, by 13½ feet wide, and 1½ feet thick. The upper part of this massive portal is carved with symbolic figures. In the centre is a figure in high-relief, the head surrounded by solar rays, and in each hand a sceptre, the end of which terminates in the head of a condor. This figure is flanked on either side by three tiers of kneeling suppliants, each of whom is winged, and bears a similar sceptre. Elsewhere are mighty blocks of stone, some 36 feet long, remains of enormous walls, standing monoliths, and in earlier times colossal statues were seen on the site. When the Spanish conquerors arrived no tradition remained regarding the founders of these structures, and their origin still remains a mystery, but that they represent the remains of some mighty prehistoric kingdom is practically admitted.

The greatest mystery of all regarding the ruins at Tiahuanaco is the selection of the site. For what reason did the prehistoric Andeans build here ? The surroundings are totally unsuited to the raising of such edifices, and the tableland upon which they are placed is at once desolate and difficult of access. The snow-line is contiguous, vegetation will not grow, and breathing at such a height is no easy matter. There is, however, reason to believe that the plateau has risen considerably since it was occupied by the Andeans.

Whence did the megalithic people who built Tiahuanaco come ? Brinton, Squier, and Markham believed them to be indigenous, but modern archæology will not countenance a hypothesis so narrow and unlikely. Some traditions state that they came from the south—that is from the direction of Bolivia ; others say that they came from the north by sea.

Now there is certainly an affinity of craftsmanship and general style between the architecture and the sculpture of

Tiahuanaco and that of Easter Island. The themes of the carvers are similar, as is the treatment of these. Of course the Peruvian work exhibits a more advanced technique, such as might be expected from a later phase of the same artistic impulse, but its general Cyclopean character is the same as that exhibited in the masonry of Easter Island—and that it is not Incan Peruvian is clear from the fact that it pre-dates this style by centuries—perhaps by millenia.

Still other myths of the Indians of the west coast of South America strengthen the impression that settlements must anciently have been made in their region by people who retained a powerful memory of destruction by deluge. The Yurukare Indians have a myth that a rod was stretched from the cavern in which the refugees from the deluge were imprisoned to gauge the height of the water, and they believe that animals are men who were transformed into their present shapes during a period of fire and flood. When all men had been destroyed by fire the god Tiri opened a tree, from which he brought various tribes until the earth was sufficiently peopled—probably an allegory of the arrival of people in canoes.

The Ipurinas of this region believe the sun is a kettle of boiling water which, falling over, once consumed the earth. Further north the Aschochimi of California had a flood myth which recounted the drowning of the world so that no man escaped. But by planting the feathers of various birds the Coyote grew a crop of men of divers tribes. The Chibchas of Colombia adored a culture-hero, Bochica, who was said to bear the world on his shoulders like another Atlas, and who, when fatigued, changed his posture, hence the phenomena of earthquakes. This tribe attributed the deluge to the overflowing of a lake through the spite of Chia, the moon goddess. This latter myth assists the theory alluded to elsewhere in the book that sin interfered in some manner with the hydrostatic propensity of the moon and was thought to cause floods and deluge. The Tupuya Indians of Bolivia believed the deluge to have been precipitated by Anatiwa, who sent fish to pull down those who had taken flight to the hill Tupimare.

How, indeed, are we to account for the presence in the north of South America of an almost completely isolated race, like the Peruvian, which enjoyed a high standard of civilization ? Civilizations, we know, do not grow up spontaneously. They are the outcome of exceedingly prolonged and accumulated endeavour on the part of countless generations.

Now it is curious to note that Peru, like Easter Island, had her Hotu Matua in Manco Ccapac. The Lifegiver, we are told, observing the deplorable condition of mankind, who seemed to exist for war and feasting alone, despatched his son, Manco Ccapac, and his sister-wife, Mama Oullo Huaca, to earth for the purpose of instructing the degraded peoples in the arts of civilized life. The heavenly pair came to earth in the neighbourhood of Lake Titicaca, and were provided with a golden wedge which they were assured would sink into the earth at the precise spot on which they should commence their missionary labours. This phenomenon occurred at Cuzco, where the wedge disappeared. The derivation of the name Cuzco, which means " Navel," or, in more modern terms, " Hub of the Universe," proves that it was regarded as a great culture centre, and we will recall that the same title was given to Easter Island. On this spot the civilizing agents pitched their camp, gathering the uncultured folk of the country around them. Whilst Manco taught the men the arts of agriculture, Mama Oullo instructed the women in those of weaving and spinning. Great numbers gathered in the vicinity of Cuzco and the foundations of a city were laid. Under the mild rule of the heavenly pair the land of Peru abounded in every desirable thing, like the Eden of Genesis. The legend of Manco Ccapac as we have it from an old Spanish source is worth giving. It is as follows :

" There (in Tiahuanaco) the creator began to raise up the people and nations that are in that region, making one of each nation in clay, and painting the dresses that each one was to wear ; those that were to wear their hair, with hair, and those that were to be shorn, with hair cut. And to each nation was given the language that was to be spoken, and the songs to be sung, and the seeds and food that they were to sow. When the creator had finished painting and making the said nations and figures of clay, he gave life and soul to each one, as well man as woman, and ordered that they should pass under the earth. Thence each nation came up in the places to which he ordered them to go. Thus they say that some came out of the caves, others issued from hills, others from fountains, others from the trunks of trees."

Let it be remarked that, like Hotu Matua, Manco Ccapac imposed a definite system of taboo on the people to whom he brought civilization. It is noticeable, too, that another myth speaks of a great flood having occurred before his advent at Tiahuanaco. This was a myth accepted by the conquering Incan Peruvians from the more ancient races whom they subdued.

And did not these Incan Peruvians resemble the ruling class of Easter Island as described by Professor Macmillan Brown, in that they were a great stone-building aristocracy who imposed on their inferiors a species of slavery unequalled for its severity before or since? The Inca was represented in the provinces by governors of the blood-royal. Officials were placed above ten thousand families, a thousand families, and even ten families, upon the principle that the rays of the sun enter everywhere, and that therefore the light of the Inca must penetrate to every corner of the empire. There was no such thing as personal freedom. Every man, woman, and child was numbered, branded, and under surveillance as much as were the llamas in the royal herds. Individual effort or enterprise was unheard of. A man's life was planned for him by the authorities from the age of five years, and even the woman whom he was to marry was selected for him by the Government officials. The age at which the people should marry was fixed at not earlier than twenty-four years for a man and eighteen for a woman. Coloured ribbons worn round the head indicated the place of a person's birth or the province to which he belonged.

Here, then, we have the civilization of Easter Island on a much larger scale, the Cyclopean stone building, the drastic taboo system, the use of quipos or knotted cords for mnemonic purposes. Peruvian tradition speaks of an immigration from the sea. Apart altogether from the theories regarding Lemurian or Oceanic immigration or temporary settlement at Grand Chimu, what should retard us from the belief that Peru drew her early culture from a sinking Lemuria?

Is it the space of the ten thousand years or so which must have elapsed between the submergence of the Lemurian continent and the suppositious date of the foundation of Peruvian civilization? But it is by no means without the likelihood that large Lemurian communities were occupying considerable land-masses in the Pacific perhaps a thousand years before the beginning of the Christian era, and he would indeed be rash who dated the mysterious ruins of Tianhuanaco as much later in origin. At the date of the arrival of the Spaniards no tradition remained regarding the founders of its structures. That they represent the remains of the capital of some mighty prehistoric kingdom is admitted.

If we digest the material contained in this chapter the result may be enlightening. Several theories are advanced regarding the cause of the submergence of Lemuria. We have seen that General Jourdy believes that America, Africa, India, and Australia formed a single great continent, whose remains permit of the restoration of its process of development. The wreck of this ancient land-mass holds exclusively the diamentiferous deposits of the globe, and is inhabited by the survivors of a primitive black race. The disappearance of a part of the primitive continent was due to the concentration in the southern hemisphere of hydrocarburates of a light and inflammable nature. Their gases, escaping through fissures in the soil, were set alight by volcanic fires in the Pliocene epoch and the escape of masses of gas thus produced under the earth hastened the sinking process.

Colonel Churchward believes the "Continent of Mu" to have been honeycombed with cavities filled with explosive gases, which, when voided, caused the supporting roofs to cave in so that the submersion of the land followed.

THE CATASTROPHE AND ITS RESULTS 199

But, as I have shown, it seems more probable that slow disintegration occurred through vast periods of time and that the fragmentary portions of the Lemurian land-masses were still further demolished by volcanic agency. The general causes of such disintegration are to be discovered in the history of oceanic geology.

As regards the results of the submergence of the several parts of Lemuria, emigration ensued in a gradual sense, regions being abandoned little by little when notoriously volcanic or threatened by submergence. The inhabitants betook themselves either to islands still existing or to the coasts of the adjoining continents, and that they had the nautical means to do so seems plain from traditional evidence, as in the case of Easter Island. The elements of Lemurian culture were thus carried to either Pacific coast, as their resemblance, though separated by thousands of miles of ocean, reveals.

The Indians of the north-west coast of America still possess many customs resembling those of the Oceanic peoples. Their art resembles that of the Maori. There are good grounds for believing that old America drew much of its culture from Asia, but, this notwithstanding, much of it also came from Oceania by way of Easter Island, especially the art of megalithic building, which the Peruvian Incas later adopted and improved upon. Many South American customs and art forms are of Oceanic origin, and that a considerable body of people from Oceania, perhaps from the Marquesas, arrived on American soil seems proved by remains at Grand Chimu and elsewhere. But we need not regard these invaders as " Polynesian " or modern.

Some of the races of the west coast of South America possessed traditions of a great flood or submergence, and some of the religious beliefs of the Peruvians seem to show that at one time they dwelt in an oceanic environment. The ruins of Titicaca and Tiahuanaco seem to point to the influence of people of " Lemurian " stock or who had imbibed a Lemurian tradition. The architectural style of Tiahuanaco and Easter Island is similar. In polity and custom the Incan Peruvians closely resembled the rulers of Easter Island. Chronology may not actually raise its barriers here, as it may be that large Lemurian communities occupied considerable land-masses in the Pacific less than a thousand years before the beginning of the Christian era.

So much, then, we gleam from the chapter under review. We must not forget that America may have received cultural impulses from Asia or Polynesia many centuries after the disappearance of Lemuria, or its main land-masses, and it is necessary that we should not confuse such cultural impulses with more ancient ones drawn direct from Lemuria itself. Indeed, it is the prevalence of late cultural impulses in the Pacific from Asia which, I believe, vitiates and overlays the evidence of Lemurian influence in Asia. That cannot be the case nearly so much as America is concerned, but caution is essential in accepting therefrom instances that may be quite late features.

CHAPTER XII

LIFE AND CIVILIZATION IN LEMURIA

FROM what has been written it will be obvious that any description of life and civilization on the Lemurian continent can be gleaned only from analogy and from the very imperfect data at our disposal. It must also be clear that any wild theories regarding its occupation by a race with superhuman attributes cannot be entertained.

We must imagine the culture of Lemuria to be that of the late Stone Age. As we have seen, all the evidence points to such a conclusion. The art and customs of Polynesia have undoubtedly been received from such a civilization, and the lack of any evidence of such artifacts as might be described as " modern " is sufficient to assure us that we are on sound grounds if we think of the Lemurian civilization when at its height as appertaining to, and achieving the standards of, the late Stone Age.

But what does this imply? The term " Stone Age " usually signifies to the general reader an atmosphere associated with the lowest savagery. In nothing could he be more mistaken, for assuredly the New Stone Age, especially in its later developments and that phase of it which immediately preceded the Bronze Age, was an epoch of very considerable culture. Indeed it differed not at all from the Bronze Age, or indeed from the Early Iron Age, save that it lacked the aid of metals. If we think then of the late Stone Age in loose general terms as a sort of Homeric era without metal, we will probably not be going very far astray.

For this age and its various manifestations all over the world, was governed by laws clear-cut and distinct, the legacy of generations of thought. It could boast of a religion and probably of a theology of high advancement from which, indeed, our modern systems of religion and thought have descended. It possessed the arts of weaving, of pottery-making, of sculpture, and painting. Indeed, in an embryo manner, it had practically all the material advantages we have to-day, with the exception of speedy locomotion.

If we consider the great American empires of Mexico and Peru and bear in mind that both of these gorgeous and intricate civilizations were without metals in the strict sense of the term, and that the early civilization of Egypt achieved its extraordinary results with stone tools and chisels which seem to have been made of tempered copper, we may be able to glean a general idea of the phase of culture emjoyed by the Lemurians. That they probably had a script or hieroglyphical system of some kind, we shall see, and we are almost driven to the conclusion that their legal code must have been based on the extraordinarily strict system of taboo obtaining until recently in Polynesia as a whole, and still flourishing in certain parts of it. The extraordinary tenacity of this system shows that it must have been of extremely ancient provenance in the Oceanic region.

The legends relating to a fair civilizing race cannot but apply to a white Lemurian aristocracy. The fact that tradition attributes the invention and practice of the arts to such a caste, makes it plain that they were regarded as a superior section of the population. What is equally important, they appear to have been the conservators of all hidden knowledge and magic.

What has been gathered together in this work concerning the traditional lore of this white race, makes it reasonably clear that at some period there existed in the Oceanic area a caste of fair people, formerly governing several large continents now submerged, who not only excogitated an extensive body of law and custom and a religion associated with an expressive mythology and ritual, celebrated in large temples, but whose degenerate descendants bequeathed these things to the incoming Polynesians.

If they possessed such a religion, ritual and mythology,

these must undoubtedly have been backed, as are all religions of any development, by a very considerable corpus of arcane wisdom and knowledge.

Now it is precisely in such arcane wisdom that Polynesian tradition is lacking. Polynesian magic is embraced in the principle of *Mana*, the belief in the existence of a reservoir of supernatural force, or perhaps, life-force, which may be resident in the Moon. *Mana* is really the idea of soul-force which may return again and again to earth, a kind of early doctrine of metempsychosis and of no very profound arcane character. Even Melanesian tradition is ahead of it in this respect, but it retains certain germs or rather intimations of an arcane cultus, as displayed in its elementary secret societies and rather primitive mysteries. But of these things Polynesian religion displays very little. True, it is, that in New Zealand certain houses or colleges of wise men, the Hui-te-Rangiora, have retained the remnants of an ancient wisdom which appears to be concerned more with nice points about the native mythology and religion, than with matters peculiarly arcane. But regarding Polynesia as a whole, there seems, so far as it is given me to see, a striking lack of the survival of such traditions as are the peculiar property of a higher caste.

What would this seem to imply? I cannot think that it signifies anything else than a very clean cut in tradition. That, in fact, an older race, who, as Mr. Cowan says, were regarded as the conservators of occult knowledge, had refused the communication of its mysteries to an incoming people whom it regarded as barbarous and unfitted to receive them. To this invading race it passed on its arts and crafts and its popular religion and mythology as well as its system of taboo, without inculcating the hidden wisdom which it possessed.

It may be asked, and with justice, how do we know that it possessed any hidden wisdom at all? We know that the people of Atlantis did possess this in some degree at least, judging from analogy of the statements made in Plato's account, and in the bull-worship which they bequeathed to the early Mediterranean peoples. But what evidence have we that the Lemurians were similarly equipped?

Apart from the traditions which uphold the belief, we find that practically every one of the regions surrounding Oceania, the ancient site of Lemuria, has either a mystery religion of its own, an ancient system of arcane wisdom, or the elements of such a system. Even the primitive tribes of Australia possess the elements of the Mysteries. Now it must be granted as a striking thing that although each of the countries surrounding the Pacific, from Kamtchatka to Australia, and from Alaska to Chile, has at least vestiges of an ancient wisdom religion, that the Pacific area itself shows only slight traces of these. Towards the Asiatic side there are, indeed, more instances of such a condition, but in the mid-Pacific mystery societies are scarcely known.

This can only be accounted for by the fact that they were suppressed, for the most part, by incoming conquerors, or that their main tenets were lost when the regions where they were chiefly cultivated foundered beneath the sea. But there can be little doubt that the professors of the ancient Lemurian Mysteries found a refuge in one or other of the lands surrounding the Pacific Ocean. An unwritten tradition current in knowledgeable occult circles supports this view and in certain societies a definite legend is handed down to initiates concerning the fate and destiny of the Lemurian schools of religion.

There are, I am aware, similar traditions which tell of the transmission of the ancient Atlantean wisdom to initiates in both Europe and America. But to speak frankly I have always been suspicious regarding these, because the whole circumstances and setting of the tradition did not square with archæological fact. But the same cannot be said regarding the Lemurian legend current in certain occult circles—circles, I may say, which are above the weakly acceptance of such notions as that which would wish us to believe that the Lemurians were capable of individual flight, or that their physical bodies were of semi-gaseous nature. Nor does the legend even refer to those whom we would call Lemurians, as Lemurians, and I hasten to add that it is not the result of any visionary process and that it has never been set down by the automatic writer. This is not to say that I believe either vision or automatic writing to be among the impossibilities, but when one has either seen or heard of many hundreds or even thousands of automatic writings relating to Atlantis and Lemuria, and when one knows that none of these agrees with the other regarding the history or circumstances of these regions, he is apt to become just a little dubious concerning their bona fides.

There is no reason whatever why the legend or account which I am about to describe should not be made public. Actually it is ancillary to, rather than of, the mysteries themselves. Of course, I tell it as it was transferred to me, as all such things are, by word of mouth, and, as I have every confidence, it was handed down to those who passed it on to me. So far as quite a clear memory of its terms serves me, it gives to understand that " many thousands of years ago " a country existed in the heart of the great ocean of the south. This country is described not as a continent, but as a large island, and I take it that those who retained the memory of it had received this from people who were themselves far from clear as to its actual position.

The nearest we can come to proof of this, indeed, is the statement that it was " many days' sail from any other land." No data whatsoever was given regarding the circumstances of life in this island sphere. A catastrophe of some kind seems to have overtaken it, but what the precise nature of this may have been was not specified.

Whatever its nature, it seems to have been sudden. Be that as it may, the rest of the story briefly related that " the sages " " sailed Westward " and re-established their mysteries " in new lands."

Vagueness, of course, is apparent, and owing to this it is with some hesitation that I have mentioned the account at all. But I think that its sketchy nature speaks more for its possible authenticity than if it had been accompanied with a great show of detail. After all, it is well-nigh impossible that a tradition transmitted orally over countless generations could have retained more than its mere framework. I may add that it seems to me to justify in some measure the traditions of Easter Island, upon which sudden catastrophe undoubtedly descended. That island was very probably one of the last refuges of the intelligentsia of Lemurian society, which would undoubtedly seek for a more lasting refuge when it became no longer habitable.

It is manifest that if Lemuria in its later phases consisted in a number of island-continents, as I think I have proved it did, there must have been vast differences between the character and customs of its inhabitants. These land-masses seem to have occupied a very considerable part of the Pacific region, and as they were separated by great distances there must have been several centres of control or even a multiplicity of states, although the homogeneity of custom which still obtains in the Pacific area would seem rather to detract from this theory.

The races of Lemuria, as we have seen, must have exhibited a considerable ethnic variety, but that they were all governed by the fair white race which their traditions so frequently allude to, has, I think, been proved beyond dispute. It seems probable, too, that the religion of the ruling caste must, in its higher aspects at least, have obtained over the entire tract or empire, and that a more popular version of it would be in vogue among the subject races.

We have observed that the life of the Polynesian and Melanesian peoples of Oceania has been conditioned very much by its alimentary side, that is by its lack of the greater food animals. The pig and poultry, in fact, constitute the chief staples of diet. We find practically the same phenomenon in Mexico and Central America, where flesh food was limited to the deer and the turkey, and latterly to the turkey alone, a circumstance which, in a measure, led to the practice of cannibalism as it did in Oceania.

But all authorities are agreed that cannibalism was practically a late introduction into Oceania, that it was, indeed, brought there by the Polynesians, and that even among them it was by no means an ancient custom is proven by the dreadful name by which they designated human food—" long pig," showing that the flesh of swine and not that of man had been their original diet and that the latter was indeed used in a ritual manner only.

There was thus no cannibalism in an earlier Oceania. On what animals, then, did the Lemurians rely for their food-supply? Doubtless before the submergence of the greater continents many animals of the marsupial class existed upon them, such as the kangaroo and wallaby.

Of cattle or sheep there are no traces in the ancient Pacific. We must then assume that the people who dwelt in this region drew their food supply either from marsupial animals or chiefly from the sea, and the preponderance of myths relating to the Ocean, and of gods connected with fishing, serves to buttress the latter notion. It would, however, be absurd to think that continental areas of very considerable size, such as those of Lemuria appear to have been, would not contain animals and birds sufficient in numbers to form a suitable food-supply for the population. And if it be asked what became of this stock, the obvious reply is that it must have been abandoned at the time when the last vestiges of Lemuria sank beneath the sea. It would have been impossible to have conveyed animals of any size in slender craft, and it is also clear that they could not have long survived on the small islands which formed the remaining vestiges of the Lemurian land-masses.

We must now consider whether or not the Lemurians possessed a system of writing. In several parts of the Pacific strange scripts still survive which certainly do not seem to have been invented by people of Polynesian origin. It is to be found in Easter Island and in Oleai, many hundreds of miles away from it. The Easter Island tradition is, that Hotu Matua, the civilizing culture-hero of the island, brought sixty-seven tablets of this writing with him. But where did he bring them from? No island possessing a script is nearer than Oleai, situated in the north-west of the Caroline group nearly 8000 miles distant. Moreover, the script brought by Hotu Matua is ideographic, whereas that in use in Oleai is syllabic in character, a much more advanced type. The Easter Island characters, if so they can be called, are written one line from left to right and the next from right to left. Nor were they used by the Easter Islanders for other than sacred purposes. Indeed there was little use for writing of any kind in Easter Island, where commands could be conveyed almost by word of mouth. The whole literature of the place, indeed, consisted of a number of prayers or hymns written in this strange script in which men and fishes and sea-fowl form ideas.

It is also strange that the great monuments of Easter Island have none of this writing carved upon them. The Easter Islanders had the genealogies of their kings and nobles written on bark cloth and wooden tablets. But although they carved pictures on the rocks they did not incise their script upon them. Leaving the Easter Island script for a moment, let us consider that found in Oleai, and still used thereon to some extent. Each of its characters represents a syllable and it is much more highly developed than that of Easter Island. Some of the syllables for which the characters stand indicate their origin, but most do not. That is, most of the characters are highly conventionalized, while some retain a resemblance to the thing to which their name or sound corresponds, as in the case of certain symbols in the script of the Maya of Central America. For example, one symbol known as *pu*, means " fish," and it is clear that the character has originated in the representation of a fish. Another, *nga*, means " bamboo," and has some remote resemblance to that wood. Only some half-dozen men on the island now know the script, as well as a few in Faraulep, an islet 100 miles distant. It must, however, have once been used over a wide area. It certainly is not of modern origin and is the product of many ages. Indeed, as Professor Macmillan Brown says : " it must have belonged to the ruling class of an empire of some extent that needed constant record of the facts of intercourse and organization."

It is absurd to think that it could have originated in a small island whose population of 600 souls are constantly menaced by famine and cyclones.

To return to the question of the Easter Island script, the examples of it are, for the most part, to be found in what is known as the Rongo-rongo, or collection of hymns and songs, genealogies and traditions, which Hotu Matua

PHOTOGRAPH OF THE SCRIPT ON THE TABLET IN THE
MUSEUM OF SANTIAGO, CHILI

is said to have brought either from the land of Marae Renga to the west, or from their earliest home, Motu Matiro Hiva in the east. The fact that the god Makemake appears pictorially in this script makes it likely that it had an Eastern origin.

Now the ancient Polynesians did not employ any script, so far as we are aware, but what was known as the Taupon-apona, or knotted-cord record, resembling the Quipu of Incan Peru, which seems to have been used for purposes of government communication. We have two instances in Polynesian legend of tame birds being sent long distances with these cord messages tied round their necks. In Tahiti bundles of little sticks of different sizes and thicknesses were used as mnemonic aids for the priests when at prayer, but no script is heard of in that region although the Quipu is used in Oleai side by side with its particular syllabary, chiefly for magical purposes.

The script of Easter Island appears to have originated in religious symbolism which had a connection with the alimentary supply, or with phallic symbols. These latter were frequently tattooed on the skins of the natives as symbols of fertility. Doubtless, tattooing was one of the first steps in the formation of written characters. There must have been a wide popular understanding of the meaning the signs conveyed, which would lend itself to the more or less ready comprehension of other symbols when they were adapted or invented. Certain signs in tattooing are of the nature of heraldic symbols and indicate the ancestry of an individual. Tattoo marks have even been used as signatures by Maori chiefs.

I have already mentioned that the figure of Makemake which appears so frequently in the script of Easter Island is a composite one, made up of parts of fish, man and bird as his status as an insular deity in a wide Oceanic tract would suggest. But he is one of the few absolutely clear symbols in the script, although even this takes various forms. There is by no means agreement as to the others. The first investigator who tried to arrive at their significance was Tepano Jaussen, Bishop of Tahiti. Some of the tablets had been sent to him and he got in touch with certain Easter Islanders who were working on his own island in the hope that some of them would have knowledge of the script. One of these pretended knowledge of them, but it seems to have been a partial understanding. In any case the Bishop abandoned the enterprise.

Meanwhile the missionaries were destroying all the wooden tablets containing the script on which they could lay hands. But when the *Mohican* expedition arrived at Easter Island in 1886, its members made inquiries regarding possible interpreters and were told of an old man, Ure Vaeiko, who was said to understand the script. But afraid to intermeddle in things religious, he made himself scarce. Later, however, he was run to earth and a glass or two of whisky made him more communicative. One of the investigators says that he interpreted the script quite fluently, but it was evident that he was not reading the characters. They substituted the photograph of another tablet for the first and found that " the same story was continued without change being discovered." Nor could Ure provide the meaning of the signs when they were copied indiscriminately. " He explained at great length that the actual value and significance of the symbols had been forgotten but the tablets were recognized by unmistakable features ... just as a person might recognize a book in a foreign language and be perfectly sure of the contents without being able to actually read it." Another native also recognized the tablets from the photographs and the description he gave of their contents agreed with that given previously by Ure, who, it turned out, had once been a royal servant and had thus frequently had opportunities of hearing the tablets read by his master.

In 1895 a M. de Harlez, a Belgian, made an effort to decipher the script. He believed that the characters represented a few mnemonic words only of each phrase or sentence. His results were far from intelligible. But it is obvious that some of the characters are conventional signs having a meaning arbitrarily fixed, while others are symbolic. Even so, they do not express a sentence, but only a suggestion of the same. That is, they are intended as an aid to memory of the hymns and other matters of tradition formerly used in the island. Indeed were these latter not remembered almost in their entirety, the tablets themselves could have little meaning. That is to say that the two were interdependent, the one on the other.

It is also fairly clear that the script had originally been used for religious pruposes, as the constant appearance of the figure of the god, Makemake, suggests. Proof of this is also to be discovered in the fact that the system was kept in the hands of the priesthood, but that they had originally come from afar seems clear enough from the statement that when they reached Easter Island, they were written, or rather painted, on bark-cloth. But bark-cloth was scarcely to be obtained on Easter Island and the inner bark of the banana stem took its place. This, however, scarcely served the purpose and recourse was had to scratching the script on planks of imported wood with an obsidian tool. The tablets were copied on this wood annually when an examination of the priests was held to see if they remembered the traditions, a ceremony which was kept up until the date of the great Peruvian raid of 1863, which practically destroyed the ancient life of Easter Island.

These tablets became a sort of sacred book, but their real significance was understood by the priesthood only and the people were wellnigh ignorant of their contents. No new tablets were ever made, other than those originally brought to the island, and it is probable that the whole significance of the characters they contained was unknown to anyone who survived the submergence of the archipelago or continent whence they were brought.

The very circumstance that this script must have originated ages before it reached Easter Island opens up a train of suggestion of the most valuable kind. That it can be Polynesian is, indeed, out of the question, as we have seen that no such Polynesian scripts ever existed. Where then did it originate, if not on one of those island-continents which formerly occupied the ocean spaces of the Pacific? It is out of the question that it could either have been developed in Easter Island or, indeed, on any other insular locality. It would seem as though it were the broken-down remains, the last vestige of a much more advanced type of writing. Not only have we the clearest evidence that it was actually brought from some other locality, but that it was the special preserve of the priestly and kingly class. This implies, of course, that it must have been so from the time it was first developed, that is for the space of untold generations. This is valuable evidence for the presence in the Pacific region of a caste of wise men who must have existed as a corporate body during a very long period of time. We know that the development of any script, no matter how elementary its character, presupposes hundreds of years of gradual growth, from the stage of mere drawing of rude pictures to that of conventional characters, and it is obvious that the system in use in Easter Island must have been evolving for centuries before it arrived in its present seat.

Now the presence of a similar though much more advanced script at Oleai, thousands of miles away in the Caroline Islands, leads to the assumption that at least two systems of writing were anciently in vogue in Oceania. That in use in the Carolines is obviously in a much later stage of development. It has reached the phase of the syllabary, that is each symbol represents a syllable, while that of Easter Island is merely mnemonic. Are we to assume that both originated in one and the same place?

This is admittedly a question of surpassing difficulty. But one thing is clear enough. Neither system owes anything to Asiatic or American sophistication. Neither resembles in the least either the Chinese or any other Asiatic system of writing on the one hand, or on the other, the Mayan or Mexican in America. It may safely be said that both are Oceanic in origin. But it is clear that each has taken a separate path of development of its own, whether or not they have sprung from the same source.

It seems fairly clear, then, that just as a separate art had been developed in the Pacific area before Polynesian times, as Professor Fenellosa shows, at least one system of writing had also been evolved.

Now a fairly high type of progress is required before even a rudimentary system of writing can be developed. That a system of writing obtained in Atlantis we have

LIFE AND CIVILIZATION IN LEMURIA 213

at least the evidence of Plato, who tells us that the laws of the island-continent were engraved on the pillar of oricalchum which stood in the Temple of Poseidon. But we have no means of knowing what the Atlantean writing was like. We are more fortunate in the case of the Lemurian script, if those of Oleai and Easter Island be its fragmentary remains.

These scripts appear to be of much the same stage of development as the Mexican (Aztec, not Maya) picture-writing, which was in a sense syllabic as well as pictorial, or that of the Hittites of Asia Minor. It had not yet reached that stage when the pictorial is entirely lost in the conventional, that is when the picture, through long usage, has grown so unlike its original model that it no longer resembles it, but takes on a different and arbitrary form. This, then, gives us a substantial clue to the cultural status of the Lemurians, and permits us to range it with that of the Egyptians and Babylonians at that particular stage of their development when as yet letters had not become hieroglyphic and conventional, but still retained much of the pictorial—that is they were in much the same cultural stage as the people of pre-dynastic Egypt or as the Aztecs of Tenochtitlan.

Mr. W. J. Thomson, an investigator, who was assisted by a native interpreter, has given the following translations of two of the Easter Island tablets.

Tablet 1. " When this island was first created and became known to our forefathers, the land was crossed with roads beautifully paved with flat stones. These stones were laid together so nicely that no rough edges were exposed. Coffee trees were growing close together along the borders of the roads. They met overhead and their branches were laced together like muscles.

" Heke was the builder of the roads, and it was he who sat in the place of honour, where the roads branched away in every direction.

" In that happy land, that beautiful land where Romaha formerly lived with his beloved Hangarva,

" Turaki used to listen to the voices of the birds and feed them.

" In that beautiful land governed the gods from Heaven, who lived in the waters when it was cold.

" There the black and white pointed spider would have mounted to Heaven, but he was held back by the bitterness of the cold."

The second tablet is headed " The Great King." It asks : " What power has the Great King on land ? He has the power to make the plants grow and to change the colour of the sky.

" All hail the power of the Great King who makes us lenient to the young plants, to admire the different colours of the sky and to behold the clouds that rise.

" All hail the power of the Great King who enables us to appreciate the blessings of bright stars, the lowering clouds, the gentle dew, the falling rain and the light of the sun and the moon.

" What power has the Great King on land ?

" He has the power to populate the earth to create both kings and subjects.

" All hail to the power of the Great King, who hath created the human beings, given authority to kings, and created loyal subjects.

" What power has the Great King ?

" He has the power to create the lobsters, whitebait, eels, ape-fish, and everything in the sea.

" What power has the Great King over the seas ?

" He hath the power to create the mighty fish that swim in deep water.

" All hail the power of the Great King who enables us to withstand the attacks of the maggots, flies, worms, fleas, and all manner of insects."

I can only say that these translations appear to me as highly dubious. I do not mean to say that they were made in bad faith, but that to wring such meanings from these symbols must have implied the use of a good deal of imagination, and Mr. Thomson must have relied greatly on his interpreter. At the same time it is not impossible that the interpreter recognized in these tablets the catch-words to well-known legends. If that be so, the first of the tablets would seem to refer to a myth of almost

LIFE AND CIVILIZATION IN LEMURIA

universal acceptance, that of the earthly paradise, lost by man's wickedness and folly. Does the spider signify some power of evil like the serpent in the story in Genesis, who aspired to a place in Heaven? In ancient Mexico the spider was the surrogate of the god of evil and cold, Tezcatlipoca, who descended from the sky, where he dwelt as a planet, by aid of a web. He was the deceiver of mankind, its sworn enemy. Here we seem to have some such figure. As regards the second tablet, its terms are obvious enough. It refers to a creative deity and the means he takes to safeguard the lives of his creatures.

In what manner, then, generally speaking, must we envisage life in ancient Lemuria in its heyday? In the first place we must think of several large continents, two of which were not far distant from each other, each having a large population, a condition which is vouched for by the existence of the remains of large stone buildings which must have occupied the activities of many thousands of people. It follows that the Lemurian land-masses must also have possessed numerous cities of considerable population, some sacred and religious centres, others commercial nuclei or ports, like Metalanim.

It is also pretty clear from the mass manner in which these cities were constructed that the work was carried out on what is known as the corvée system, that is, that, as in the case of the Egyptian pyramids, large numbers of men were brigaded for the purpose and fed by grain or other stores which had been hoarded for some years previously. This implies a species of slavery, and the existence of millions of coloured people in Lemuria who were for the most part segregated from the aristocratic whites, points to the probability that this slave labour was chiefly drawn from their numbers. That the laws governing them were of the strictest possible character may be implied from the existence of a taboo system of extraordinary severity.

Of kings and rulers we hear again and again in the traditions and legends of the sunken Lemuria, and the presence of extensive religious edifices also signifies the existence of a large and powerful priesthood. Nor can we dispense with the supposition of a widespread system of trade or barter, which in its turn presupposes a numerous commercial class. That the arts and crafts were in the hands of castes, probably hereditary, is also likely, considering the chary manner in which they were handed down to the late-comers in the Pacific area.

The existence of a script as well as of undertakings of such magnitude in the way of building is eloquent of the prevalence of an official and clerical class, as well as of a system of communication. That an economy which depended upon the compulsion of its people to heavy tasks would not have safeguarded itself by the formation of a large standing army is scarcely to be thought of, and that agriculture must have been in a flourishing condition to permit of the upkeep of large bodies of labourers and their overseers naturally follows.

Another conclusion which in the circumstances seems irresistible is that the royalty and aristocracy of Lemuria led an existence of the most luxurious character. Great undertakings in building construction are rarely engaged in unless the power which directs them finds itself in material circumstances the most flourishing. The traditions of the wickedness of these people is perhaps a memory of the soulless selfishness of an aristocracy glutted with power which failed to recognize its duty to the wretched people under its control. Perhaps after the catastrophe popular anarchy supervened and in the sequel a maddened democracy, leaderless and without tradition, plumbed the depths of licence and degradation, as is invariably the way with an ignorant and unorganized proletariat, until at last its wild career ended in almost utter barbarism.

Now of what particular culture is the picture of Lemurian society I have tried to draw from the known facts most reminiscent? I may say that the conclusions I have arrived at concerning the state of Lemurian society appear to me as arbitrarily dictated by the data at our disposal. Does the culture they reveal not bear a closer resemblance to that of Incan Peru than to any other known system of human economy?

For here we observe a polity and social custom almost

identical with that of Incan Peru—the harsh almost tyrannous rule of an aristocracy bent above all things on the erection of large megalithic buildings, the exaltation of royalty and the priesthood. Of course such parallels have frequently been drawn between civilizations, as for example betwixt Egypt and Peru, where the general circumstances were much the same, without much justification, or without recognition of the fact that, though it may not be difficult to prove resemblances, it cannot be easy to prove authoritative penetration of custom or tradition after a prolonged lapse of time. Yet proved it has been, in many instances, and I believe we have here another. It cannot but arouse intelligent reflection that the nearest of the Pacific Islands to the Peruvian coast, even though it be far distant, possessed at one time a culture having a resemblance so exceedingly close to the megalithic civilization of the Incan age.

Surely such a consideration makes it plain that between Peru and Easter Island there flourished at one period a great continental land possessed of a culture from which both of these regions received their own. As we proceed westward from Easter Island the megalithic culture continues, but its types and models have less resemblance to that of the Peruvian than the stone-working of Easter Island. Nevertheless we cannot regard the Incan Peruvian otherwise than as the modern and late descendant of the megalithic culture of the Pacific, although that at Tiahuanaco might well serve as typical of a more archaic stage.[1] We are thus faced with some such conclusion as that which would infer a series of development where a sunken land-mass (that of Davis?) had generated a great megalithic art which at a later date it had transferred to the Tiahuanaco region, which in its turn had centuries still later resolved itself into the Incan Peruvian. The stone culture at Easter Island, it would seem, must have had its inception earlier than that which gave its impetus to the art of Tiahuanaco. The megalithic art of the Marquesas generally resembles that of Easter Island, as do those of

[1] The gateway at Tiahuanaco has frequently been compared with the trilithon at Nukualofa in the Tonga Islands.

Hawaii and Fiji in a lesser degree. It is only when we reach Samoa and the New Hebrides that any actual difference in character becomes apparent, and that is due to Asiatic influence, though even in distant Metalanim in Micronesia the megalithic character of the architecture persists, although its more modern provenance is obvious.

It would seem then that we must consider the sunken continent which lay between Easter Island and Peru as having first fostered the characteristics of the megalithic culture of the Pacific, as the eastward trend of its development, as of its script, is certainly of later occurrence. Must we then regard this as the original Lemuria? It is my own belief that we must. I have never thought that the hypothesis of a Lemuria lying in the Indian Ocean or further eastward in Oceania held any real weight, and that is why I have not sought to burden these pages with much proof concerning its existence from African or Asiatic sources. I do not say that such a sub-continent never existed. Indeed I believe that it did, but that it could have ever been more than an Afro-Asiatic area of overflow, with little character of its own, I cannot conceive. My preferences are for a strictly Oceanic and Pacific series of continents lying between South America and New Guinea, and with an eastward-westward tendency of cultural direction rather than the opposite. Thus it follows that I cannot accept the westward-lying Lemuria of Haeckel, Sclater, and others as being the veridical Lemuria, or other than a sub-continent. For me the most ancient of the Lemurias lies submerged in the Southern Pacific between Easter Island and Peru.

The careful reader will have divined that I have sought to build up proof of the former existence of several oikoumenoi or continental land-masses in the Pacific from the consideration of different kinds of evidence, archæological, racial, and geological. This evidence it is my intention to collate in the final chapter, in an endeavour to arrive at definite conclusions regarding the number and locality of the Lemurian sub-continents and their relative antiquity.

Crystallizing the evidence in this chapter, it is clear that any description of life on Lemuria can be gleaned from analogy only. The culture of Lemuria was that of the late Stone Age. This does not imply a state of savagery, as the cultures of Mexico and early Egypt show.

The evidence leads to the assumption of the former existence in Oceania of a caste of fair people formerly governing several continents now submerged, who instituted an extensive body of law and custom and a religion celebrated in spacious temples, and whose degenerate descendants bequeathed these things in some measure to the incoming Polynesians. If they possessed such a religion it follows that it must have been accompanied, like all religions, by a body of arcane wisdom.

But Polynesian tradition, on the whole, is lacking in arcane knowledge. This seems to signify, more or less, a clean cut with tradition, that an older race has withheld its mysteries from barbarous invaders, to whom, however, it passed on the knowledge of its mythology, its arts and crafts, and its system of taboo.

That this older race did possess such wisdom is clear from the circumstance that the regions surrounding Lemuria, even Australia, all possess the elements of the Mysteries. An unwritten tradition current in knowledgeable occult circles supports the view. It states that " many thousands of years ago " a country, a great island existed in the great ocean of the south, " many days' sail from any other land." Catastrophe overtook it, and its " sages " " sailed westward," and re-established their mysteries " in new lands."

As Lemuria, in its later phases, consisted of a number of island continents there must have been vast differences in the character and customs of its inhabitants. Its races must have exhibited much ethnic variety, but were all governed by the fair white ruling caste. The recognized religion, too, must have been the faith of that caste.

The food of the Lemurians may have been drawn from marsupial animals and from the sea, but the main sources of their food supply must naturally have vanished with the land on which they dwelt. Animals of any size could not have been conveyed in slender craft.

The scripts or systems of writing still preserved in the

Pacific area do not seem to have been of Polynesian origin. That of Easter Island is ideographic, while that obtaining in the Carolines is syllabic, a great advance. The first was employed for religious purposes only. Both must have been used by the ruling class of an empire of some extent where organization was necessary. They could not have originated on small islands with a population of a few hundreds only. That of Easter Island seems to have had an Eastern origin. The Polynesians proper never employed a script.

The script in question must have been in use for ages before it reached Easter Island, was the special preserve of the priestly class and must have been developed elsewhere. This provides valuable evidence of the presence of a caste of wise men in Oceania during a very long period of time. That both scripts are of Oceanic origin and owe nothing to any other system of writing is also clear, although each has taken a separate path of development of its own, whether or not they have sprung from the same source, which seems doubtful. Just, as Fenellosa shows, a separate art had been evolved in the Pacific, so had a separate method of writing. Its type supplies us with a substantial clue to the cultural status of the Lemurians. If we believe it impossible that any script should have survived so long, we should remember that the Egyptian lasted for five thousand years and that our own is its direct descendant.

We must think of several Lemurian continents, each having a large population with great cities built of stone in the Cyclopean manner, large numbers of men being brigaded for their construction. This implies a species of slavery and a strict and even severe code of laws. Royalty, nobility, and a powerful priesthood must also have existed, and a large commercial class as well as an official class. A standing army to safeguard the nobility would be necessary and agriculture must have been in a flourishing condition to support the masses of the workers and a luxurious aristocracy.

This culture bears a closer resemblance to that of Incan Peru than any other known type, and it also resembles that anciently obtaining in Easter Island. We are left, then, with the hypothesis that at one period a great continental land, possessed of a culture from which each of these regions received its own, lay somewhere betwixt them, the Peruvian culture representing its most modern phase, and that of Easter Island a more ancient relationship. Was this continent the lost Davis Land? The megalithic building which originated on this continent spread over the whole Oceanic region, although it met in places with other influences, and it seems to me that its place of provenance was the original Lemuria. The probability is that there formerly existed a series of continents lying between South America and New Guinea, and with an eastward-westward tendency of cultural direction rather than the opposite.

CHAPTER XIII

ATLANTIS AND LEMURIA

WAS there communication between Atlantis and Lemuria, did the two great civilized centres of the ancient world, now hidden from human eyes, actually enjoy the contacts of culture and perhaps of commerce ?

The prospect opens up a vista of extraordinary interest. Our ignorance of what was taking place on this earth some ten thousand years ago or more, if the European area be excepted, is profound. We know that at that era men who possessed a certain degree of civilization existed in Western Europe, that they were painters and sculptors of high achievement, and that they must have been cognisant of more than the elements of law and organized religion.

That the culture they maintained, the Aurignacian, was at least thirteen thousand years older in its origin than the date with which we are dealing, and that it suddenly appeared in Europe as almost fully developed about twenty-three thousand years before the beginning of the Christian era is established, and is recognized by all pre-historians as beyond question. It was followed by the Azilian. But, with a very natural hesitancy, our foremost authorities refuse to tender any opinion as to the area of its origin.

In my *Problem of Atlantis* I have already adduced evidence in support of the theory that the Aurignacian civilization of France and Spain had an Atlantean background. But what proofs or even surmises can be advanced to assist the belief that an Atlantis in which an early type of civilization flourished had any intercourse with an equally civilized Lemuria ?

At the first glance the theory appears as preposterous.

Not only did large tracts of ocean intervene betwixt the now submerged continents, but the whole stretch of America as well, at that period (some twelve thousand years ago) almost certainly in a semi-desert state, and, according to all the evidence, in an uninhabited condition.

If communication be looked for by way of the other side of the globe it certainly appears as a consideration much more feasible. The head of one of the Lemurian land-masses must have been within comparatively easy distance of Java, if, indeed, that island were not actually a part of it. Access to India, the Persian Gulf and thus to Egypt and the Mediterranean must therefore have been possible, and once that were reached the rest would be a matter of time and occasion.

It is not necessary to infer direct communication between Lemuria and Atlantis, that is a regular coming and going of their merchants or inhabitants, the setting forth of fixed expeditions and so forth. These would, in the circumstances, have necessitated journeys which might well have occupied a lifetime, and, in the light of our present knowledge, are scarcely to be considered seriously. When we recall the extraordinary difficulties and hardships of early European travellers and explorers in Asia and elsewhere, of Marco Polo and John de Plano-Carpini, for example, we can hardly credit any considered and organised communication between an Atlantis still in the Stone Age, however advanced in art and thought, and a Lemuria in a similar condition.

No, what we must rather envisage is the drift and flow of culture from one continent to another, the slow process of many centuries. Ancient China knew only dimly of Rome, though she profited considerably from Byzantine, Egyptian and Indian art, ancient Mexico and Peru knew not of each other, yet assuredly exchanged, in the course of ages, many ideas and inventions. Ideas and arts were communicated in early times, slowly, by a hand-to-hand process, over many extensive distances, and myths and artifacts, tools, and even slaves and captives have been known to travel thousands of miles from the areas of their origin by exchange or barter.

Thus the old Azilian bone harpoon, with its several barbs, which probably originated in Atlantis, was currently in use in the Oceanic area only half a century ago. The peoples of Oceania wore feather head-dresses of Azilian type, their stone masonry closely resembles that of the Azilians, and such drawings as they have made display a certain likeness to Azilian art.

It will be interesting to see whether what I have called "the Atlantis Culture-complex" can in any way be applied to the circumstances of Oceanic culture. If it can, that would go far to establish the hypothesis of an ancient communication on a firm basis.

In my *History of Atlantis* I brought forward the theory that a slow cultural penetration drifted eastward and westward from the area of the now submerged continent. Every great civilization has been distinguished by a very definite group of cultural and customary manifestations and practices, and I showed that what I called "the Atlantean Culture-complex" had penetrated on one side to Europe and the other to America, that is that a certain complex or group of inventions, customs and ideas was to be found along a parallel extended east and west from the former site of Atlantis. To quote my own words:

"The principal elements which distinguished the Atlantean culture-complex are the practice of mummification, the practice of witchcraft, the presence of the pyramid, head-flattening, the couvade, the use of three-pointed stones, the existence of certain definite traditions of cataclysm, and several other minor cultural and traditional evidences. The main argument is that these are all to be found collectively confined within an area stretching from the western coasts of Europe to the eastern shores of America, and embracing the western European islands and the Antilles. So far as I am aware, these elements are not to be found associated with each other in any other part of the world. This seems to supply the surest kind of proof that they must have emanated from some Atlantic area now submerged, which formerly acted as a link between east and west, and whence these customs were distributed eastward and westward respectively."

It will be observed that I here limit the presence of this particular culture-complex to a definite area, and may I say at once that I do not expect to find that culture-complex reflected in its entirety in the Pacific region. But should it be found that certain of its parts have penetrated there, and that these parts are associated one with another, it may be possible to infer a certain degree of borrowing between Lemuria and Atlantis, especially if the cultural elements can be traced as links over the intervening spaces and can be shown to be of great antiquity.

Now it is clear that witchcraft, as we know it in Europe, was not practised in Oceania, but head-flattening, mummification, the pyramid and the couvade are all found in the Oceanic area.

There is, of course, a school, led by Professor Elliot Smith and Mr. Perry, which believes that the pyramid and the mummy and other cultural products of thought believed to have been invented in Egypt, were carried round the world by a race of culture-heroes known as "the Children of the Sun." These people were pearl-fishers and builders of irrigation terraces, and wherever we find traces of pearl-fishing and terrace-building we may be sure, they tell us, the Children of the Sun have settled.

But mummification and the pyramid in their early stages are a good deal older than Egypt, and the likelihood is that these early stages originated in the Aurignacian Age, as all the evidence goes to show. That the Aurignacians were responsible for the beginnings of Egyptian civilization is almost certainly proved by the presence of Solutrean flint-work, a phase of Aurignacian, in Egypt, and that the practice of embalming was communicated to the Aurignacian people of Spain by their racial congeners in the Canary Islands is scarcely to be questioned, or it may be more correct to say that in its early stages mummification was brought to Spain from the Canaries, the vestiges of Atlantis, by way of an ancient land-bridge.

But the idea of the preservation of the body after death as found, for example, in the Torres Straits, is relatively weak in Oceania, compared with its manifestations in America and Egypt. The strength and universality of the idea in America and its presence in the West India Islands, shows that it advanced westward from some site betwixt the Canaries and the West Indian archipelago, whereas its extension from Egypt, where it was derivative, and distant from its place of origin, is weak in an easterly and south-easterly direction. Only vestiges of the practice of ritual embalming are to be found in India and China, a fact which should surely give some pause to the vivacious protagonists of the hypothesis of " the Children of the Sun."

But in Oceania the pyramid, on a small scale, is well represented. The same criticism has, however, to be applied to its presence there as is employed with reference to the art of mummification. It is when we go west from Atlantis that we find the pyramid, especially in Mexico, the Mound region and in Peru, on a large scale of building, thus demonstrating that the initial urge of pyramid-building took a westerly direction rather than an eastward trend.

It is beside the point to object that American pyramids are of late development. They exhibit a masonic technique equally as old at least as those of Egypt, and may well have been the comparatively late work of a people driven to the mainland from a disintegrating and now sunken semi-continental area in the West Atlantic, the area I have called Antillia, which, I believe, maintained the culture of Atlantis up to a relatively late period. The whole tradition of Maya and Mexican culture is eloquent of such immigration.

The touchstone of the question, it seems to me, is the presence of vestigial pyramids on Easter Island. The comparative proximity of this isolated island to America and its remoteness from Asia and the other insular groups seems eloquent of the western character of its pyramidal architecture. The vestiges of its pyramids are Cyclopean and thus of early technique, and resemble those found in that part of the Mexican coast formerly inhabited by tribes of Maya origin.

This seems to show that the Lemurian civilization might to some extent have been sophisticated by the Atlantean. The trend of early civilization appears to have been east-

A MARAE OF TAHITI AS REPRESENTED IN *THE VOYAGE OF THE DUFF*, 1799

ward and westward from Atlantis, rather than in both directions from Lemuria. Indeed, the probability is that it ringed the globe at an early date. But for reasons I have given in the chapter on the civilization of Lemuria, I prefer to think that the masonry of Peru was in the main of Lemurian origin, and that if Antillian or Neo-Atlantean building methods reached Lemuria at all they did so at a time when masonry there was well established and had a character of its own, which was only partially influenced by the invading style. In any case, Neo-Atlantean building fashions did not greatly affect Peru, where, however, the pyramid form may have come directly from Antillia.

This is not to say that Lemuria possessed no civilization of its own. The mere fact that the cultures of ancient China and America possessed so many things in common is eloquent of a common Lemurian origin. That civilization made its way by sea from China or Cambodia to Peru and Central America about the seventh century was long held as axiomatic by a certain school of Americanists, but the subsequent discovery in Peru and Guatemala of remains greatly more ancient than that period, proved the hollowness of this hypothesis.

I believe that many of the circumstances of early culture may have been carried from one or other of the Lemurian land-masses to China and Peru. The question of the early development of the great civilization of China holds, indeed, a profound mystery. Its extraordinarily unique and egregious character is surely indicative of a most ancient settlement.

But to return to our Atlantean culture-complex. We have found the pyramid and the mummy in Oceania, if in a vestigial sense only. Do we find head-flattening ? In the New Hebrides the head is moulded by the wearing of bandages and an ovoid shape is thus produced. In some parts of the Hawaiian group the practice of squeezing the head of a child so that it may take this shape, is still indulged in. In the Cook Islands the women massage the infant's head from birth to train it to this form. The cradle-board for flattening the brow is in use in Penrhyn Island. Moulding is the process employed in French

Oceania. The Maoris of New Zealand also massage the head in infancy.

Says Professor Macmillan Brown, writing on the native custom of head-flattening : " It is tolerably clear that the custom was universal amongst the Polynesians. It is also clear that it was because they admired the round, domed head with sloping brow that they took such trouble with the child's skull during the plastic stage, and that this was not the natural head-form. But it must have been the natural head-form of some racial elements that had come into the central Pacific ; else there would have been no model to follow in the moulding process. It also stands to reason that these invaders were conquering warriors, who constituted the new aristocracy ; it is never from the subjects that a people's ideal of beauty is taken, but from the superiors."

But it also " stands to reason " that the Polynesians may have adopted the process from a more civilized people whom they conquered. However that may be, we find head-flattening, another sign of the Atlantis culture-complex, in the area of old Lemuria. Oceania is also rich in the couvade. That is, we find most of the " apparatus " of this theory in that area.

And mark that we find little of it in Asia, whence the Polynesians and Melanesians are thought by some authorities to have come. Asia exhibits only small vestiges of embalmment, no pyramids, and little head-shaping unless among the Tartars.

We find, then, the most salient and outstanding characteristics of what we know of the Atlantean culture in the Lemurian area. We find that area cut off from such customs almost absolutely on the Asiatic side, though in contact with them on the American side. We have also seen that, according to all the available evidence, communication between Atlantis and Lemuria via America seems preposterous, and that, if it did occur at all, it must have taken place by way of Asia.

" Seems preposterous." Quite. But so many things in archæology have at first sight seemed preposterous. All the evidence, preposterous or not, points to a communication of the Atlantis culture-complex to Lemurian Oceania via America. In other words, the Atlantis culture-complex has a clear run from Spain, which anciently possessed every one of its features, and still can boast of some, to the Sandwich Islands and the Cook Islands and New Zealand by way of the Canaries, the West India Islands, and Mexico, or half the breadth of the globe, whereas in the Orient the culture-complex is not found in its collective entirety, but in a patchy, isolated, and vestigial fashion only.

It is also of importance to add that this complex is discovered at its most consistent, almost in a straight geographical line. It deviates scarcely at all to north or south if regarded in its entirety. That implies that mummification, the pyramid, head-flattening, the couvade and traditions of cataclysm (as apart from mere flood stories) are found together in an almost direct line from Spain to Hawaii. The further west we go toward the Hawaiian limit, the more embalmment weakens, the pyramid grows, the couvade becomes more common, witchcraft dwindles and head-flattening and tattooing persevere.

Therefore we find the pyramid, or its technique of colossal stone building, the couvade and head-flattening and tattooing an almost constant and associated cultural group in place, if not always in time. These, be it noted, are the signs of a most ancient civilization. Nowhere else are they associated but on the line Spain–Sandwich Islands.

It seems to me then that we are almost compelled, whether we like it or not—and personally, I avouch myself as almost averse from such an acceptance—to agree that communication of some description must have taken place between Atlantis and Lemuria at a very early period. The chief difficulty I find in accepting such a contact is that of premising the existence of a Central American civilization very much older than any I had envisaged.

But I believe an adequate explanation is forthcoming. As I have said elsewhere, it seems probable that the sub-continent of Antillia, the western " doublet " of Atlantis, survived that island for many centuries. Indeed it still persists fragmentally in the West Indian Islands. That

Antillia had much the same culture as Atlantis must be presumed, and that it was connected with it terrestrially by a chain of islands, has been proved in my *Atlantis in America*.

That Antillean man, on the submergence of his main continental mass, found refuge on the American mainland seems proven. It may well have happened that Antillia, as a sub-continent, was not finally submerged until some 2100 years ago. The last vestiges of the last land-bridge which connected Britain with Europe existed until 3000 years ago, or, more properly speaking, its main mass then underwent submergence, the Frisian Islands constituting its last remains. The Antillean region is one of notorious seismic instability. Be that as it may, we find about the year 200 B.C., or 2100 years ago, abundant traces of the invasion of American soil by a race possessing the highest artistic capacities of a culture which can, in many ways, be linked with the Aurignacian. In a word, the phenomenon of the Aurignacian invasion of Europe was repeated on American soil at a later date, and accompanied by the manifestations of an Aurignacian art which had developed during the intervening centuries, as might be expected, but which had never lost its basic resemblance to original forms. Such sudden appearances in Europe and America of cultures so closely allied, though divided by many centuries of time, cannot be fortuitous.

The carriers of the culture in question were the Maya, the origin of whom is, according to archæologists, shrouded in a mystery quite as dense as that which surrounds the provenance of the Aurignacians.

The clearest proof of the Atlantean-Antillean origin of American civilization is to be found in the culture and traditions of the Maya race of Guatemala, Chiapas, and Yucatan. This great and truly advanced people appear suddenly in Central America with a culture fully developed, an elaborate hieroglyphic system, a religion eloquent of high theological concepts, and an architecture which rivals, if it does not surpass, that of Egypt or Sumeria.

The roots of Maya civilization are not to be encountered on American soil. No steps in the evolution of its writing, religion, or architecture can be traced in the regions in which its monuments are found, and though competent authorities recognize new phases and aspects in its artforms subsequent to their entrance to Central Africa, the complete absence of all primary evolutionary forms proves conclusively that Maya art was not originally conceived on American soil. Where not a link with the humbler forms of art, handicraft, or custom is to be found, it seems only rational to look for the beginnings of their culture and art elsewhere.

Indeed, the very earliest specimens of Maya art, architecture and handicraft known to us, exhibit the sure traces of degeneration. Here is an art and a philosophy so rich, so overripe, as to approach senility and disintegration. Its forms were stereotyped, its ideas rooted in convention. Its society resembled that of the China of half a century ago, a community passionately conservative in its ideals, hastening to decay.

Maya civilization makes its first appearance in Central America in the centuries immediately preceding the Christian era, roughly about 200 B.C. Its earliest dated monuments cannot with safety be ascribed to a more remote period. No sooner did it take root in Central American soil than it began to send forth vigorous shoots. Regarding the precise place of its first settlement, authoritative opinion is practically agreed. The general character of the architectural remains in the region lying between the Bay of Tabasco and the foot of the Cordilleras, and watered by the River Usumacinta and the Rio de la Pasion in the state of Chiapas, points conclusively to this district as its cradle, and the archaic type of the hieroglyphs upon its monuments as well as the early dates these contain, give this theory something of finality. The oldest known centres of Maya life are probably Tikal and Peten in Eastern Guatemala. It is believed that the development of the Maya states in Chiapas and Guatemala continued for seven or eight hundred years, or until the close of the sixth century A.D., about which time disaster seems to have come upon them with tragic suddenness.

The Antillean origin of the Maya civilization has been

stressed by many authorities, who believed their culture to have had its beginnings in the West Indies. Columbus alludes to the peaceable and civilized character of the inhabitants of these islands. They possessed very considerable maritime skill, and those of the Bahamas had a regular commerce with Florida. The Caribs of the Lesser Antilles penetrated to the heart of Brazil and strongly resembled the Maya in appearance and culture. Both flattened the skull in infancy, had the same burial customs, and some of the gods of the Antilles strongly resemble those of the Maya. The Maya language, too, has been classified by Beuchat and others as of Antillean origin.

But perhaps the best and most sufficient test of the relationship of the Maya and Mexicans with the Antillean region is to be discovered in the surprising traditions they have left us which refer to their colonization of Central America and Mexico.

A wealth of tradition regarding a westerly and trans-oceanic connection existed in ancient Mexico and Central America. This centred round the great mythic figure of the culture hero, Quetzalcoatl (Feathered-snake) and his people, the Toltecs, the civilizing race who are believed to have entered Mexico in peaceful invasion, and to have sown the ideas of culture among its barbarous peoples.

We seem, then, to have here an adequate explanation of the manner in which the Atlantean culture-complex found its way via America to Oceania and Old Lemuria. The narrow isthmus on which the Maya founded their Atlantean civilization in Central America would readily lend itself as a point of departure for the dissemination of that culture throughout Oceania. However that may be, such a theory necessitates the relegation of Maya beginnings in America to an era considerably older than 200 B.C. By that date there was no Lemuria in existence.

The acceptance of the dissemination of the Atlantis culture-complex in Oceania—itself manifestly the home of a culture of great antiquity—compels us to believe that it came to the Pacific area some thousands of years ago, by way of Antillia and Central America, whether these regions were then civilized or not. Many good authorities believe that they were civilized. Must we accept their dicta ?

I believe that we must, or how can we account for the presence of an Atlantean customary code in Oceania ? I admit that such an acceptance vitiates my whole opinion concerning the Maya civilization, which, I had always believed, arrived in Central America quite shortly before the beginning of the Christian era.

It is apparent, then, that we must look for a much more ancient civilization on American soil than anything some of us had previously believed in. Some American archæologists have been led to the conclusion that it harked back to five or even ten thousand years before the Christian era. Its chronology, as expressed in its hieroglyphic monuments, assuredly does, if it be not altogether mythical.

But I hasten to say that that does not imply that we must accept the notions of Le Plongeon or the Abbé Brasseur de Bourbourg, which were obviously founded on conclusions the most unscientific.

To summarize, it is not necessary to infer direct communication between Lemuria and Atlantis, but rather the drift and flow of culture during many centuries. We find the Azilian bone harpoon in the Oceanic area, the Azilian feather head-dress, and other " Atlantean " features. We also find many instances of what I have called " the Atlantean culture-complex " in the Lemurian area, in some cases associated together, such as head-flattering, mummification, the pyramid and the couvade.

But mummification is relatively weak in Oceania ; the pyramid, if on a small scale, is, however, well represented, and exhibits a masonic technique as old as that of Egypt. The touchstone of the matter is the presence of vestigial pyramids on Easter Island. But for reasons I have given in the chapter on the Civilization of Lemuria I prefer to think that Lemurian methods of building were only partially affected by the Antillean or Neo-Atlantean.

Head-flattening, an Atlantean custom, is well developed in Oceania, and the area is rich in the couvade. Indeed we find most of the " apparatus " of the Atlantean couplex in Oceania, more or less, though not in Asia. That is, the area is cut off from such customs on the Asiatic side, though in contact with them on the American.

Although contact between Atlantis and Lemuria on the American side seems " preposterous " the evidence is in favour of it and not as regards communication by way of Asia. The Atlantis culture-complex, in some of its phases, has a clear run from Spain to the Sandwich Islands, the Cook Islands and New Zealand by way of the Canaries, the West India Islands and Mexico—that is, it runs in an almost straight geographical line from Spain to Hawaii. The further west we go towards the Hawaiian limit, the more embalmment weakens, the pyramid grows, the couvade becomes common and head-flattening perseveres until the Asiatic coasts are reached.

The acceptance of this theory premises the existence of a Central American civilization very much older than any as yet agreed upon, a civilization founded by Antillean man. In a word, the phenomenon of the Aurignacian invasion of Europe was repeated on American soil at a much later date.

CHAPTER XIV

CONCLUSIONS

THE reader will have observed that piece by piece out of the available evidence a workable hypothesis of a Lemurian continent has gradually unfolded itself quite naturally and almost automatically. " Let the evidence speak for itself," is the best advice one can offer a protagonist, and I claim that, through no skill or sapience on my part, the theory of a formerly existing series of Pacific land-masses has, with its several branches, grown from what Omar Khayyam might have called " the soil of consideration " as naturally as might a tree, which has divers boughs, but is still one growth, from the soil terrestrial.

For myself the most surprising thing is that in the course of writing this book it has become clear that the myth of Lemuria in its Polynesian form, and the myth of Atlantis as told by Plato, have a common basis. This in itself I regard as a discovery of some moment. It has, of course, long been recognized that the myths of Ys, Lyonesse, Cardigan Bay, and many others which relate to the submergence of land have a similar basis—the idea that popular or individual evil-doing roused the gods to their destruction and submergence in the depths of ocean.

But why should the gods have submerged these particular regions ? Many deities visit their people with afflictions in ancient myth because of sin or contumaciousness, yet do not drown their lands for ever, and it is to be particularly noted that in all cases where such a myth of submergence is found, submergence has actually taken place, as geological research has proved.

If this is so in the case of a dozen or more localities in Europe, Asia, and America, a number of which are to be found in our own island, is it so illogical to apply the general rule to Atlantis and Lemuria ? There is nothing absurd in crediting a great gradual crumbling and subsidence in Cardigan Bay or on the coast of Norfolk, where the remains of submerged towns and villages may even yet be seen at low water. That is an everyday affair enough. But when one is asked to believe that entire continents have so crumbled and disappeared, leaving only vestigial islands, the very magnitude of the conditions he is invited to consider engenders a dubious frame of mind.

Possibly doubt, if not derision, is aroused by the presentation of the case by those enthusiasts who believe that the ancient continents of the Atlantic and Pacific plunged into the abyss of ocean in the course of a single day and night, and who appeal to Father Plato as their authority for the statement. But we have to remember that it is governed by the previous clause that catastrophe followed "after there had been exceeding great earthquakes and floods," thus showing that Atlantis did not go down by the head in one vast and unparalleled dive to the awful orchestra of elemental wrath in thunder-peal and volcano's roar, as some good folk with Transpontine proclivities seem to believe. A prolonged process of attrition is certain, but that cumulative calamity, induced in the case of Atlantis by the continual lapse of the most treacherous ocean-bed in the northern hemisphere, must have ended in a final, if gradual, crash and ruin I am willing to believe, although I feel that the submersion was effected to " slow music " rather than to more dramatic trumpet-blasts and the beatings of Vulcan's atabals.

But how are we to account for the similarity of the myths of Atlantis and Lemuria ? By the same process, of course, by which we account for that of Ys and Cardigan, or their resemblance to the myths, now growing up, of the former and present subsidences in Norfolk or Oceania. The subsidence took place, and men must account for it, must try to discover a reason of some sort for a catastrophe so appalling, and the reason they arrive at is ever of the same kind.

When unpleasant things, great or small, occur, we have

always with us the people who warned us that if we did not mend our ways " something " would happen. That " something " is not always particularly specified, but the amateur and professional Jeremiahs among us are never at a loss for melancholy prospect and retrospect. And are not the professional prophets and Cassandras invariably persons gifted with more than extraordinary powers of menace, derision, and lung-power ? Dreadful self-centred old men and tiresome withered women have in all ages indicated to all peoples that if they continued on the purple path of pleasure a frightful fate would overtake them and they have seized upon social, racial, or meteorological menaces to support their threats of ruin.

More philosophically, it is the duty of a priesthood, however primitive, to keep the balance between God and man, to preserve the cosmic economy, real or imaginary, from infringement by reckless or impious persons, and the spectacle of widespread popular impiety must inevitably appear to its ministers as a monstrous interference with and invasion of the " cosmic symphony." To them, man's chief end is the worship or placation of the gods, and as " sin " interferes with this and derogates from it, it will bring down the punishment of the gods.

It is clear, too, that to the primitive mind pleasure of any sort is regarded as bringing in its train dreadful sequelæ, especially if it be of a marked and rapturous character. Particularly is this the case with amorous pleasure. Delight awakes the jealousy and rancour of the gods, as many an ancient myth makes plain. Equally so, do pomp and pride. Man must not arrogate to himself the joys of heaven, or imitate its hauteurs. This idea crystallized at last in the belief that it was " wicked " or " sinful " for man to enjoy himself too deeply and doubtless the physical weakness, nausea, and disgust which follow on debauch or orgy strengthened the belief, until it came to be thought that human profligacy had a direct and blighting effect on the powers and economy of nature. From such a notion it is merely a step to a belief in the wholesale destruction of nations or countries by outraged deity.

But the " reason " afforded by myth for destruction is of secondary importance to the fact of the destruction itself. It is merely ætiological, or explanatory of it. It matters little that we are told that Atlantis, or Lemuria, or Ys were submerged because of the wickedness of their inhabitants. It matters much that we are told that they *were* submerged. The accompanying warning only helps to indicate and fortify the fact, and to assure us that wherever we hear of the submergence of a land because of its flagitiousness we may be certain such a cataclysm actually took place. That is a fact of importance to the consideration of the whole study of sunken localities. We know that submergence occurred in certain localities, and we are told that it occurred because of the sins of the inhabitants. If we hear, then, that because of the sins of its inhabitants another area has been submerged, we are surely justified in surmising, at least, that sink it actually did. There is no myth which has not its background of reality.

Coming to more ponderable proof, we have seen that many Pacific islands have disappeared within living memory, and that a mass of tradition of subsidence too frequent and widespread to be void of significance exists regarding Oceanic lands formerly existing and which became submerged.

From the archæological evidence we learned that Oceania was inhabited while continental conditions still prevailed, and that its many archaic monuments are classed by good authorities as beyond the powers of the present native races, who are ignorant of their origin. Isolated structures are found in certain islands, no traces of masonry existing in the neighbouring isles. The architecture of Ponape, Yap, and Easter Island particularly is eloquent of the erection of buildings while continental conditions still persisted or shortly after their cessation.

From the traditional evidence we glean that in Hawaii and Samoa a myth of world chaos and destruction known as " Po " obtained, while another speaks of a land " the fount of civilization and religious dispensation," which became lost or hidden because of sin. The Marquesans believed the early world to extend from Vavau to Hawaii, the myths of the Maori of New Zealand referred to a land called Mataaho which had been destroyed by flood, while the Hawaiians maintained the tradition of a former continent stretching from Hawaii and including Samoa, New Zealand, and Fiji, which sank and left only its mountain-tops as islands which were inhabited by a dwarf race.

We have seen that the struggle between the elements of fire and water is a marked feature of Oceanic myth. The chief Plutonic deity of Oceania is a fair-haired god who exhorted his people to " keep their skins white like their minds," meaning, of course, that they should not intermarry with darker races. The people of Easter Island preserved a tradition that they had come from a submerged area. The Maori and other Polynesians believed the Country of the Dead to lie underneath the sea. It was a land of fair-haired folk who practised weaving and wood-carving.

It is obvious that those Polynesian myths of submergence and cataclysm had their origin in Lemurian tradition, as by the period of Polynesian settlement in Oceania its greatest time of seismic violence had long passed. No continents have been submerged since then, though islands have, and it remains as a logical consequence that the numerous myths of continents formerly existing must be a legacy from an older Oceanic race. In any case it is probable that the Polynesians discovered little more than mere generally widespread archipelagic conditions on their entrance to Oceania, unless in the neighbourhood of Easter Island or Davis Land.

As we have seen, the clearest traces of the previous occupation of the Pacific area by a fair-haired race exist, as does the evidence for its survival in many places. Hawaii, the New Hebrides, Nez Zealand, and Micronesia all possess traditions and actual vestiges of this race, who dwelt in secluded regions and were frequently regarded as supernatural beings. With this evidence we must associate the traditions of a fair race dwelling beneath the sea (who cultivated the arts, especially weaving and wood-carving, and who were regarded as wise men and enchanters, possessing abnormal powers) as bearing upon the fact of the submergence of the principal areas in which they must have lived. According to the tradition quoted by Mr. Cowan, the submarine world in which these blond people dwelt was regarded by the Polynesians as the home of occult knowledge, and the Maori of New Zealand modelled the economy of their *Hui-te-Rangiora*, or Houses of Wisdom, on those of the fair race which they had dispossessed in New Zealand.

This fair race, it is clear, cannot have passed through the western Oceanic area inhabited by the dark races. Had it been so they must have lost those physical characteristics which they still possess.

The customary evidence I do not regard as very conclusive owing to the great lapse of time which has passed since Lemurian conditions must have obtained. The folklore and customs of the native races who inhabit the region about Zimbabwe in East Africa, for example, exhibit almost no traces of its former civilization, and it is scarcely to be expected that the Pacific area could show many evidences of Lemurian custom after a very much longer passage of time.

The theory of Fenellosa regarding a very ancient unity of art-form in the Pacific is of high evidential value. Although the balance of authority in geological science is on the side of the former existence of Lemuria, I feel that its testimony is greatly inferior in value to that afforded by tradition, which, after all, has an equal claim to be an "exact" science. Indeed, the findings of traditional science, as a general rule, are much more susceptible of rational deduction than those of geology, whose foremost professors seem incapable of agreement almost on the very elements of their subject; such, for example, as the question of the permanence of ocean basins.

It is especially to be remarked that the several races of Oceania coincide in their positions with its more pronounced geographical divisions, and this induces the belief that the races at an early period may have effected a settlement on several great Pacific land-masses while these were in a more markedly archipelagic condition than they now

CONCLUSIONS 241

are. The biological evidence, like the geological, seems much too contradictory and chaotic to permit of rational scientific conclusion.

As the result of submergence over a prolonged period gradual emigration ensued, regions when notoriously volcanic or unstable being abandoned. That their inhabitants had the nautical means to reach other insular localities cannot be doubted when the general evidence from ancient and extensive navigation in the Pacific is taken into account, though it is not necessary to premise any very extensive degree of navigation. The elements of the Lemurian civilization may then have been carried to either Pacific coast. Ancient America drew much of its civilization from Lemuria, by way of the Easter Island archipelago or land-mass, especially as regards megalithic building, which the Peruvian Incas later adapted and improved upon.

Many South American customs and art-forms are of Oceanic origin, and that a body of people from Oceania arrived and settled at Grand Chimu in Peru seems to be proved. The architectures of Easter Island and Incan Peru seem, in some respects, almost identical, especially in the case of the burial platform at Vinapu, Easter Island, where the cutting and laying of the stone is precisely the same as in numerous examples of Incan masonry.. The ruins of Titicaca also display Oceanic characteristics. Here chronology may not actually raise its barriers, as large Lemurian communities may have occupied considerable land-masses in the Pacific less than a thousand years before the beginning of the Christian era, which is well inside the chronological limit fixed by Fenellosa for the dispersal of Pacific art.

Piecing together the evidence in order that we may arrive at some comprehension of life as it may have been in Lemuria, we seem to have good proof of the former existence in Oceania of a caste of fair people governing several land-masses now submerged, who were remarkable chiefly for their arcane knowledge and their prowess as builders, and who possessed a religion the rites of which they celebrated in spacious temples, and a script which seems to have been a possession of the priestly class.

Sifting and compressing the evidence, it seems to me that we must accept the following conclusions.

(1) That several sub-continents, land-masses, or large archipelagoes now submerged, formerly existed in the Pacific area. More than one of these (Davis Land) may have persisted, at least in archipelagic form, until the seventeenth century of our era.

(2) I believe these several areas to have been:

(a) A land-mass or archipelago in the vicinity of Easter Island. This, I think, was the land seen by Davis, and known as Davis Land, which appears to have foundered not very long after he observed it in 1687.

(b) A great continent stretching from the Sandwich group to, and including, New Zealand.

(c) Another stretching from New Caledonia to Sumatra.[1] The theory of these two latter masses coincides, as regards the first, both with the traditional evidence and the ethnographical situation, while, as regards the second, the racial position applies—a surprising and valuable result.

(d) Three other sunken land-masses, or archipelagoes, once the nuclei of considerable " empires," occupied areas about Ponape, Oleai and Yap. I believe the masses in the vicinity of Pitcairn Island to have been more of an archipelagic character. The same applies to the Marquesas.

I believe the oldest or more cultured of these empires to have been situated in what may be called for the sake of convenience, " Davis Land." I am led to that conclusion by the well-founded evidence that the course of ancient civilization in Oceania is from east to west and not in the contrary direction, and that the architecture of Easter Island, the " religious nucleus " of Davis Land, exhibits actual correspondence with that of Peru.

Moreover there is sound evidence that this early easterly continent, which was known to Polynesian tradition as Motu Matira Hiva, was the original home of a cultured white race. Furthermore, it seems probable that it remained longer than any other among the land-masses

[1] As I have said, I have not dealt more particularly with this area from the cultural or traditional side, as I believe Asiatic proximity to have overlaid or obscured the evidence. Nor is it necessary to believe that Lemuria was exclusively a sub-Asiatic continent.

above water, and may have been known even to the late Polynesians, who took long voyages, as its observation by Davis in 1687 would lead us to suppose.

I believe, then, that this land-mass or archipelago early developed a civilization of its own, which it communicated by degrees to the other Lemurian sub-continents or archipelagoes.

I am aware that Professor Macmillan Brown prefers a Marquesan origin for Peruvian architecture. He thinks that it would not have been easy for voyagers from a point so far north as Easter Island to reach the American coast, as they must first have had to sail far south into the latitude of the " occasional Westerlies." Moreover, Easter Island possessed a script, and South America can boast of no system of writing. We must, he thinks, look to the Marquesas or Pitcairn Island before we encounter a combination of such stonework and statuary as are to be found in Peru, for example at Tiahuanaco.

But I feel that the masonry at Easter Island has affinities with a much greater number of Peruvian examples of masonry than with Tiahuanaco, and on that I would chiefly base my opinion that the later Incan architecture had its origin in that Davis Land of which Easter Island was either the last remnant or the insular religious centre. And it is possibly just because it formed such a religious centre that the script characteristic of it was to be found there and there alone, and not in a colonial settlement in Peru. As regards the difficulties of approach, Easter Island is much nearer the coast of Peru than any other land, now existing or previously existing.

Such, then, are my conclusions. It must remain for future research to discover more precisely the actual character and type of Lemurian civilization, but I think I have at least been able to indicate the geographical position of its several remnants and especially of its oldest and most important cultural centre. I feel, too, that I have succeeded in proving the similarity of its myth with that of Atlantis, a revelation of some importance, I believe, capable of profound repercussions on the whole study of submerged localities.

With these novel and, I think, weighty, conclusions to guide us, we may then, with some confidence, approach the further consideration of the whole subject in a more practical manner than has hitherto been possible, and I need not say that in doing so I shall be only too happy to avail myself of any assistance or suggestion which other students may feel disposed to extend to me—such aid, indeed, as I have to thank hundreds of readers in all parts of the world for in the case of my previous endeavours to cast light on the difficult problem of Atlantis.

INDEX

A

Agassiz, on upheaval in the Pacific basin, 150-1
America, Asiatic settlements in, 186 ff.; Polynesian influences in, 189 ff.
Antillia, its culture, 229-32
Araki, floating island of, 20-1
Art, Pacific forms of, 119 ff.
Asiatic influence in America, 186 ff.
Atlantis and Lemuria, similarity of myths of, 236 ff.; was there communication between ? 222
Atlantis culture-complex, can it be applied to Oceanic culture ? 224 ff.; scope of its influence, 229 ff.
Atlantis, parallels with, 68
Atlantis, resemblance of its myth to that of Lemuria, 59-62
Australia and South America, continental connection between, 166 ff.; 178-9.
Australian zoological region, 164 ff.
Austro-Malayan zoological sub-region, 165-6.

B

Biology, evidence from, 163 ff.
Birds and continental connections, 167; of New Guinea, 170-1
Birds, wingless, the problem of, 175
Blandford, H. F., his conclusions on former existence of Lemuria, 142-3

Blavatsky, Madame, on the Lemurian theory, 86-90
Bolatu, the isle of immortality, 56
Brown, J. Macmillan, on theory of a Pacific continent, 151-3
Browning, K., on the Lemurians, 94-6
Buddhism in America, 188

C

Caroline Islands, monuments of, 32
Cataclysm, myths of, 47 ff., 58-9; 71-2; explanation of, 61-2
Celebes, zoological problem of the, 172
China, art of resembles that of the Pacific, 119 ff.
Churchward, Col. James, on the Lemurian theory, 91-4; his theory of savagery, 114 ff.
Conclusions, general, 235 ff.; summarised, 242
Continents, the several Lemurian, 218
Continents, myths of sunken, 19, 38, 47 ff., 54, 59, 71, 152; explanation of, 61-2; submerged, 83. See also Geology
Continental connection between Australia and South America, 166 ff.; between Peru and Easter Island, 217-18
Culture of Lemuria, its importation into Asia and America, 185 ff.; parallel between that of Easter Island and Peru, 197 ff.

Culture-myths, resemblance between those of Peru and Easter Island, 196-7
Custom, evidence from, 111 ff.; in Oceania, developed in separate environments, 114

D

Darwin, Charles, on subsidence in the Pacific, 147 ff.
Davis Land, 22, 41, 86

E

Earth's surface, instability of, 131
Easter Island, 22, 23, 29, 39-43, 58-9; native name of, 85; native script of, 207 ff.; resemblance of its masonry to the Peruvian, 189; 194 ff.
Elevation of land, 20; myths of, 56; 130 ff.

F

Fair native race of Oceania, 57, 59, 71, 76; 79-82; 113; 125-6; 202 ff.
Father-right in Oceania, 111-12
Fenellosa, his theory of the influence of Pacific art, 119 ff.
Fiji, monuments of, 29; flood myth of, 51-2
Fishes, intercommunication of, between continents, 168-9
Flood myths, 67-8; 191 ff.; 195 ff. See also Cataclysm
Funafuti, boring of the volcano of by Sollas and David, 131.

G

Gardiner, Starkie, on Lemurian hypothesis, 141-2

Gatsepar, island of, 24-5
Geikie, Sir A., on submarine outlines of Pacific Ocean, 143 ff.; criticism of Darwin's theory of subsidence, 150
Geology, of Lemuria, 128 ff.; time and, 129-30
Grand Chimu, Peru, possible Polynesian or Lemurian settlement there, 190 ff.
Guppy, H. B., on continental condition of Fiji Islands, 155-6

H

Haeckel on the Lemurian origin of the human race, 102 ff.; on the Lemurian theory, 136 ff.
Hartlaub on Lemurian hypothesis, 140-1
Hawaii, antiquities of, 28, 29; myths of, 19, 47, 49, 50, 53 ff.
Head-flattening in Oceania, 227-8
Heilprin, A., on Lemuria, 177-8
Hivaoa, island of, in Marquesas group, stone images of, 39
Hotu Matua, myth of, 19, 23, 40-3
Hutton, on biological evidence for Lemurian theory, 163

I

Islands, appearing suddenly in the Pacific Ocean, 145 ff.; 148; disappearing, 135, 161-2; lost, search for by Polynesians, 50-51; Peruvian tale of a sunken, 192; submerged, 19, 20, 23, 38, 134 ff.

J

Jacolliot, Louis, on the Lemurian theory, 97-9

INDEX

Japanese influence in Pacific, 37
Jourdy, General, his theory of the destruction of Lemuria, 182 ff.
Juan Fernandez, discovers land in Pacific now lost, 22-3

K

Kane, a god of Hawaii, myth of, 47; chant of, 48-50, 53-4
Kihawahine, a Polynesian god, 64

L

Land, distribution of, 78
Lemuria, the name, 18; wreck of known as Po, 48, 60 ff.; resemblance of its myth to that of Atlantis, 59-62; Col. J. Churchward on, 91-4; its destruction, 114 ff.; geology of, 130 ff.; epoch of its floreat, 130; disappearance of its sub-continents, 182 ff.; cause of its submergence, 182 ff.; arcane tradition concerning, 204-6; food-supply of, 206-7; life in reconstructed, 201, 215 ff.; the original, 218; the myth of explained, 238
Lemuria and Atlantis, similarity of their myths, 235 ff.; was there communication between? 222 ff.
Lemurian civilisation closely resembles that of Incan Peruvian, 217-8
Lemurian race, 37; Steiner on, 90-1; Browning on, 94-6; variety of the, 99; origin of the, 100-2; supposed fragments in America, 104 ff.; its descent into savagery, 114 ff.; its retention of the arts, 117; emigration of, 184; its settlements in Peru, 190-3; its arcane knowledge, 203 ff.
Lemurian origin of Pacific myth, 70

M

Makemake, god of Easter Island, 58
Malden Island, 37
Mangaia, lost island of, 23
Maori, carved lintel, 31
Maori myths, 59, 79-85
Marquesans, myths of the, 50; expeditions from in search of lost islands, 50; their myth of the Flood, 52-3
Mataora, a Polynesian god, 59
Maui, a god of the Maori, 56-9, 67
Maya, civilisation of the, 230 ff.; traditions of origin, 232
Melanesia, stone monuments of, 31
Menehune, a dwarf white race, 55, 76
Metalanim, ruinous city in Caroline Islands, 24, 33-7
Micronesia, antiquities of, 32; mythology of, 57-8
Moerenhout, on statues and submergence myth of Raivaivai, 38
Moriori, ancient race of New Zealand, 29 ff.
Mother-right in Oceania, 111-12
Motu Motiro Hiva, a sunken empire, 59
Mummification, 225

N

Negrito race, 36; its disposal in Oceania, 78

INDEX

New Caledonia, monuments of, 31
New Guinea, antiquities, of, 32
New Hebrides, monuments of, 31-2
New Zealand, aboriginal races of, 83-5; antiquities of, 29, 30, 31; myths of, 50; Oceania or continental, 174-5; its fauna, 175-6

O

Oleai, island of, 24, 42; native script of, 209

P

Pacific Islands, botanical isolation of, 176-7
Pacific Ocean, submarine outlines of the, 143 ff.
Patupaiarehe, or fair race of New Zealand, 76, 81, 82
Pele, a volcanic deity, 56, 66
Peru, masonry of resembles that of Easter Island, 189; Lemurian settlements in, 190, 193-4; resemblance of its civilization to that of the Lemurians, 217-18
Phantom Island, Keuhelani, 55
Po, or chaos, the wreck of Lemuria, 48, 59, 60-1, 71
Polynesia, stone manuments of, 28, 29 ff.
Polynesians, mythology of, 64 ff.; origins of the, 21, 77, 100
Polynesian influence in America, 186 ff.; 189 ff.; settlement in Peru, 190; zoological sub-region, 166 ff.
Ponape, island of, 24, 32, 42, 78
Pyramids in the Pacific, 226

R

Raivaivai, island of, Austral group, 29, 38, 39
Rua-Haku, Ocean god of Society Islands, myth of, 52

S

Samoa, monuments of, 29
Sandwich Islands, zoology of, 172-3
Savagery, descent of Lemurians into, 114 ff.
Sclater, W. L., on Austral mammalia, 178
Scripts of the Pacific, 207 ff.
Sin, the sense of in Lemurian and Atlantean myth, 61-2, 68-70
Society Islands, myth of the deluge, 52
Sollas, Professor, bores the atoll of Funafuti, 131
Solomon Islands, antiquities of, 28
Steiner, Rudolf, on the Lemurians, 90
Stone monuments of Pacific area, 28-32
Submarine eruptions in the Pacific Ocean, 144 ff.
Submergences of land in Pacific, 19, 21, 22, 23, 25, 37, 38, 58, 59; proofs of, 130 ff., 134 ff.; Haeckel on, 136, 155, 182 ff. See Geology

T

Taboo in Oceania, 113-14
Tahiti, pyramids, of, 29
Tangaroa, a plutonic deity, 56-7
Tattooing in Oceania, 121 ff.
Thomson, J. W., his translations of the Easter Island script, 213-15

INDEX

Tiahuanaco, Peruvian prehistoric site, 194–5; masonry of resembles that of Easter Island, 195

Timor, group, zoology of the, 171–2

V

Volcanic myths, 57–8

W

Wafer, observes Davis Land, 22

Wallace, Alfred Russel, on the Lemurian hypothesis, 138 ff.; inconsistencies in his arguments, 164–5

Wegener, his theory of floating continents, 153–4; on Lemurian, 154–5

Whiro, a storm-god, 68

Women, taboo on among the Polynesians, 113–14

Y

Yap, island of, 25, 32, 42

ORDER FROM YOUR FAVORITE BOOKSELLER OR CALL FOR OUR FREE CATALOG

Of Heaven and Earth: Essays Presented at the First Sitchin Studies Day, edited by Zecharia Sitchin. ISBN 1-885395-17-5 • 164 pages • 5 1/2 x 8 1/2 • trade paper • illustrated • $14.95

God Games: What Do You Do Forever?, by Neil Freer. ISBN 1-885395-39-6 • 312 pages • 6 x 9 • trade paper • $19.95

Space Travelers and the Genesis of the Human Form: Evidence of Intelligent Contact in the Solar System, by Joan d'Arc. ISBN 1-58509-127-8 • 208 pages • 6 x 9 • trade paper • illustrated • $18.95

Humanity's Extraterrestrial Origins: ET Influences on Humankind's Biological and Cultural Evolution, by Dr. Arthur David Horn with Lynette Mallory-Horn. ISBN 3-931652-31-9 • 373 pages • 6 x 9 • trade paper • $17.00

Past Shock: The Origin of Religion and Its Impact on the Human Soul, by Jack Barranger. ISBN 1-885395-08-6 • 126 pages • 6 x 9 • trade paper • illustrated • $12.95

Flying Serpents and Dragons: The Story of Mankind's Reptilian Past, by R.A. Boulay. ISBN 1-885395-38-8 • 276 pages • 6 x 9 • trade paper • illustrated • $19.95

Triumph of the Human Spirit: The Greatest Achievements of the Human Soul and How Its Power Can Change Your Life, by Paul Tice. ISBN 1-885395-57-4 • 295 pages • 6 x 9 • trade paper • illustrated • $19.95

Mysteries Explored: The Search for Human Origins, UFOs, and Religious Beginnings, by Jack Barranger and Paul Tice. ISBN 1-58509-101-4 • 104 pages • 6 x 9 • trade paper • $12.95

Mushrooms and Mankind: The Impact of Mushrooms on Human Consciousness and Religion, by James Arthur. ISBN 1-58509-151-0 • 180 pages • 6 x 9 • trade paper • $16.95

Vril or Vital Magnetism, with an Introduction by Paul Tice. ISBN 1-58509-030-1 • 124 pages • 5 1/2 x 8 1/2 • trade paper • $12.95

The Odic Force: Letters on Od and Magnetism, by Karl von Reichenbach. ISBN 1-58509-001-8 • 192 pages • 6 x 9 • trade paper • $15.95

The New Revelation: The Coming of a New Spiritual Paradigm, by Arthur Conan Doyle. ISBN 1-58509-220-7 • 124 pages • 6 x 9 • trade paper • $12.95

The Astral World: Its Scenes, Dwellers, and Phenomena, by Swami Panchadasi. ISBN 1-58509-071-9 • 104 pages • 6 x 9 • trade paper • $11.95

Reason and Belief: The Impact of Scientific Discovery on Religious and Spiritual Faith, by Sir Oliver Lodge. ISBN 1-58509-226-6 • 180 pages • 6 x 9 • trade paper • $17.95

William Blake: A Biography, by Basil De Selincourt. ISBN 1-58509-225-8 • 384 pages • 6 x 9 • trade paper • $28.95

The Divine Pymander: And Other Writings of Hermes Trismegistus, translated by John D. Chambers. ISBN 1-58509-046-8 • 196 pages • 6 x 9 • trade paper • $16.95

Theosophy and The Secret Doctrine, by Harriet L. Henderson. Includes *H.P. Blavatsky: An Outline of Her Life*, by Herbert Whyte, ISBN 1-58509-075-1 • 132 pages • 6 x 9 • trade paper • $13.95

The Light of Egypt, Volume One: The Science of the Soul and the Stars, by Thomas H. Burgoyne. ISBN 1-58509-051-4 • 320 pages • 6 x 9 • trade paper • illustrated • $24.95

The Light of Egypt, Volume Two: The Science of the Soul and the Stars, by Thomas H. Burgoyne. ISBN 1-58509-052-2 • 224 pages • 6 x 9 • trade paper • illustrated • $17.95

The Jumping Frog and 18 Other Stories: 19 Unforgettable Mark Twain Stories, by Mark Twain. ISBN 1-58509-200-2 • 128 pages • 6 x 9 • trade paper • $12.95

The Devil's Dictionary: A Guidebook for Cynics, by Ambrose Bierce. ISBN 1-58509-016-6 • 144 pages • 6 x 9 • trade paper • $12.95

The Smoky God: Or The Voyage to the Inner World, by Willis George Emerson. ISBN 1-58509-067-0 • 184 pages • 6 x 9 • trade paper • illustrated • $15.95

A Short History of the World, by H.G. Wells. ISBN 1-58509-211-8 • 320 pages • 6 x 9 • trade paper • $24.95

The Voyages and Discoveries of the Companions of Columbus, by Washington Irving. ISBN 1-58509-500-1 • 352 pages • 6 x 9 • hard cover • $39.95

History of Baalbek, by Michel Alouf. ISBN 1-58509-063-8 • 196 pages • 5 x 8 • trade paper • illustrated • $15.95

Ancient Egyptian Masonry: The Building Craft, by Sommers Clarke and R. Engelback. ISBN 1-58509-059-X • 350 pages • 6 x 9 • trade paper • illustrated • $26.95

That Old Time Religion: The Story of Religious Foundations, by Jordan Maxwell and Paul Tice. ISBN 1-58509-100-6 • 220 pages • 6 x 9 • trade paper • $19.95

Jumpin' Jehovah: Exposing the Atrocities of the Old Testament God, by Paul Tice. ISBN 1-58509-102-2 • 104 pages • 6 x 9 • trade paper • $12.95

The Book of Enoch: A Work of Visionary Revelation and Prophecy, Revealing Divine Secrets and Fantastic Information about Creation, Salvation, Heaven and Hell, translated by R. H. Charles. ISBN 1-58509-019-0 • 152 pages • 5 1/2 x 8 1/2 • trade paper • $13.95

The Book of Enoch: Translated from the Editor's Ethiopic Text and Edited with an Enlarged Introduction, Notes and Indexes, Together with a Reprint of the Greek Fragments, edited by R. H. Charles. ISBN 1-58509-080-8 • 448 pages • 6 x 9 • trade paper • $34.95

The Book of the Secrets of Enoch, translated from the Slavonic by W. R. Morfill. Edited, with Introduction and Notes by R. H. Charles. ISBN 1-58509-020-4 • 148 pages • 5 1/2 x 8 1/2 • trade paper • $13.95

Enuma Elish: The Seven Tablets of Creation, Volume One, by L. W. King. ISBN 1-58509-041-7 • 236 pages • 6 x 9 • trade paper • illustrated • $18.95

Enuma Elish: The Seven Tablets of Creation, Volume Two, by L. W. King. ISBN 1-58509-042-5 • 260 pages • 6 x 9 • trade paper • illustrated • $19.95

Enuma Elish, Volumes One and Two: The Seven Tablets of Creation, by L. W. King. Two volumes from above bound as one. ISBN 1-58509-043-3 • 496 pages • 6 x 9 • trade paper • illustrated • $38.90

The Archko Volume: Documents that Claim Proof to the Life, Death, and Resurrection of Christ, by Drs. McIntosh and Twyman. ISBN 1-58509-082-4 • 248 pages • 6 x 9 • trade paper • $20.95

The Lost Language of Symbolism: An Inquiry into the Origin of Certain Letters, Words, Names, Fairy-Tales, Folklore, and Mythologies, by Harold Bayley. ISBN 1-58509-070-0 • 384 pages • 6 x 9 • trade paper • $27.95

The Book of Jasher: A Suppressed Book that was Removed from the Bible, Referred to in Joshua and Second Samuel, translated by Albinus Alcuin (800 AD). ISBN 1-58509-081-6 • 304 pages • 6 x 9 • trade paper • $24.95

The Bible's Most Embarrassing Moments, with an Introduction by Paul Tice. ISBN 1-58509-025-5 • 172 pages • 5 x 8 • trade paper • $14.95

History of the Cross: The Pagan Origin and Idolatrous Adoption and Worship of the Image, by Henry Dana Ward. ISBN 1-58509-056-5 • 104 pages • 6 x 9 • trade paper • illustrated • $11.95

Was Jesus Influenced by Buddhism? A Comparative Study of the Lives and Thoughts of Gautama and Jesus, by Dwight Goddard. ISBN 1-58509-027-1 • 252 pages • 6 x 9 • trade paper • $19.95

History of the Christian Religion to the Year Two Hundred, by Charles B. Waite. ISBN 1-885395-15-9 • 556 pages • 6 x 9 • hard cover • $25.00

Symbols, Sex, and the Stars, by Ernest Busenbark. ISBN 1-885395-19-1 • 396 pages • 5 1/2 x 8 1/2 • trade paper • $22.95

History of the First Council of Nice: A World's Christian Convention, A.D. 325, by Dean Dudley. ISBN 1-58509-023-9 • 132 pages • 5 1/2 x 8 1/2 • trade paper • $12.95

The World's Sixteen Crucified Saviors, by Kersey Graves. ISBN 1-58509-018-2 • 436 pages • 5 1/2 x 8 1/2 • trade paper • $29.95

If you liked this book, you may want to order its companion by Lewis Spence, also available from The Book Tree.

THE PROBLEM OF ATLANTIS

The research in this book covers all available evidence known for Atlantis by the author and bears out the fact that such a place must have existed beyond any doubt.

Spence reveals supporting evidence from many disciplines including geology, archaeology, mythology, anthropology, biology, linguistics (including word origins), and the transmission of various customs. He also does a compelling job in detailing the various myths and legends of the Aztecs, Brazilian Indians and the North American Indians, and how they fully support the existence of Atlantis. In writing this book Spence was clearly ahead of his time. ISBN 1-58509-089-1 • 6 x 9 • paper • 280 pages • $22.95

Also by Lewis Spence

ATLANTIS IN AMERICA

In this book Spence puts forth evidence that Atlantis was located in the Western hemisphere—in and around Central America.

He does an impressive job of detective work by comparing Indian myths from various lands including Peru, Brazil, Central America, North America, and the Atlantean story from the philosopher, Plato. Many of the myths he covers duplicate themselves in various cultures, leading one to believe that they must have had a common source. That source, according to Spence, was Atlantis. This is one book that should not be missed. ISBN 1-885395-97-3 • 6 x 9 • paper • 248 pages • $19.95

Order from your favorite bookseller of call 1-800-700-TREE 24 hrs to order by credit card or to request our free catalog.

www.ingramcontent.com/pod-product-compliance
Lightning Source LLC
Chambersburg PA
CBHW030137170426
43199CB00008B/97